THE ECONOMICS
OF PRODUCTION

THE ECONOMICS OF PRODUCTION

BRUCE R. BEATTIE
C. ROBERT TAYLOR
Montana State University

JOHN WILEY & SONS
New York • Chichester • Brisbane • Toronto • Singapore

Library of Congress Cataloging in Publication Data:

Beattie, Bruce R.
The economics of production.

Includes bibliographies and index.
1. Production (Economic theory)   I. Taylor, C. R.
(Charles Robert), 1946–   II. Title.

HB241.B43 1985   338.5.   84-17432
ISBN 0-471-80810-5

Printed in the United States of America

10 9 8 7 6 5 4 3 2

DEDICATION
To Gail and Claireda

PREFACE

The Economics of Production was written as a textbook for courses in production economics theory and the theory of the firm. The book is aimed at first-year graduate students and advanced undergraduates in economics and agricultural economics.

In writing this text we were motivated by two concerns: (1) we wanted the final product to be readable and student-oriented; and (2) we believed technical aspects of production and input-side issues should be given equal standing with the common notions of production costs, product supply, and other output-side issues found in most microeconomic theory texts. To meet our first concern, we have written the book in an informal style; we have also developed in considerable detail mathematical derivations and have amply sprinkled the text with intuitive motivations for the principles and ideas that evolve from these derivations. Although we have refrained from referring to the mathematical proofs in the text as "shade tree," that is clearly their nature in some instances. Mathematical purists will no doubt have concerns, but we believe that our sometimes casual use of mathematics will yield results that will be insightful to the *beginning* graduate student—especially those with a meager mathematical background. The level of mathematics presumed is that of A. C. Chiang's *Fundamental Methods of Mathematical Economics* (1974).

Most of the chapters are organized along similar lines: development proceeds from a single output, single variable factor case to the single output, two-factor case, to the single output, several-factor case. Multiple output situations are not introduced until Chapter 5. Perfectly competitive and imperfectly competitive market structures are treated together. Generally, we have discussed the monopoly and/or monopsony model most fully, and presented the perfectly competitive situation as a special case. Concepts and supporting arguments develop from the general to the specific, for we believe that this approach enables students to deal comfortably with all technical and economic (product demand and factor supply) forces. Moreover, this approach has the pedagogical advantage of producing fewer surprises and fewer inappropriate generalizations.

We have used geometry extensively, both two- and three-dimensional graphs, to enable students to make the transition from the more familiar geometric/intuitive form of economic reasoning to the less familiar abstract mathematical approach. Upon completion of the text, students should be able to capture and hold the complementarities of both approaches. Finally, at the end of each chapter there is a list of suggested readings, including published works cited in the chapter, and a set of relevant problems (except for Chapter 1).

Our second concern is addressed in a number of ways. First, at least one-half of the book is devoted to technical aspects of production economic theory and input-side issues. Further, throughout the book, attention is given to the technical and economic implications of several production functions that are commonly used in applied work—the quadratic, the Cobb–Douglas, the transcendental, and the constant elasticity of substitution functions. Tables are provided at the end of each chapter to summarize important technical and economic properties of these production functions; some less widely known production function specifications are given at the end of Chapter 2.

There are but six chapters in the book. Our intention was to provide the essential fundamentals of production economics theory and to cover those fundamentals in considerable detail. We believe the book is ideally suited for a one semester course, if covered totally, and that it can be adapted to a quarter system quite easily by judicious bypassing of certain sections. The introductory chapter provides general background and motivation for the subject matter and focuses on some basic definitions, assumptions and the production determining forces. Chapter 2 is devoted to technical, as opposed to economic, aspects of production, namely, properties of production functions. Possible optional sections in this chapter are Sections 2.2.d, 2.2.k, 2.3, and 2.5.

Chapter 3 deals with economic aspects of production, focusing on factors of production. Sections that might be omitted in this chapter to conserve class time are Sections 3.1.c, 3.3, 3.4, and 3.5. Careful attention is given to both conditional and ordinary derived factor demand and to the homogeneity and symmetry properties of factor demand functions.

The subject of Chapter 4 is also on economic aspects of single product production, but covered from the traditional output-side perspective. Chapter 4 is the most compact chapter in the book. We believe that all sections of this chapter should be covered, even for courses on a quarter system. If something must be omitted here, the most likely candidate is Section 4.5. A special strength of this chapter compared to treatments in other textbooks is the thorough development of linkages between the input-side and the output-side of production economics theory. Again, much attention is paid to derivation of product supply and the properties and comparative statics of product supply and factor demand.

Chapter 5 addresses multiproduct production as a logical extension of Chapters 3 and 4. An extended introduction in this chapter deals with proper conceptualization of the multiproduct framework, with emphasis on factor allocability, separability and jointness. For the instructor who is severely restricted for time, we believe Chapter 5 (except for Section 5.1) can be sacrificed. In fact, we argue in Chapter 5 that most of the important applied production problems can be handled using the conventional (although extended) single product, multifactor framework, but with the products linked through resource constraints, nonallocability of factors, or jointness of production. Optional sections in Chapter 5 are Sections 5.3 and 5.4.

Chapter 6 presents the economics of production from a duality perspective. We believe that this chapter is a must for a contemporary treatment of the theory of the firm. However, it is the last chapter because we believe that the power, beauty, analytical leverage, and shortcomings of duality theory as a conceptual framework for economic analysis can only be appreciated by those who first fully understand the primal approach of Chapters 2 through 5. Unlike some authors, we do not view duality as an alternative way of learning economic theory; rather, it is an embellishment of the standard primal approach. Possible optional sections in Chapter 6 are Sections 6.4 and 6.6.

In an effort such as this there are many people to acknowledge. In particular, we are in considerable debt to our former teachers: W. G. Brown, A. N. Halter, and L. C. Rixe (Beattie); and E. R. Swanson and J. C. Headley (Taylor). Professors Brown, Headley, and Swanson further provided numerous helpful comments on an earlier draft of the manuscript. Many graduate students and colleagues at the University of Kentucky, University of Illinois, Texas A & M University, and Montana State University provided encouragement, untold helpful suggestions, and corrections of outright errors in numerous earlier versions of class notes. Finally, we greatly appreciate the major effort and unfailing sense of humor of our typists, Dianne DeSalvo and Judy Harrison.

Bruce R. Beattie
C. Robert Taylor

CONTENTS

GLOSSARY OF SYMBOLS AND ABBREVIATIONS

Common notation used in this book is set out below:

y	is the amount of the product produced (output)
x	is the amount of a factor used (input)
p	is product price
r	is factor price
TPP	is total physical product
APP	is average physical product
MPP	is marginal physical productivity
MP	is marginal product
TVP	is total value product
AVP	is average value product
MVP	is marginal value productivity
VMP	is value of the marginal productivity
c	is variable factor cost
C	is total factor cost
$\tilde{c}$	is indirect factor cost
AFC	is average factor cost
MFC	is marginal factor cost
π	is profit
$\tilde{\pi}$	is indirect profit
RTS	is the rate of technical substitution (marginal rate of substitution)
E	is partial elasticity of production
ϵ	is the function coefficient
ξ	is the quasifunction coefficient
x_i^*	is demand for the ith factor
x_i^c	is conditional demand for the ith factor
VC	is variable cost (in terms of output)
TC	is total cost
ATC	is average total cost

AVC	is average variable cost
MC	is marginal cost
TR	is total revenue
$\tilde{R}$	is indirect total revenue
AR	is average revenue
MR	is marginal revenue
y_j^*	is supply of the jth product
y_j^c	is conditional supply of the jth product
RPT	is the rate of product transformation
$\dfrac{dy}{dx}, y', f'$	are first derivatives
$\dfrac{d^2y}{dx^2}$	is a second derivative
$\dfrac{\partial y}{\partial x_1}, f_1$	are first-order partial derivatives
$\dfrac{\partial^2 y}{\partial x_1^2}, f_{11}$	are second-order own-partial derivatives
$\dfrac{\partial^2 y}{\partial x_1 \partial x_2}, f_{12}$	are second-order, cross-partial derivatives

Any of the above abbreviations when preceded with L refer to the corresponding Lagrangean formulation. In addition to the above, several Greek symbols are used throughout the text, including:

α	alpha	η	eta	ξ	xi
β	beta	θ	theta	π	pi
γ	gamma	λ	lambda	σ, Σ	sigma
δ, Δ	delta	μ	mu	ϕ	phi
ϵ	epsilon	ν	nu	ψ	psi

THE ECONOMICS
OF PRODUCTION

CHAPTER 1   INTRODUCTION

Production economics is concerned with choice among alternative production processes, namely, enterprise selection and resource allocation. How much and what to produce and the optimal combination of resources are key issues in any production problem, whether at the level of an individual firm, an entire industry, or society. Production economics concerns not only production choices but, more importantly, how choices are influenced by changes in technical and economic circumstances.

Because many production and decision processes have considerable complexity, economists have found it useful to employ abstract deductive reasoning to formulate theories of firm-level decision making. These theories or decision rules, if you will, are based on given assumptions, behavioral postulates, and initial conditions. Accordingly, theories represent simplifications and generalizations of reality. By abstracting from particulars, we find elements that many situations have in common. In addition to providing considerable insight into economic processes, theory serves a useful role in guiding empirical studies and in interpreting results of empirical studies.

This book makes extensive use of the mathematical language, primarily calculus and algebra. Where possible, algebraic concepts and arguments are related to less abstract, and more familiar, geometric interpretation. All theory presented in this book is cast in a comparative static framework, with decisions assumed to be made in an environment of certainty. Of course, this deviates considerably from many actual decision problems in that it ignores dynamic forces, learning, and risk and uncertainty; but to understand these more complicated theories, it is essential that we fully understand comparative static theories and concepts under certainty.

1.1 OUTLINE OF TEXT

In the remainder of this chapter, definitions and assumptions essential to understanding production economics are presented. The following chapter discusses the technical aspects of production, with emphasis on the productivity functions and related concepts such as factor elasticity, the function coefficient, returns to scale, homogeneity, isoclines, ridgelines, and stages of production. The objective of Chapter 2 is to become familiar with concepts, methods, and terminology used to characterize response surfaces. An appreciation and intuitive feel for how technical considerations impinge on economic choices of producers is the desired outcome.

Chapter 3 focuses on economic aspects of production (in combination with technical aspects) from an input perspective. Concepts of factor supply and product demand are incorporated with technical aspects in a profit maximization setting. Economic principles are deduced in terms of optimal input usage, culminating with implications for factor demand. Concepts such as price flexibility, the economic region of production, factor expansion path, and economic interdependence of factors are introduced.

Chapter 4 also deals with economic aspects of production but from an output-side perspective. Conditions for profit maximization are derived in terms of marginal revenue and marginal cost, and implications for product supply are deduced. Careful attention is given to drawing output-side/input-side linkages; that is, establishing the intimate relationship between the cost functions and the production function.

Whereas previous chapters deal with a single product, Chapter 5 presents technical and economic aspects of multiproduct production. Such concepts as production possibilities curves, rate of product transformation, output expansion path, and product interdependence are considered.

The final chapter develops the dual approach to production theory. Having labored through Chapters 3, 4, and 5 the beginning student will, no doubt, be frustrated with the difficulty of deriving optimal solutions, factor demand functions, product supply functions, and comparative statics for all but the most simple production functions and factor supply and product demand assumptions. The traditional approach used in Chapters 3, 4, and 5 is known as the primal approach, problem or setup. In Chapter 6 the duality framework simplifies considerably the mechanics of factor demand, product supply and comparative statics. Duality is a powerful tool of particular benefit to the individual that thoroughly understands the rigors and frustrations of the primal problem.

Having noted what we will find in this book, it is perhaps equally important to know what we will not find. Two most important areas of production economics theory, especially for applied economists, are multiperiod (polyperiodic) production and production under uncertainty. Virtually no real world production processes operate in an environment of certainty. Frequently entrepreneurs do not know with certainty the price they will receive for their product once produced, the price they will have to pay for inputs purchased, and/or the success they will have in converting inputs into output. Also few production processes are timeless or truly monoperiodic; decisions and input usage in one production period are seldom independent of earlier or subsequent production periods. The complexities of a dynamic and uncertain world are real and pose important problems. Therefore, the very complexity of the real world suggests that most of us should proceed carefully, one step at a time.

We begin where we must, with some basic definitions and assumptions.

1.2 DEFINITIONS

Several terms used in production economics have meanings that may differ from common usage. So, to avoid potential confusion, we adopt the following definitions.

> **Definition 1.1** *Production* is the process of combining and coordinating materials and forces (inputs, factors, resources, or productive services) in the creation of some good or service (output or product).

The terms *input* and *output* only have meaning in connection with a particular production process. Note that an output from one production process can be an input to another production process, or it can be a final consumer good.

An abstract representation of the production process is given by the production function.

> **Definition 1.2** A *production function* is a quantitative or mathematical description of the various technical production possibilities faced by a firm. The production function gives the maximum output(s) in physical terms for each level of the inputs in physical terms.

Mathematical specification of the production function can range from simple algebraic functions, such as a quadratic function relating corn yield to nitrogen fertilization rate, to highly complex systems of equations, such as a detailed model of corn plant growth and response to nitrogen fertilization. The degree of mathematical complexity of the production function depends on the production process and on the degree of accuracy desired.

In the specification of a production function, differentiation between fixed and variable factors is important.

> **Definition 1.3** Given a production period, *variable factors* are factors of production, the levels of which may be augmented or diminished during that period; *fixed factors* are those factors whose levels cannot (or will not) be altered during the production period.

Thus, the distinction between fixed and variable factors depends on the length of the production period.

> **Definition 1.4** The *long run* is a production period in which all n factors are considered variable, whereas 1 to $(n - 1)$ factors are variable in the *short run*.

The conventional terms, *long run* and *short run*, can be confusing for the uninitiated. If n factors are pertinent in describing a production process, then a production period sufficiently long that all n factors may be varied is referred to as the *long run*. The term *short run* unfortunately covers a multitude of possible cases, ranging from a production period in which a single factor is variable to a production period in which all but one factor is variable. Thus, we have many possible short-run cases.

In length-of-run considerations, technology is generally assumed constant or at least exogenously specified. That is, we use length-of-run terminology principally in reference to the number of variable factors, disallowing change in the production parameters describing or specifying the production technology. We do, however, consider some comparative static implications of changing technological parameters. Clearly the longer the length of run the more erroneous the fixed technology assumption becomes. In fact, in poly-period problems it is entirely possible that production parameters as well as fixed-factor and exogenous variable levels could change. Accordingly, economists frequently incorporate the possibility of changing technology in their modeling efforts.

With many economic events, and especially with a mathematical approach to optimization, we are interested in necessary and sufficient conditions for the event.

> **Definition 1.5** A *necessary condition* is a circumstance the absence of which precludes a particular event or outcome. A *sufficient* condition is a circumstance the presence of which ensures the event.

For example, with a calculus approach to optimization, the first-order condition ($dy/dx = 0$) and the second-order condition ($d^2y/dx^2 < 0$) are each necessary conditions for a local maximum of the unconstrained function, $y = f(x)$. Taken together they are sufficient. That is, if $dy/dx \neq 0$ *or* $d^2y/dx^2 > 0$, a maximum solution is precluded.[1] And if $dy/dx = 0$ *and* $d^2y/dx^2 < 0$ at the critical x (the value of x, where $dy/dx = 0$), a maximum is ensured. But if $dy/dx = 0$ and $d^2y/dx^2 > 0$, we have a minimum.

If all necessary conditions except one are satisfied then satisfaction of the final necessary condition is sufficient to ensure the event. Accordingly, one often finds economists referring to the second-order condition as the sufficient condition because they have implicitly assumed satisfaction of the first-order condition. However, there is no reason why we could not just as well call the first-order condition sufficient *given* satisfaction of the second-order condition. The important thing to remember is that satisfaction of first- and second-order conditions are both *necessary* and *taken together* they are *sufficient*. Necessary and sufficient conditions for optimization will be discussed in more detail in subsequent chapters.

1.3 ASSUMPTIONS

Unless stated otherwise, several key assumptions are made throughout this text.

---

[1]The sufficient condition given by this example is incomplete in the sense that the outcome $d^2y/dx^2 = 0$ is not considered (e.g., consider the problem of maximizing $y = a - (x - 2)^4$). When a zero second derivative is encountered, higher derivatives must be examined. For additional discussion, see Chiang, (1974, p. 258) (see Selected Bibliography at end of chapter for references).

Assumption 1.1 The production process is *monoperiodic*. That is, a firm's production activity is so arranged that production in one time period is entirely separate or independent of production in preceding and subsequent time periods.

This assumption rules out dynamic aspects that characterize some production processes, such as insect control in one crop year that influences the insect population in the next crop year. It should be cautioned that if such dynamic aspects characterize the production process, successive application of one-period optimum input rates will not optimize a firm's multiperiod objective function.

Assumption 1.2 All *inputs and outputs* of the firm are *homogeneous* in the sense that there are no quality differences for different levels of a particular input or output.

In both theory and empirical studies, Assumption 1.2 can be relaxed, but the mathematical derivations and resulting economic principles are much more complex. Heterogeneous outputs and inputs can be introduced by specifying a multidimensioned production function that accounts for quality as well as quantity.

Assumption 1.3 The production function is given by a single, *twice continuously differentiable* function.

Assuming a continuous production function abstracts from reality in some cases. For example, if output is measured as number of automobiles, we obviously cannot have 3.789 functioning automobiles. Although the continuity assumption may not be realistic in all cases, economic principles and theories can be more neatly demonstrated in the continuous case. Economic principles for inputs and outputs that are not continuous are the same as for the continuous case, except that they are expressed as lumpy changes rather than infinitesimal (infinitely small but nonzero) changes. The reader interested in a formal discussion of continuity should consult Chiang (1974).

Assumption 1.4 The production function and product and factor price relationships are known with *certainty*.

This assumption says that the entrepreneur's expectations regarding input–output transformations and product and factor price relationships are known with a subjective or objective probability of one.

Assumption 1.5 *Funds available* for purchase of variable factors of production *do not limit* such *purchases*.

On occasion, this assumption will be relaxed to show how operating capital constraints influence optimal decisions.

Assumption 1.6 The *goal* of the firm is *to maximize profit*, or in some instances to minimize the cost of producing a specified level of output, subject to technical and economic constraints and forces.

Entrepreneurs may have different objectives, such as the maximization of profit, wealth maximization, sales maximization, earning a specified percentage return on capital, producing a given level of output at minimum cost, maximizing output for a given cost outlay, or maximizing a utility function. We focus mainly on the conditions for maximum profit, as this is a plausible goal for many firms, especially those that are operating in a competitive economic system.[2]

In discussing the goal or behavioral postulate of the firm it is appropriate to consider the concept of rationality. To the economist a *rational* action is a choice or action (observed behavior) that is consistent with a prescribed behavioral postulate attributed to the economic actor. When offering prescriptive advice to decision makers and policy makers, applied economists should always make clear the assumed goal on which their prescriptions are based. Furthermore, we should be cognizant that our suggested prescriptions may very well be irrelevant and go unheeded if for no other reason than the actors are behaving in accordance with a different goal. Again, one of the areas where economists may often be misled by their analyses is when their model fails to formally account for uncertainty.[3]

1.4 THE PRODUCTION DETERMINING FORCES

In his classic book, *A Study on the Pure Theory of Production,* Sune Carlson notes that four forces interact to effectively determine the actions of the profit maximizing firm—technical knowledge, product demand, factor supply, and capital supply. These four forces influence the entrepreneur's decisions regarding what to produce and what methods of production to use.

Technical knowledge is knowledge of the possible combinations of the productive services and output associated therewith. This knowledge is summarized in the production function.

Product demand to the individual firm appears as a continuous series of possible price–quantity combinations, the character of which depends on the firm's market position. It is not price as it appears in the market (presently or at time of sales) but the entrepreneur's price expectation at planning (choice) time that represents the production determining force. The student should

---

[2]For students of finance, we should note that profit maximization is a special case of wealth maximization. Profit maximization abstracts from several complicating features of wealth maximization, for example, tax considerations and depreciation of durable inputs. (Recall we are limiting ourselves to monoperiodic production.) We do not argue that profit maximization is the most likely goal of most firms. In fact, we are inclined to favor a goal of maximization of expected net present utility to the decision maker cast in a polyperiodic and uncertainty framework. However, a serious attempt to formally develop a theory of the firm along these lines is beyond the scope of this text.

[3]An additionally complicating factor concerning the concept of rationality is that it also has a "level of aggregation" dimension. Note that we define rationality in the context of an individual economic actor or decision maker. What is optimal for an individual (rational action) may not be optimal in some larger societal context. For example, if a decision maker's action imposes uncompensated costs on others, then what is rational behavior on the part of the decision maker may be nonoptimal from society's viewpoint (e.g., pollution). Nevertheless, an economist would call the observed (decision maker) behavior rational.

note that at this point no assumption concerning the nature of the firm's product market (market power) has been made other than that price is a function of output. From time to time (in fact, frequently) the assumption that price is constant will be used to simplify the analysis.

Factor supply appears to the individual firm as a continuous series of price–quantity combinations. Again, it is not price actually prevailing at any particular date, but the entrepreneur's anticipation that represents the production determining force.

Upon completion of this book the student should realize that perfect competition in product and factor markets is merely a special case of imperfect competition and that the *general* optimizing conditions are the same. That is, if we state optimizing conditions and adopt terms descriptive of the general case, then all special market cases will be covered.

The firm's *supply situation regarding capital funds* represents the fourth force. We will most often assume that funds available for purchase of variable factors are unlimited to the firm; that is, the firm is not constrained to a level of factor usage and output less than that implied by the unconstrained solution. Thus, this production determining force is not given major attention in this book. However, the student is cautioned to remember that it is nevertheless a force to be reckoned with—certainly your professor of finance will not want you to disregard it.

One of the aims of this book is to impress upon the student of production economics the need to be aware that more than one force is at work when considering a truly general theory of the firm. Too often we are tempted to overgeneralize the result of some special case that was deduced by assuming away one or more of the production determining forces. Most often this is seen when concepts, terminology, and assertions appropriate only to the perfectly competitive case are used in a more general context, or when firm-level postulated supply and demand model specifications are inconsistent with reasonably well-behaved production functions.

A final justification for emphasizing the product demand and input supply forces and concepts (i.e., deriving and discussing optimality conditions first in terms of the general or imperfectly competitive case and only subsequently in terms of the special or perfectly competitive case) is that production economics has macro as well as micro implications and application. Often economists are called upon to provide positive analyses of the economic consequences of public policy on economic sectors (industries), regions and/or society as a whole. While we would be clearly remiss to imply that aggregate analysis is a mere straightforward extension of an imperfectly competitive firm-level model, it is clear that for many aggregate analyses to assume that product and factor prices are unaffected in the aggregate for a perfectly competitive industry is often inappropriate. Accordingly, the student with interests in economic policy will find it advantageous to become conversant with the concepts and terminology of the imperfectly competitive case and with thinking in terms of several forces (technical and economic) interacting simultaneously.

1.5 SELECTED BIBLIOGRAPHY

Carlson, S. *A Study on the Pure Theory of Production*. New York: Sentry Press, 1965. This is a classic textbook on production economics that was first published in 1939. Chapter 1 provides a good introduction to the general theory of the firm.

Chiang, A. C. *Fundamental Methods of Mathematical Economics*. New York: McGraw-Hill, 1974. The first 12 chapters of this book provide an excellent mathematical background for the material covered in this book.

Heady, E. O. *Economics of Agricultural Production and Resource Use*. New York: Prentice-Hall, 1952. This book is usually referred to as the "Bible" of agricultural production economics; the book is credited with bringing neoclassical microeconomic theory to bear on agricultural production problems. Although the book is now dated, the introductory chapter should be read and the remainder of the book scanned. The book is particularly rich in empirical examples.

CHAPTER 2

TECHNICAL ASPECTS OF PRODUCTION: THE PRODUCTIVITY FUNCTIONS

This chapter explores in considerable detail the production economist's abstract representation of a production process or technical force which was alluded to in Section 1.4. All production choices and economic decision rules are conditional on the underlying physical properties of the production process. That is, there are certain physical input–input, input–output, and output–output transformations that may not be altered in a given decision framework.

It is convenient to assume that the entrepreneur's technical knowledge and realities of the production process are embodied in the production function. The purpose of this chapter is to identify and examine those characteristics or properties that are typical of production processes and that are convenient pedagogical devices for economic analysis.

Accordingly, things economic, like prices, budgets, value, and cost, will be introduced in later chapters. The focus here is exclusively on physical relationships and properties from both an algebraic and geometric perspective, with the aim of gaining a mental image and intuitive feel for how technical considerations impinge on economic choices of producers. We begin with the single-variable factor case, then move to the two-factor model, and finally extend the ideas and concepts to an s-variable factor framework.

2.1 ONE PRODUCT, ONE-VARIABLE FACTOR RELATIONSHIPS

It is assumed that the technical relationship between a variable factor of production and output can be represented by a *production function*, which is mathematically expressed as

$$y = f(x_1|x_2) \qquad (2.1)$$

where y denotes output, x_1 is the variable factor of production (input) and x_2 is a (the) fixed factor, and f is a function. To simplify notation, output for a fixed production period and a given plant with only a single-variable factor is represented by

$$y = f(x) \qquad (2.2)$$

The fixed factor, x_2, is assumed but, for notational convenience, is not written down. Since output is measured in physical rather than pecuniary terms, y is also referred to as *total physical product* (*TPP*).

Another important physical concept is *average physical product* (*APP*), defined as

$$APP \equiv \frac{y}{x} \equiv \frac{f(x)}{x} \tag{2.3}$$

A third and most important physical concept is *marginal physical productivity* (*MPP*). *MPP* is defined as

$$MPP \equiv \frac{d(TPP)}{dx} \equiv \frac{dy}{dx} \equiv \frac{df(x)}{dx} \equiv f'(x) \tag{2.4}$$

The marginal productivity function gives the exact rate of change of the total product function for an infinitesimal change in the factor. That is, marginal productivity is the slope of the total product function evaluated at a particular level of the variable factor.

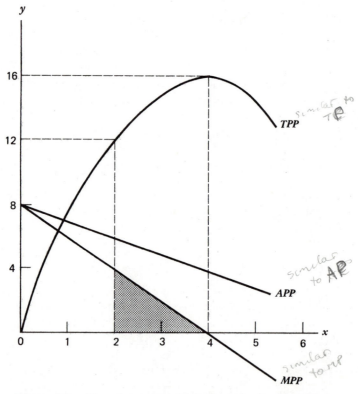

Figure 2.1. Plot of the productivity functions for the production function, $y = 8x - x^2$.

Although much of our economic literature uses the terms marginal product and marginal productivity interchangeably, it is important to distinguish between these terms to avoid ambiguity. *Marginal productivity* (*MPP*) is defined as $MPP \equiv df(x)/dx \equiv f'(x)$, whereas *marginal product* (*MP*) is defined as $MP \equiv dy$ or $MP \equiv \Delta y$, depending on whether the change in x is arbitrarily small or lumpy. The relationship between marginal productivity, $f'(x)$, and marginal product, dy, is given by the total differential,

$$dy = f'(x)\, dx \qquad (2.5)$$

where dx can take on any specified value as long as it is sufficiently small to be in the neighborhood of zero (but not equal to zero). Thus, marginal product is given by the product of marginal productivity and dx. In the case of a lumpy change in x, Δx, marginal productivity times Δx, $f'(x)\,\Delta x$, approximates Δy; marginal product in the lumpy case is exactly given by $\Delta y = y^1 - y^0 = f(x^1) - f(x^0)$ for the change $\Delta x = x^1 - x^0$.

As a specific example of the concepts discussed thus far, consider the production function,

$$TPP \equiv y = 8x - x^2 \qquad (2.6)$$

The average physical product function is

$$APP = 8 - x \qquad (2.7)$$

and the marginal physical productivity function is

$$MPP \equiv \frac{dy}{dx} = 8 - 2x \qquad (2.8)$$

The above productivity functions are graphically illustrated in Figure 2.1.[1]

Given production function (2.6), let us consider a lumpy change in x from $x = 2$ to $x = 4$ ($\Delta x = 4 - 2 = 2$). The marginal product from this two-unit change in x can be calculated in two ways. One way is to compute the difference in total physical product for the two input levels:

$$MP = \Delta y = TPP_{(x=4)} - TPP_{(x=2)}$$
$$= [8 \cdot 4 - (4)^2] - [8 \cdot 2 - (2)^2] = 16 - 12 = 4 \qquad (2.9)$$

---

[1]Mathematical purists will object to our plotting of *TPP*, *APP*, and *MPP* on a single vertical axis since they represent different units. *TPP* is a quantity, *APP* is an average quantity, and *MPP* is a *rate of change*. Nevertheless, we think that it is instructive to evaluate all three functions on the same axes.

which is the difference in *TPP* in Figure 2.1. The second way to compute the change in *TPP* is to integrate marginal productivity over the range $x = 2$ to $x = 4$:

$$MP = \Delta y = \int_2^4 MPP \, dx = \int_2^4 (8 - 2x) \, dx$$

$$= \int_2^4 8 \, dx - \int_2^4 2x \, dx = 8x\big|_2^4 - x^2\big|_2^4$$

$$= (32 - 16) - (4^2 - (2)^2) = 4 \tag{2.10}$$

which is the shaded area in Figure 2.1.

Both procedures, (2.9) and (2.10), give us an exact measure of marginal product associated with a two-unit change in x. Note that the marginal product from this change can be *approximated* by the product of Δx and marginal productivity evaluated at a particular value of x between 2 and 4. For example, at $x = 3$, the midpoint of the incremental change in x,

$$MP \simeq MPP_{(x=3)} \, \Delta x = 2 \cdot 2 = 4 \tag{2.11}$$

In this case, the approximation is exact because the *MPP* curve is linear, and we evaluated *MPP* at the midpoint.

2.1.a Elasticity of Production

A fourth physical concept encountered in production economics is that of elasticity of production. Typically there are two physical elasticity concepts found in production economics literature—factor elasticity (partial elasticity of production) and the function coefficient (total elasticity of production). In this section we limit our discussion to factor elasticity. Factor elasticity is concerned with changes as only *one* factor is varied and all others are held constant, whereas the function coefficient (total elasticity of production) deals with the case where *all* factors are varied in fixed proportions.

The *factor elasticity*, *E*, for our single-variable-input production function, $f(x)$, is defined as

$$E \equiv \frac{\% \text{ change in output}}{\% \text{ change in input}} \equiv \frac{dy/y}{dx/x} = \frac{dy}{dx}\frac{x}{y}$$

$$= MPP \frac{1}{APP} = \frac{MPP}{APP} \tag{2.12}$$

E is a measure of the percentage change in output in response to an infinitesimal percentage change in a factor given that all other factors are held fixed. If *E* is greater than one, an increase in the input level will result in a more than proportionate increase in output; for $E < 1$ the proportionate increase in output is less than that of input; and for $E = 1$ the proportionate

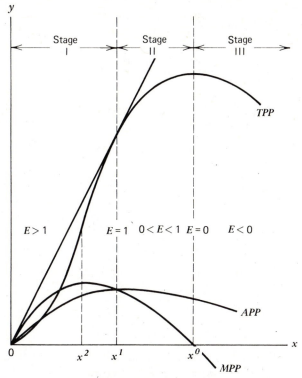

Figure 2.2. Classical three-stage textbook production function and marginal and average curves—single factor variation.

increases are equal. In the single-variable factor case, we have only one such elasticity as indeed we are assuming all but one factor fixed.

2.1.b Geometry of the Technical Functions

To illustrate the geometry of the various technical functions, consider the classical three-stage textbook case shown in Figure 2.2. The three *stages of production* are noted as Stage I, Stage II, and Stage III. The rightmost vertical dashed line (x^0) is the boundary between Stages II and III. The locus of x^0 is associated with maximum *TPP*, which occurs when *MPP* = 0; that is,

$$\frac{d\,TPP}{dx} \equiv MPP = 0 \qquad (2.13)$$

To ensure that (2.13) is associated with a maximum rather than a minimum, we must determine if the *TPP* function is strictly concave[2] in the neighborhood

---

[2]Readers who are not familiar with the concept of concavity should read Section 2.4 before completing this section.

of the x for which $MPP = 0$. The easiest way to check for concavity is to apply the second derivative test: TPP is concave if

$$\frac{d^2TPP}{dx^2} \equiv \frac{d\,MPP}{dx} \leq 0 \qquad (2.14)$$

If (2.14) holds with strict inequality (i.e., $<$, rather than $\leq$), the TPP function is strictly concave; that is, TPP is increasing at a decreasing rate, or decreasing at an increasing rate, as x increases in the neighborhood of the solution to $MPP = 0$.[3]

In Figure 2.2, x^2 indicates the x level for which marginal productivity is maximum. This occurs when

$$\frac{d\,MPP}{dx} = 0 \qquad (2.15)$$

and

$$\frac{d^2MPP}{dx^2} < 0 \qquad (2.16)$$

The phenomenon described by conditions (2.13) through (2.16) is that of the *law of diminishing marginal returns*, which unfortunately is commonly referred to simply as the *law of diminishing returns*. The modifying adjective, *marginal*, is essential to avoid ambiguity because we note that APP does not everywhere decline when MPP declines.

Notice that when MPP is a maximum, TPP has an inflection point. The inflection point occurs where TPP changes from increasing at an increasing rate to increasing at a decreasing rate; that is, the second derivative of TPP with respect to x is zero at x^2. This is expected since

$$\frac{d^2TPP}{dx^2} \equiv \frac{d\,MPP}{dx} \qquad (2.17)$$

and since $d\,MPP/dx = 0$ at maximum MPP.

Stages I and II are delineated by the point where average product is a maximum—at x^I; that is,

$$\frac{d\,APP}{dx} = 0 \qquad (2.18)$$

---

[3]Years ago, one of the authors had an instructor in a first calculus course who had a clever way to remember the sign on the second derivative test. If one were caught in a rainstorm and had two cups, one sitting upright and one upside down, which would catch a *positive* quantity of water?

and

$$\frac{d^2 APP}{dx^2} < 0 \tag{2.19}$$

Note that at x^1, *APP* and *MPP* are equal. Recall that marginal productivity is the slope of tangent lines along the production function. The slope of the tangent line depicted in Figure 2.2 is not only a measure of *MPP* but, *because* it happens to pass through the origin, it also is a measure of the average product at x^1. Furthermore, we know that *APP* must be maximum at this point because the ray line (a straight line passing through the origin) depicted in Figure 2.2 has the greatest possible slope of all possible ray lines intersecting (or tangent to) *TPP*.

Consider further the relationship of *MPP* to *APP*—again referring to Figure 2.2. *MPP* is greater than (lies above) *APP* until APP attains its maximum value; *MPP* equals *APP* when *APP* is maximum; and *MPP* is less than (lies below) *APP* beyond the point where *APP* is maximum. This can be explained as follows. As we increase *x* moving from the origin, *MPP* is increasing and each additional unit of *x* adds proportionally more to *TPP* and thus *APP* is increasing. But because the intramarginal units[4] as well as the marginal unit are included in the calculation of *APP*, *MPP* will lie above *APP*. (*APP*, by definition, is the sum of successive marginal products divided by *x*.) Then, as we move beyond the point where *MPP* is maximum, *APP* does not immediately begin to decline because of the intramarginal units included in *APP*. Finally at some point, *MPP* and *APP* are just balanced, after which continued declining *MPP* pulls *APP* down.

A formal proof of the above assertion follows. We know that the following identities hold between *MPP*, *TPP*, and *APP*:

$$MPP \equiv \frac{d\ TPP}{dx} = \frac{d(x\ APP)}{dx} \tag{2.20}$$

Applying the product rule for differentiation, we obtain

$$MPP = APP + x\frac{d\ APP}{dx} \tag{2.21}$$

---

[4]Intramarginal units refer to the marginal product associated with units of *x* to the left of the value of *x* under consideration.

So, assuming second-order condition (2.19) is satisfied, we find that

$$\frac{d\,APP}{dx} > 0 \Rightarrow MPP > APP$$

$$\frac{d\,APP}{dx} = 0 \Rightarrow MPP = APP \qquad (2.22)$$

$$\frac{d\,APP}{dx} < 0 \Rightarrow MPP < APP$$

(The symbol $\Rightarrow$ is read *implies*.) An alternative approach to proving the relationship between *APP* and *MPP*, which we will leave to the reader, is to use the quotient rule for derivatives to examine

$$\frac{d\,APP}{dx} = \frac{d(TPP/x)}{dx} \qquad (2.23)$$

To prove the factor elasticity relationships shown in Figure 2.2, recall (2.12) which establishes that $E = MPP/APP$. Translating the relationships in (2.22) and knowledge about *MPP* into elasticity terms, it must be that

$E > 1$ when $MPP > APP$

$E = 1$ when *APP* is maximum ($MPP = APP$)

$E < 1$ when $MPP < APP$ (2.24)

$E = 0$ when *TPP* is maximum ($MPP = 0$)

$E < 0$ when $MPP < 0$

Thus, the magnitude of the factor elasticity can be used to delineate the various technical stages of production. That is, $E > 1$ in Stage I, $0 < E < 1$ in Stage II, and $E < 0$ in Stage III. We will find this property especially useful in considering stages of production, symmetry of stages, and the economic region of production for the two-variable factor model.

2.2 ONE PRODUCT, TWO-VARIABLE FACTOR RELATIONSHIPS

For the case of two-variable factors, we denote the production function by

$$y = f(x_1, x_2) \qquad (2.25)$$

where y is the quantity of output and x_1 and x_2 are factors of production. That is, we presume that there are only two factors, one or both of which may be varied and either or neither of which may be considered fixed.

One of the pedagogical advantages of the two-factor model is that the ambiguity between long run and short run is reduced compared to production models with many factors. Recall from Chapter 1 that for an n-factor model it is possible to have many different short-run situations by merely specifying alternative factors as fixed. However, for the two-factor model there are only two possible short-run cases in addition to the usual single long-run situation. That is, the short-run options for (2.25) are limited to

$$y = f(x_1|x_2) \text{ and } y = f(x_2|x_1) \tag{2.26}$$

We should note that the two-factor production function model is commonly assumed in economic literature. Often x_1 is taken to represent capital and x_2 to represent labor, and it is assumed that all possible production inputs can be "captured" in the generic terms, capital and labor. Accordingly, the reader will find that a thorough understanding of the two-factor model will be invaluable in reading and interpreting both the theoretical and applied literature of economics. In Section 2.3 we extend and generalize ideas and concepts of the two-factor model to n dimensions.

An example of a two-factor production function is illustrated in the three-dimensional representations in Figure 2.3. Readers who are not familiar with three-dimensional diagrams may find it easier to visualize the production surface as a smooth mountain. The x_1 and x_2 axes can be thought of as valleys, with the origin of the graph represented by the intersection of the valleys. Output can be viewed as altitude. Suppose we are in valley x_2 and hike up the surface, moving parallel to valley x_1. As our altitude increases, we are moving along a single-factor production function like that illustrated by the line where x_2 is held constant at x_2^0 in Figure 2.3b. As we begin our climb, altitude may (although it need not) increase at an increasing rate, then increase at a decreasing rate. Finally, we reach the point where altitude begins to decrease (Stage III), which is not shown in Figure 2.3b, but which can be seen in Figure 2.3a.

If we begin our hike at the origin, moving in a straight line but *not* parallel to either valley, increases in altitude show the effects of varying both factors, x_1 and x_2, in fixed proportions (Figure 2.3c). This concept is discussed in Section 2.2.h. If we walk around the mountain without changing altitude, we are tracing out an isoquant or constant-output curve (Figure 2.3d). This concept is discussed in the next section.

Average and marginal productivity concepts associated with two-factor production functions are similar to the one-factor case, because as we vary one factor, the other variable factor is held constant. Thus, the average product functions are

$$APP_1 \equiv \frac{y}{x_1} \equiv \frac{f(x_1,x_2)}{x_1} \tag{2.27}$$

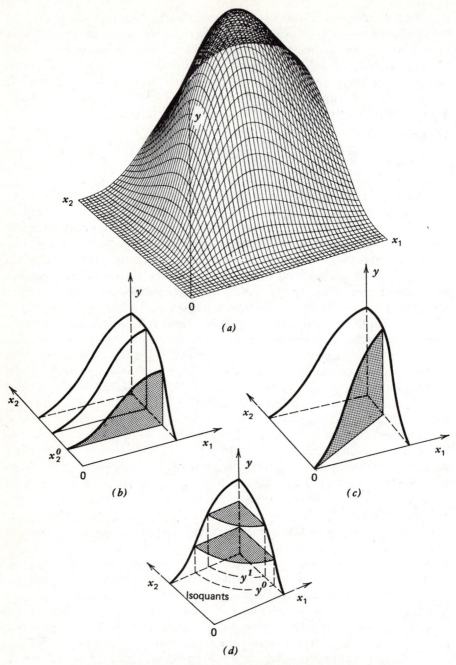

Figure 2.3. An illustration of a production function for two variable factors. (*a*) Three-dimensional representation. (*b*) Single-factor variation slice. (*c*) Proportional-factor variation slice. (*d*) Output-constant slice.

and

$$APP_2 \equiv \frac{y}{x_2} \equiv \frac{f(x_1,x_2)}{x_2} \tag{2.28}$$

and the marginal productivity functions are

$$MPP_1 \equiv \frac{\partial TPP}{\partial x_1} \equiv \frac{\partial y}{\partial x_1} \equiv \frac{\partial f(x_1,x_2)}{\partial x_1} \equiv f_1 \tag{2.29}$$

and

$$MPP_2 \equiv \frac{\partial TPP}{\partial x_2} \equiv \frac{\partial y}{\partial x_2} \equiv \frac{\partial f(x_1,x_2)}{\partial x_2} \equiv f_2 \tag{2.30}$$

Note that equations 2.29 and 2.30 are based on partial derivatives (denoted by backward sixes) and not total derivatives. In (2.30), MPP_2 is defined as $\partial y/\partial x_2$ which means that we take the derivative of $f(x_1,x_2)$ holding x_1 constant. All of the expressions in (2.29) and (2.30) are alternative ways of representing the marginal productivity of x_1 and x_2, respectively. The shorthand notation, f_1 and f_2, is especially convenient and widely used.

    If we allow both x_1 and x_2 to vary by arbitrary (but arbitrarily small) amounts dx_1 and dx_2, then the change in output is given by the total differential,

$$dy = f_1\,dx_1 + f_2\,dx_2 \tag{2.31}$$

where, again, f_1 and f_2 are the marginal productivities of x_1 and x_2, respectively. As in the single-variable factor case, dy is the *marginal product*, but in this case it is associated with changes dx_1 and dx_2. However, when there is more than one variable factor, the "total" marginal product is the sum of marginal products attributable to each of the factors individually, that is, $f_1\,dx_1$ and $f_2\,dx_2$. To graphically illustrate these concepts, consider lumpy changes Δx_1 and Δx_2. Then $\Delta y_1 \simeq f_1\,\Delta x_1$ (marginal product due to changing x_1, holding x_2 constant) and $\Delta y_2 \simeq f_2\,\Delta x_2$ (marginal product due to x_2, holding x_1 constant). Suppose you are at some point on the production surface and wish to move to another point further up the hill, say from point A to C in Figure 2.4. The total change in altitude ("total" marginal product) is given by Δy which for the stout-hearted mountain climber is most directly attained along the dashed line directly from A to C. There are, of course, many routes from A to C. In particular we are interested in a geometric mental image of (2.31). Consider stepping off first parallel to the x_1 axis; that is, let's climb heading due east (holding x_2 constant). Our gain in altitude, Δy_1, is the marginal product attributable to changing x_1 by Δx_1. We are now at point B. Now turn 90° to the north and climb to C holding x_1 constant (parallel to the x_2

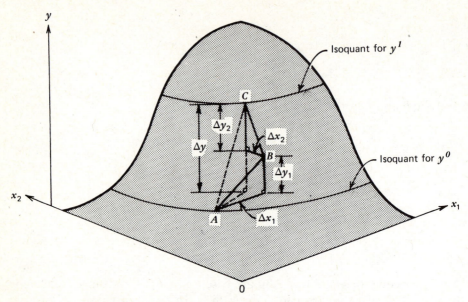

Figure 2.4. A three-dimensional graph showing marginal product when both factors are varied.

axis). Our gain in altitude from this maneuver is Δy_2. The sum of Δy_1 and Δy_2 equals Δy. Letting Δx_1 and Δx_2 approach arbitrarily small values results in dy, as shown in equation 2.31.

MPP_i and APP_i are usually, although not necessarily, functions of both factors. That is, the marginal productivity and the average product of a factor depend not only upon the usage level of the factor in question, but also upon the level of the other factor as well. Let us consider some specific examples, using some common mathematical specifications for production functions. In the examples, and throughout the book, the convention is adopted that parameters carry their own sign. While a particular sign is often required for a function to exhibit desirable properties, in principle, the parameters, A, a_1, a_2, b_1, b_2, and so on can be positive, negative, or zero.

Example 2.1   For the linear production function,

$$y = b_1 x_1 + b_2 x_2 \qquad (2.32)$$

we have

$$MPP_1 = b_1 \qquad (2.33)$$

and

$$MPP_2 = b_2 \qquad (2.34)$$

Obviously the linear model leaves something to be desired for most production problems, since the marginal productivities are constant.

Example 2.2   For the quadratic production function,[5]

$$y = a_1x_1 + a_2x_2 + \tfrac{1}{2}b_1x_1^2 + \tfrac{1}{2}b_2x_2^2 + b_3x_1x_2 \tag{2.35}$$

we have

$$MPP_1 = a_1 + b_1x_1 + b_3x_2 \tag{2.36}$$

and

$$MPP_2 = a_2 + b_2x_2 + b_3x_1 \tag{2.37}$$

Note that MPP_1 (MPP_2) would not be a function of x_2 (x_1) if the interaction term were deleted from (2.35), in other words, if $b_3 = 0$.

Example 2.3   With a generalized Cobb–Douglas production function,

$$y = Ax_1^{b_1}x_2^{b_2} \tag{2.38}$$

we have

$$MPP_1 = Ab_1x_1^{b_1-1}x_2^{b_2} \tag{2.39}$$

and

$$MPP_2 = Ab_2x_1^{b_1}x_2^{b_2-1} \tag{2.40}$$

It is often convenient to express (2.39) and (2.40) in terms of y. Rewriting (2.39) we get

$$MPP_1 = \frac{b_1Ax_1^{b_1}x_2^{b_2}}{x_1} = \frac{b_1y}{x_1} \tag{2.41}$$

Similarly,

$$MPP_2 = \frac{b_2y}{x_2} \tag{2.42}$$

---

[5]The parameters b_1 and b_2 in (2.35) are multiplied by $\tfrac{1}{2}$ to simplify terms of the derivatives of the function as in (2.36) and (2.37).

Example 2.4 Consider the transcendental production function,

$$y = Ax_1^{a_1}e^{b_1x_1}x_2^{a_2}e^{b_2x_2} \tag{2.43}$$

So,

$$
\begin{aligned}
MPP_1 = {} & Aa_1x_1^{a_1-1}e^{b_1x_1}x_2^{a_2}e^{b_2x_2} \\
& + Ab_1x_1^{a_1}e^{b_1x_1}x_2^{a_2}e^{b_2x_2}
\end{aligned} \tag{2.44}
$$

which can be simplified to

$$MPP_1 = y(b_1 + a_1x_1^{-1}) \tag{2.45}$$

Similarly,

$$MPP_2 = y(b_2 + a_2x_2^{-1}) \tag{2.46}$$

Example 2.5 Consider the constant elasticity of substitution (CES) production function,

$$y = A[bx_1^{-g} + (1 - b)x_2^{-g}]^{-(v/g)} \tag{2.47}$$

where v is a homogeneity parameter (see Section 2.2.i). Thus,

$$MPP_1 = \left(-\frac{v}{g}\right)A[bx_1^{-g} + (1 - b)x_2^{-g}]^{-(v/g)-1}(-gbx_1^{-g-1}) \tag{2.48}$$

which simplifies to (see Henderson and Quandt for $v = 1$, p. 112)

$$MPP_1 = bvA^{-g/v}y^{(v+g)/v}x_1^{-(g+1)} \tag{2.49}$$

Similarly,

$$MPP_2 = (1 - b)vA^{-g/v}y^{(v+g)/v}x_2^{-(g+1)} \tag{2.50}$$

2.2.a Isoquants

An *isoquant* or production indifference curve is a curve that combines all factor combinations which give the same output. The equation of an isoquant is given by the production function when output is held constant. The usual way of expressing the isoquant equation is

$$x_2 = f^{-1}(x_1, y) \tag{2.51}$$

where f^{-1} denotes the mathematical operation (inverse function) required to express the production function in terms of x_2 as a function of x_1 and y.

Example 2.6 An isoquant for a Cobb–Douglas production function is obtained by solving (2.38) for x_2:

$$x_2 = A^{(-1/b_2)} x_1^{(-b_1/b_2)} y^{(1/b_2)} \qquad (2.52)$$

For a given value of y, say y^0, and given parameter values, we can plug various values of x_1 into (2.52) and find associated x_2 values, thereby finding points on the y^0 isoquant.

Plotting isoquants is a convenient method for compressing three dimensions into two. To see this, refer back to Figure 2.3*d*, then to Figure 2.5. Recall that a particular isoquant is traced out by walking around the mountain, without changing altitude.

A family of isoquants is given by a particular production function (Figure 2.5)—we merely need to change the value of y to obtain another isoquant. Also note that the family of isoquants can be expressed as x_2 as a function of x_1 and y, or by expressing x_1 as a function of x_2 and y. We adopt the convention, $x_2 = f^{-1}(x_1,y)$, as we prefer to plot x_1 on the horizontal axis and x_2 on the vertical.

2.2.b Rate of Technical Substitution

The slope of the tangent line to a point on an isoquant is the rate at which one factor must be substituted for the other factor in order to maintain the same output level. The negative of the slope of the isoquant is defined as the

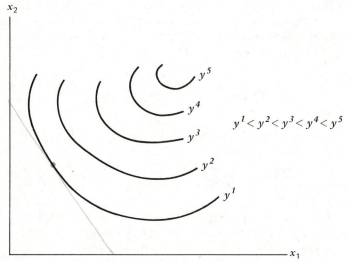

Figure 2.5. A family of isoquants.

rate of technical substitution (RTS). For the family of isoquants expressed by $x_2 = f^{-1}(x_1, y)$,

$$RTS_{12} \equiv - \frac{dx_2}{dx_1} \tag{2.53}$$

where y is held constant. (RTS_{12} is read as the rate of technical substitution of factor one for factor two.)

To derive RTS, consider the total differential of the production function:

$$dy = f_1 \, dx_1 + f_2 \, dx_2 \tag{2.54}$$

Since the change in output, dy, is zero along an isoquant, we have

$$0 = f_1 \, dx_1 + f_2 \, dx_2 \tag{2.55}$$

Therefore, the slope of the isoquant is

$$\frac{dx_2}{dx_1} = - \frac{f_1}{f_2} \tag{2.56}$$

which is the negative of the ratio of marginal productivities. The rate of technical substitution is generally stated in positive terms, so

$$RTS_{12} \equiv - \frac{dx_2}{dx_1} = \frac{f_1}{f_2} \tag{2.57}$$

An example of RTS_{12} is shown in Figure 2.6.

The nature of the rate of change of the slope of the isoquant, d^2x_2/dx_1^2, establishes the convexity or lack thereof of the isoquants. To express this second derivative in terms of partial derivatives of the production function, consider the total differential of (2.56):

$$d(dx_2/dx_1) = \frac{\partial(-f_1/f_2)}{\partial x_1} \, dx_1 + \frac{\partial(-f_1/f_2)}{\partial x_2} \, dx_2 \tag{2.58}$$

Dividing both sides of (2.58) by dx_1, we have

$$\frac{d(dx_2/dx_1)}{dx_1} \equiv \frac{d^2x_2}{dx_1^2} = \frac{\partial(-f_1/f_2)}{\partial x_1} + \frac{\partial(-f_1/f_2)}{\partial x_2} \frac{dx_2}{dx_1} \tag{2.59}$$

Since we wish to hold y constant, (2.56) must be substituted for the last term in (2.59); making this substitution and using the quotient rule for partial derivatives gives

$$\frac{d^2x_2}{dx_1^2} = -\frac{f_2 f_{11} - f_1 f_{21}}{f_2^2} - \frac{f_2 f_{12} - f_1 f_{22}}{f_2^2}\left(-\frac{f_1}{f_2}\right),$$

$$= \frac{-f_2 f_{11} + f_1 f_{21}}{f_2^2} + \frac{f_1 f_2 f_{12} - f_1^2 f_{22}}{f_2^3}$$

$$= \frac{-f_2^2 f_{11} + f_1 f_2 f_{21} + f_1 f_2 f_{12} - f_1^2 f_{22}}{f_2^3} \tag{2.60}$$

where f_{11}, f_{22}, f_{12}, and f_{21} are second-order partial derivatives of the production function. For example, f_{12} is the rate of change of f_1 as x_2 is varied, in other words, the rate of change of MPP_1, in response to a change in x_2.

From Young's theorem, we know that a cross-partial derivative is invariant with respect to the order of differentiation; therefore, $f_{12} = f_{21}$ and (2.60) can be simplified to

$$\frac{d^2x_2}{dx_1^2} = \frac{-f_2^2 f_{11} + 2f_1 f_2 f_{12} - f_1^2 f_{22}}{f_2^3} \tag{2.61}$$

If the isoquants are to be convex toward the horizontal axis (or origin) in the region of positive marginal productivity, the sign of (2.61) must be positive. Given $f_2 > 0$, the numerator of (2.61) must be positive for (2.61) to be positive; a positive sign on the numerator of (2.61) is the condition for quasi-concavity of $f(x_1, x_2)$ (see Section 2.4). Before interpreting (2.61) and (2.56) in terms of alternative isoquant patterns, we note that the evaluation (signing) of (2.61)

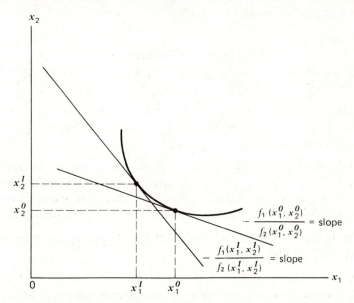

Figure 2.6.   Slope of an isoquant (slope of tangent line) is negative of RTS_{12}.

is not always an easy task. Fortunately, for some functions, there is an easier way to consider the slope and convexity of the isoquants.

Note that for the two-factor case,

$$\frac{dx_2}{dx_1}\bigg|\, dy = 0 \equiv \frac{\partial x_2}{\partial x_1} \tag{2.62}$$

and

$$\frac{d^2 x_2}{dx_1^2}\bigg|\, dy = 0 \equiv \frac{\partial^2 x_2}{\partial x_1^2} \tag{2.63}$$

That is, dx_2/dx_1 and d^2x_2/dx_1^2 *given* the side condition that y is held constant (i.e., dy set equal to zero) is mathematically equivalent to taking the corresponding partial derivatives of the isoquant equation (2.51). For some production functions, reexpressing $y = f(x_1,x_2)$ as $x_2 = f^{-1}(x_1,y)$ is an easy task. In such cases, it is likely easier to obtain and sign $\partial x_2/\partial x_1$ and $\partial^2 x_2/\partial x_1^2$ than to determine and sign all the first- and second-order partial derivatives in (2.56) and (2.61), thereby simplifying the determination of slope and convexity considerably.[6]

The reader is encouraged to determine the slope and the convexity of the isoquants for the generalized Cobb–Douglas production function (2.38) using each of these two ways to see that the results are the same; that is, (a) calculate dx_2/dx_1 by (2.56) and d^2x_2/dx_1^2 by (2.61) and (b) calculate $\partial x_2/\partial x_1$ and $\partial^2 x_2/\partial x_1^2$ using (2.52), the isoquant equation.

2.2.c Isoquant Patterns

Given the slope of the isoquant and its rate of change, the nature of the isoquant pattern can be deduced.

Case I If $dx_2/dx_1 < 0$ and $d^2x_2/dx_1^2 > 0$, the isoquants are negatively sloped and convex to the origin. This is a case of *imperfect factor substitutability* (see Figure 2.7a).

Case II If $dx_2/dx_1 < 0$ and $d^2x_2/dx_1^2 = 0$, the isoquants are straight lines and the production process is characterized by *perfect factor substitutability* (see Figure 2.7b). In this case, isoquants are not necessarily parallel, but they cannot intersect in the positive quadrant.

Case III If $dx_2/dx_1 < 0$ and $d^2x_2/dx_1^2 < 0$, the isoquants are concave to the origin (see Figure 2.7c).

---

[6]The enterprising student may be tempted to try an even simpler procedure using (2.56) to get the slope and then using (2.63) to examine convexity. Don't do it—trouble! Note that (2.56) is a function of x_1 *and* x_2. To take the partial of (2.56) with respect to x_1 and call it $\partial^2 x_2/\partial x_1^2$ is inappropriate because y is not formally held constant—in fact, it does not appear in (2.56)—and x_2 appears on the right-hand side of (2.56).

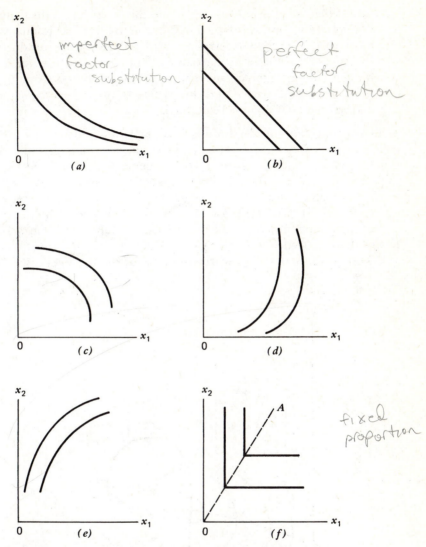

Figure 2.7. Some alternative isoquant patterns. (a) Case I. (b) Case II. (c) Case III. (d) Case IV. (e) Case V. (f) Case VI.

Case IV If $dx_2/dx_1 > 0$ and $d^2x_2/dx_1^2 > 0$, the isoquants are positively sloped and convex with respect to the x_1 axis (see Figure 2.7d).

Case V If $dx_2/dx_1 > 0$ and $d^2x_2/dx_1^2 < 0$, the isoquants are positively sloped and convex to the x_2 axis (see Figure 2.7e).

Case VI When the inputs must always be combined in fixed proportions, there is *no factor substitutability* (Figure 2.7f). The only factor combinations that are relevant lie on the ray line $0A$; the marginal productivity of x_1 below $0A$ is zero and the marginal productivity of x_2 above $0A$ is zero. A production function that exhibits isoquants of this type is commonly referred to as a fixed proportion production function or a Leontief production function. Note that the isoquants for this case are not consistent with our assumption of continuous first- and second-partial derivatives; that is, notice that dx_2/dx_1 and d^2x_2/dx_1^2 are not everywhere defined.

A single production surface showing Cases I, III, IV, and V is given in Figure 2.8. In the remainder of this text, we will be concerned largely with negatively sloped, convex isoquants (Case I). For the general case shown in Figure 2.8, the other areas (Cases III, IV, and V) are not relevant for economic analysis because the same output can be produced with a lesser amount of at least one factor. If Case II, Case III, Case IV, or Case V holds *for all* values of x_1 and x_2, economic optimization results in a corner solution (Section 3.4), which means that we need consider only one of the factors since the optimal level of the other is zero. Finally, the case of no factor substitution (Case VI) is best

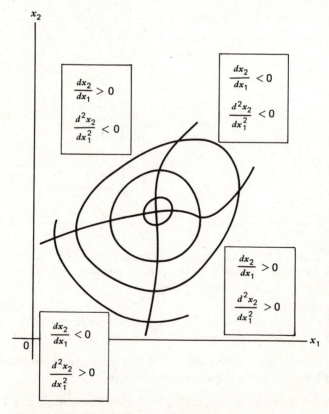

Figure 2.8. A production surface showing areas of positively and negatively sloped isoquants.

analyzed with linear programming techniques (see, e.g., Henderson and Quandt, Section 5.7) rather than the calculus techniques used in this text. Again, most subsequent discussion will focus on the negatively sloped, convex, and smoothly curved (i.e., continuous first-derivative) portions of the isoquants.

Economists' use of the term, factor substitutability, to refer to isoquant patterns is a bit unfortunate because it often conveys the wrong message to physical scientists. For example, we usually find imperfect factor substitutability between nitrogen and phosphorus fertilizer in corn production. However, this does not mean that nitrogen and phosphorus "substitute" for each other in a chemical sense; it only means that isoquants are convex to the origin. In this case the convexity of isoquants results from some type of biochemical *interaction* of the factors and not from factor substitution as such. The moral of this is to carefully define terminology to avoid alienating your physical scientist friends—some of whom you may one day wish to call upon for data.

2.2.d Elasticity of Factor Substitution

The elasticity of factor substitution, σ, is defined as the proportionate rate of change of the input ratio divided by the proportionate rate of change in RTS:

$$\sigma \equiv \frac{d(x_2/x_1)}{(x_2/x_1)} \bigg/ \frac{d(f_1/f_2)}{(f_1/f_2)}$$

$$= \frac{(f_1/f_2)}{(x_2/x_1)} \cdot \frac{d(x_2/x_1)}{d(f_1/f_2)} \tag{2.64}$$

The value of σ lies between zero and infinity for convex isoquants. The larger σ, the greater the degree of substitutability between the two inputs. If σ is infinite, x_1 and x_2 are perfect substitutes (Case II, Section 2.2c); if $\sigma = 0$, x_1 and x_2 must be used in fixed proportions (Case VI).

Equation 2.64 can be expressed as a function of factor quantities and partial derivatives of the production function as follows. First, consider the total differential, $d(x_2/x_1)$:

$$d(x_2/x_1) = \frac{\partial(x_2/x_1)}{\partial x_1} dx_1 + \frac{\partial(x_2/x_1)}{\partial x_2} dx_2$$

$$= \frac{-x_2}{x_1^2} dx_1 + \frac{x_1}{x_1^2} dx_2 = (-x_2 \, dx_1 + x_1 \, dx_2)/x_1^2 \tag{2.65}$$

Since $dx_2 = -(f_1/f_2) dx_1$, we get

$$d(x_2/x_1) = \left(-x_2 - \frac{x_1 f_1}{f_2}\right) dx_1/x_1^2 \tag{2.66}$$

Now consider the total differential, $d(f_1/f_2)$:

$$d(f_1/f_2) = \frac{\partial(f_1/f_2)}{\partial x_1} dx_1 + \frac{\partial(f_1/f_2)}{\partial x_2} dx_2 \qquad (2.67)$$

Again, since $dx_2 = -(f_1/f_2) dx_1$, we obtain

$$d(f_1/f_2) = \left[\frac{\partial(f_1/f_2)}{\partial x_1} - \left(\frac{f_1}{f_2}\right) \frac{\partial(f_1/f_2)}{\partial x_2} \right] dx_1 \qquad (2.68)$$

Substituting (2.66) and (2.68) into (2.64) for appropriate terms and rearranging yields

$$\sigma = \frac{f_1/f_2}{x_1^2(x_2/x_1)} \frac{-(x_2 + x_1 f_1/f_2)}{-\left[\dfrac{\partial(f_1/f_2)}{\partial x_2} (f_1/f_2) - \dfrac{\partial(f_1/f_2)}{\partial x_1} \right]}$$

$$= \frac{f_1(f_1 x_1 + f_2 x_2)}{f_2^2 x_1 x_2 \left[\dfrac{\partial(f_1/f_2)}{\partial x_2} (f_1/f_2) - \dfrac{\partial(f_1/f_2)}{\partial x_1} \right]}$$

$$= \frac{f_1(f_1 x_1 + f_2 x_2)}{f_2 x_1 x_2 \left[f_1 \dfrac{\partial(f_1/f_2)}{\partial x_2} - f_2 \dfrac{\partial(f_1/f_2)}{\partial x_1} \right]} \qquad (2.69)$$

Evaluating the terms in brackets, we obtain

$$f_1 \left(\frac{f_2 f_{12} - f_1 f_{22}}{f_2^2} \right) - f_2 \left(\frac{f_2 f_{11} - f_1 f_{21}}{f_2^2} \right)$$

$$= (f_1 f_2 f_{12} - f_1^2 f_{22} - f_2^2 f_{11} + f_1 f_2 f_{21})/f_2^2$$

$$= (2 f_1 f_2 f_{12} - f_1^2 f_{22} - f_2^2 f_{11})/f_2^2 \qquad (2.70)$$

Hence,

$$\sigma = \frac{f_1 f_2 (f_1 x_1 + f_2 x_2)}{x_1 x_2 (2 f_1 f_2 f_{12} - f_1^2 f_{22} - f_2^2 f_{11})} \qquad (2.71)$$

First, we note (as was asserted earlier) that σ is positive when $(2 f_1 f_2 f_{12} - f_1^2 f_{22} - f_2^2 f_{11})$ is positive, which is the case for a quasi-concave production function which implies convex isoquants. In general, we would expect σ to vary from point-to-point on the production surface; that is, we would expect *variable elasticity of substitution* (VES) production functions. However, σ is constant for some production functions; such functions are appropriately referred to as *constant elasticity of substitution* (CES) production functions. For some functions, such as a Cobb–Douglas, σ is constant and equal to unity.

2.2.e Isoclines and Ridgelines

An *isocline* is a line connecting points that have the same rate of technical substitution; that is, it is the locus of equal slopes. The equation of an isocline is given by

$$RTS_{12} \equiv -\frac{dx_2}{dx_1} = \frac{f_1}{f_2} = k \tag{2.72}$$

where k is an arbitrary constant. Since f_1 and f_2 are functions of x_1 and x_2, (2.72) may be expressed as

$$x_2 = h(x_1) \tag{2.73}$$

In Figure 2.9, A, B, and C are isoclines. There is an infinite number of isoclines for every family of isoquants.

A *ridgeline* is an isocline connecting points of zero slope or points of

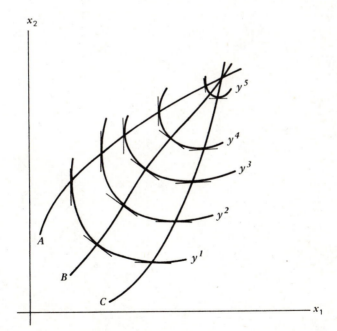

Figure 2.9. Isoclines and ridgelines for a three-stage production function.

undefined slope. In Figure 2.9, A and C are ridgelines. Ridgeline C is given by $RTS_{12} = 0$, which occurs when $f_1 = 0$; that is,

$$RTS_{12} = \frac{f_1}{f_2} = \frac{0}{f_2} = 0 \quad \text{or} \quad RTS_{21} = \frac{f_2}{0} = \text{undefined} \quad (2.74)$$

and ridgeline A is given by

$$RTS_{12} = \frac{f_1}{f_2} = \frac{f_1}{0} = \text{undefined} \quad \text{or} \quad RTS_{21} = \frac{0}{f_1} = 0 \quad (2.75)$$

For x_1 to the right of ridgeline C, $RTS_{12} < 0$ since $f_1 < 0$. Thus, the area to the right of ridgeline C is Stage III for x_1 and above ridgeline A is Stage III for x_2. Consequently, ridgelines are important because they bound the economic (rational) region of production to the extent that areas of negative marginal productivity are excluded (see Figure 2.10). A complete discussion of the economic region of production is developed in Chapter 3.

2.2.f Factor Interdependence

In this section we are concerned with the *technical* interrelationship between factors of production. Factor interdependence in an economic sense will be discussed when we consider factor demand functions.

Two factors are *technically independent* if the marginal productivity of one is not a function of the other factor. Worded another way, factors are technically independent if the *MPP* of one is not altered as the quantity of the other is changed.

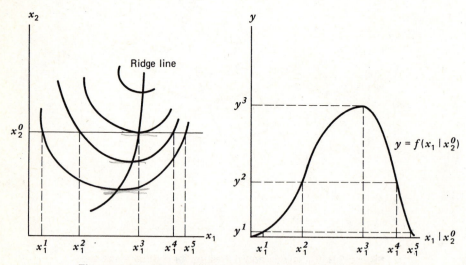

Figure 2.10. Relationship between isoquant (two-variable factor) diagram and single-variable factor diagram showing correspondence of ridgeline and maximum *TPP*.

Given $y = f(x_1, x_2)$, we have three types of technical interrelationships.

Case I If $\dfrac{\partial^2 y}{\partial x_1 \partial x_2} \equiv \dfrac{\partial}{\partial x_1}\left(\dfrac{\partial y}{\partial x_2}\right) \equiv f_{12} = f_{21} > 0$, then x_1 and x_2 are technically complementary. The term, complementary, is appealing because as shown in Figure 2.11a the marginal productivity of x_2 is enhanced at all levels of x_2 as x_1 is increased.

Case II If $f_{12} = 0$, then x_1 and x_2 are technically independent. That is, the marginal productivity of x_2 is not affected by changes in the level of x_1 (Figure 2.11b).

Case III If $f_{12} < 0$, then x_1 and x_2 are technically competitive. In this case x_1 and x_2 are said to be competitive because increasing x_1 reduces the marginal productivity of x_2 for all x_2 (Figure 2.11c).

There is some ambiguity in economic jargon regarding the concept of technical interdependence because the same or similar terminology is often

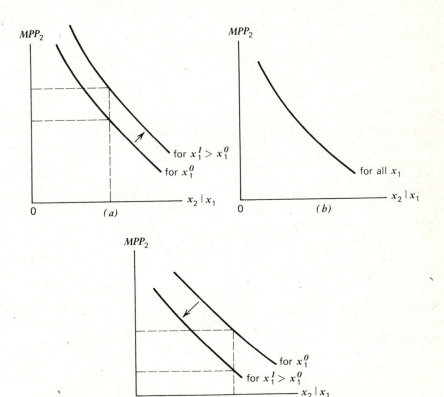

Figure 2.11. Geometric interpretation of technical complementarity, independence, and competitiveness. (a) Technically complementary factors. (b) Technically independent factors. (c) Technically competitive factors.

used in describing the nature of isoquant patterns. In Section 2.2.c, we purposely refrained from associating the concept of complementarity with right angle isoquants as do some authors. The case of right angle isoquants was identified as "no factor substitutability" because the shape of an isoquant has to do with factor–factor *substitutability* rather than factor–factor *interdependence*. In the former, output is held constant, while for the latter, it is not. Thus, it seems advisable to adopt different terminology for each concept.

The primary importance of technical interdependence is manifested in applied studies. If our knowledge of the production process indicates that factors have a particular type of technical interdependence, then we do not want to represent the production process by a functional form that imposes another type of technical interdependence.

Example 2.7 Consider the case of a generalized Cobb–Douglas production function,

$$y = A x_1^{b_1} x_2^{b_2} \tag{2.76}$$

for which

$$f_{12} = A b_1 b_2 x_1^{b_1 - 1} x_2^{b_2 - 1} \tag{2.77}$$

Since $f_{12} > 0$ for A, b_1, b_2, x_1, $x_2 > 0$, the Cobb–Douglas production function can only be used to represent technically complementary factors. So, in an applied study, one certainly would not want to represent a production process by this functional form if the factors were believed to be technically independent or competitive for any values of $x_1, x_2 > 0$.

Example 2.8 The transcendental production function exhibits all three types of technical interdependence as well as three stages of production for each factor. The functional form is

$$y = A x_1^{a_1} e^{b_1 x_1} x_2^{a_2} e^{b_2 x_2} \tag{2.78}$$

and $A > 0$, $a_1, a_2 > 1$ and $b_1, b_2 < 0$ for the function to represent a typical production surface (see Table 2.1 at end of chapter). To ascertain areas of technical complementarity, independence, and competitiveness, let us assume that $A = 1$, $a_1 = 2$, $a_2 = 3$, $b_1 = -1$, and $b_2 = -1$. Thus,

$$y = x_1^2 e^{-x_1} x_2^3 e^{-x_2} \tag{2.79}$$

and

$$\frac{\partial y}{\partial x_1} = [x_1^2(-e^{-x_1}) + 2x_1 e^{-x_1}] x_2^3 e^{-x_2} \tag{2.80}$$

To ascertain if MPP_1 increases, decreases, or remains unchanged as x_2 is changed, we must look at the sign of f_{12}. Taking the partial derivative of (2.80) with respect to x_2 gives

$$
\begin{aligned}
f_{12} &= (-x_1^2 e^{-x_1} + 2x_1 e^{-x_1})[x_2^3(-e^{-x_2}) + 3x_2^2 e^{-x_2}] \\
&= e^{-x_1} e^{-x_2}(2x_1 - x_1^2)(3x_2^2 - x_2^3) \\
&= \frac{(2x_1 - x_1^2)(3x_2^2 - x_2^3)}{e^{x_1} e^{x_2}}
\end{aligned}
\tag{2.81}
$$

Since the denominator is always positive for $x_1 > 0$ and $x_2 > 0$, we must examine the numerator to determine the sign of f_{12}. First consider the values of x_1 and x_2 that will make $f_{12} = 0$. If $x_1 = 0$ or $x_1 = 2$, the first term in brackets of (2.81) is zero; thus, $f_{12} = 0$. Or, if $x_2 = 0$ or $x_2 = 3$, the second term in brackets is zero and $f_{12} = 0$. Thus, x_1 and x_2 are technically independent if $x_1 = 0$, $x_1 = 2$, $x_2 = 0$, or $x_2 = 3$. Inspection of (2.81) will reveal that x_1 and x_2 are technically competitive if $x_1 > 2$ and $x_2 < 3$ or if $x_1 < 2$ and $x_2 > 3$. Similarly, it can be seen that x_1 and x_2 are technically complementary if $x_1 > 2$ and $x_2 > 3$ or if $x_1 < 2$ and $x_2 < 3$.

As an aside, notice from (2.80) that at $x_1 = 2$ the marginal productivity of x_1 is zero. It turns out for this example that the loci of points where the factors are technically independent are the ridgelines. Within the ridgelines the factors are technically complementary, and outside the ridgelines (those areas where the isoquants are positively sloped) the factors are technically competitive (see Figure 2.12a). The reader is cautioned, however, not to jump to the conclusion that this is generally the case. Consider for a moment the rigeline, isoquant, and technical interdependence possibilities for the quadratic model (2.35). For the case of $b_3 > 0$ (b_3 being the coefficient on the interaction term) the factors are everywhere technically complementary; yet the ridgelines are positively sloped and linear with a global maximum in the $x_1, x_2 > 0$ quadrant (see Figure 2.12b). For the case of $b_3 < 0$, the factors are everywhere technically competitive with negatively sloped and linear ridgelines which intersect in the $x_1, x_2 > 0$ quadrant (Figure 2.12c). Finally, for $b_3 = 0$ the factors stand everywhere as technically independent of each other (Figure 2.12d) and the isoquant and ridgeline pattern is similar to that of the transcendental function (Figure 2.12a).

Several technical interdependence and other ideas can be gleaned from Examples 2.7 and 2.8. First, from Example 2.8, we see that a single production function (e.g., the transcendental) can exhibit all three categories of technical interdependence between two factors depending on the factor levels. It is important to note, however, that a production function need not (in fact, many do not) exhibit all three interdependence categories, witness the Cobb–Douglas function in Example 2.7. Example 2.8 revealed that the nature of factor interdependence could flip–flop totally, in the case of quadratic functions, solely on the basis of the sign of a single parameter. Finally, Example

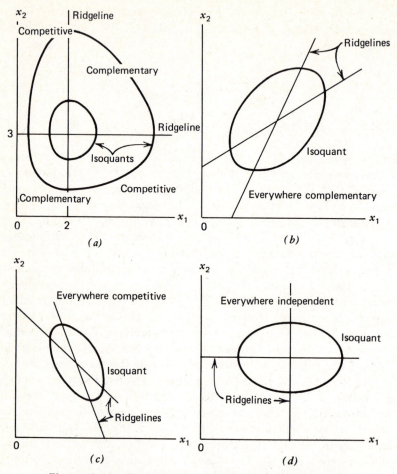

Figure 2.12. Technical interdependence, isoquant, and ridgeline properties for the transcendental and for three forms of the quadratic production function. (a) Transcendental function. (b) Quadratic function with $b_3 > 0$. (c) Quadratic function with $b_3 < 0$. (d) Quadratic function with $b_3 = 0$.

2.8 reminds us that it is risky to draw general conclusions from specific examples—a tendency that for many of us is difficult to resist. Such inductive processes are useful in suggesting hypotheses, but are seldom of value in establishing general conclusions.

2.2.g Elasticities of Production

Partial elasticity of production with respect to a particular factor is a measure of the proportional change in output resulting from a given proportional change in that factor when the other factor is held constant. In mathematical notation, partial elasticities of production are defined by

$$E_1 \equiv \frac{\partial y}{\partial x_1} \cdot \frac{x_1}{y} = \frac{MPP_1}{APP_1} \qquad (2.82)$$

and

$$E_2 \equiv \frac{\partial y}{\partial x_2} \cdot \frac{x_2}{y} = \frac{MPP_2}{APP_2} \qquad (2.83)$$

From these definitions it can be seen that, as in the single input case, values for partial elasticities are related to features of the productivity functions (see Figure 2.13). Figure 2.13 is the same as Figure 2.2 except that we now explicitly note that x_2 is held constant and the productivity curves and elasticity and stage notation are appropriately subscripted with 1.

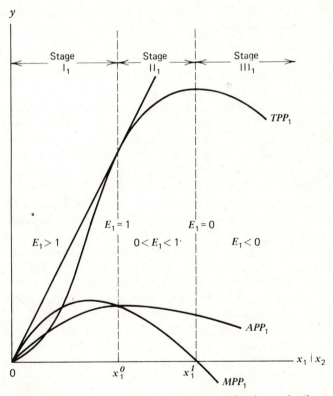

Figure 2.13. Classical three-stage textbook production function and marginal and average curves—single factor variation.

Given that x_2 is held constant, we have the following:

$E_1 > 1$ for $0 < x_1 < x_1^0$,   where x_1^0 is associated with maximum APP_1

$E_1 = 1$ for $x_1 = x_1^0$

$0 < E_1 < 1$ for $x_1^0 < x_1 < x_1^l$,   where x_1^l is associated with maximum TPP_1

$E_1 = 0$ for $x_1 = x_1^l$

$E_1 < 0$ for $x_1 > x_1^l$

Relationships for E_2 given that x_1 is held constant are similar to the above cases, except that the subscript 1 should be replaced by the subscript 2 throughout.

In order to geometrically consider the concept of partial elasticity of production in x_1, x_2 space, *isoelasticity contours* are a useful device. Consider Figure 2.14. Panel *a* shows two isoquants; in particular note that when x_2 is held constant first at x_2^0 and then at x_2^l the level of x_1 where the right most ridgeline is encountered is at x_1^0 and x_1^l, respectively. Let the output levels associated with (x_1^0, x_2^0) and (x_1^l, x_2^l) be y^0 and y^l, respectively. Now in panel *b* envision the single-factor variation TPP_1 curves for x_1 given x_2 fixed alternatively at x_2^0 and x_2^l, in other words, $TPP_1(x_2 = x_2^0)$ and $TPP_1(x_2 = x_2^l)$. Note that the distances ox_1^0 and ox_1^l in panels *a*, *b*, and *c* are the same, and they occur at the point where the isoquants have zero slope (panel *a*) and TPP_1s are maximum (panel *b*). From Figure 2.13 and earlier discussions we know in panel *b* that $E_1 = 0$ at x_1^0 when x_2 is fixed at x_2^0 and that $E_1 = 0$ also at x_1^l when x_2 is fixed at x_2^l. In panel *c*, if we extend the perpendicular loci associated with x_1^0 and x_1^l and locate points where $x_2 = x_2^0$ and $x_2 = x_2^l$, we have identified two points on the isoelasticity contour, where $E_1 = 0$ which is our familiar ridge-line of panel *a*. Similarly if we drop perpendiculars to panel *c* from those points in panel *b* where APP_1 is maximum (where the rayline is tangent to the production function), and locate points where these perpendiculars intersect x_2^0 and x_2^l in panel *c*, we have identified two points on the isoelasticity contour where $E_1 = 1$.

Of course, there are an infinite number of isoelasticity contours, but these two are of particular interest. In panel *c*, what do we know when we are left of the line $E_1 = 1$? We know we must be in Stage I for x_1, because $E_1 > 1$. If we are between $E_1 = 1$ and $E_1 = 0$, we are in Stage II for x_1, and to the right of $E_1 = 0$ ($E_1 < 0$) is Stage III for x_1.

Suppose we were to repeat the process presented in Figure 2.14 by holding x_1 constant and consider single-factor variation for x_2. With some persistence, and a little luck, we would construct a diagram like the one in Figure 2.15 for our textbook three-stage, two-variable factor production function.[7]

---

[7]The reader is cautioned not to be overly optimistic about mathematically specifying and estimating such a production function for any particular application. Most mathematical production function models that are amenable to estimation, and that are analytically manageable, are more restrictive than the general function depicted in Figure 2.15.

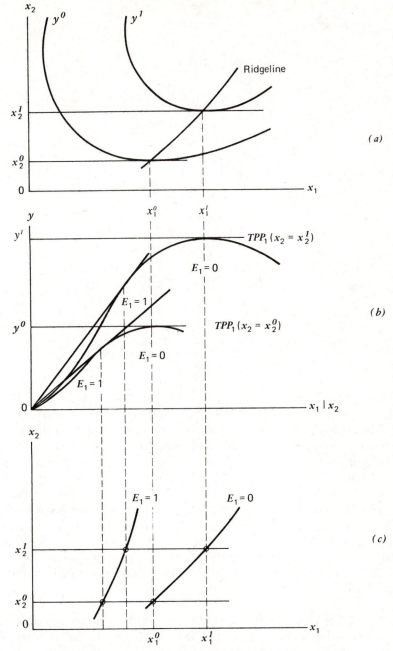

Figure 2.14. Geometrical derivation of iso-partial-elasticity contours for x_1. (a) Isoquant pattern. (b) Total product curves. (c) Iso-partial-elasticity contours.

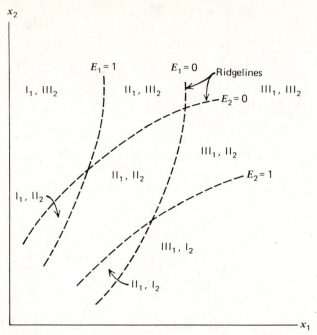

Figure 2.15. Key isoelasticity contours and stages of production for the classic textbook production function.

Stages of production for x_1 and x_2 are noted I_1, II_1, III_1, and I_2, II_2, III_2, respectively. Recall that $E_1 = 1$ is the locus of points where APP_1 is maximum; $E_1 = 0$ locates points where MPP_1 is zero (a ridgeline); $E_2 = 1$ denotes APP_2 is maximum; and $E_2 = 0$ is the other ridgeline (where MPP_2 is zero). The point where $E_1 = E_2 = 0$ is the global maximum of our hypothetical function.

Note that in Figure 2.15, I_1 does not everywhere correspond to III_2 and vice versa. That is, Stages I and III are *not* symmetric for this function. Also note that the area enclosed by the ridgelines (the area enclosed by $E_1 = 0$ and $E_2 = 0$ between the origin and the point $E_1 = E_2 = 0$) is *not* exclusively Stage II, contrary to the assertion of several textbooks (see, for example, Gould and Ferguson, 1980, p. 159). We will return to these troublesome revelations after developing the idea of the function coefficient and some related topics.

2.2.h The Function Coefficient and Returns to Scale

The function coefficient, ϵ, measures the proportional change in output resulting from a unit proportional change in *all* inputs; that is, ϵ is the percentage change in output as all inputs are varied in some fixed proportion. Thus, the function coefficient is a *long-run* concept whereas partial elasticity of production is a *short-run* idea. The function coefficient is mathematically defined as

$$\epsilon \equiv (dy/y)/(dx_k/x_k) \tag{2.84}$$

where

$$\frac{dx_k}{x_k} = \frac{dx_1}{x_1} = \frac{dx_2}{x_2} \tag{2.85}$$

assuming a two-factor model. That is, ϵ is the percentage change in output divided by the percentage change in either input, where the percentage change in both inputs is the same.

Because of the condition that *all* (both) inputs be expanded in fixed proportion, the function coefficient is a measure of the *returns to scale* exhibited by the function. If ϵ is a function of x_1 and x_2 (the general case), then the return to scale differs at alternative points on the production surface. On the other hand, if ϵ does not depend on x_1 and x_2, but is constant everywhere on the surface, the function exhibits *constant proportional returns* (a homogeneous function). Finally, if $\epsilon = 1$, we have the special case of *constant returns to scale*. More on these ideas will be presented later.

The function coefficient for the two-factor model is related to the partial elasticities of production by the formula,

$$A x_1^{.5} x_2^{.5}$$

$$\epsilon = E_1 + E_2 \tag{2.86}$$

To verify this assertion, consider (2.84). We know that

$$dy = f_1 dx_1 + f_2 dx_2 \tag{2.87}$$

Assuming $k = 1$, substitution of (2.87) into (2.84) for dy gives

$$\epsilon = \frac{(f_1 dx_1 + f_2 dx_2)}{dx_1} \frac{x_1}{y}$$

$$= \left(f_1 + f_2 \frac{dx_2}{dx_1} \right) \frac{x_1}{y}$$

$$= f_1 \frac{x_1}{y} + f_2 \frac{dx_2}{dx_1} \frac{x_1}{y} \tag{2.88}$$

However, if $dx_1/x_1 = dx_2/x_2$ as assumed, then $dx_2/dx_1 = x_2/x_1$ and

$$\epsilon = f_1 \frac{x_1}{y} + f_2 \frac{x_2}{x_1} \frac{x_1}{y}$$

$$= f_1 \frac{x_1}{y} + f_2 \frac{x_2}{y}$$

$$= \frac{MPP_1}{APP_1} + \frac{MPP_2}{APP_2} = E_1 + E_2 = \epsilon = k \tag{2.89}$$

$$k = b_1 + b_2$$

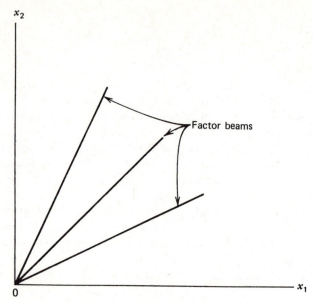

Figure 2.16. Example factor beams.

as was to be shown. Accordingly, the function coefficient may be thought of as the *total elasticity of production,* as it takes into account the change in output as x_1 is varied given x_2 constant *plus* the change in output as x_2 is varied given a level of x_1, or vice versa. It allows us to consider the change in output for cases of *long-run* multiple-input variation.[8]

Again, the function coefficient, ϵ, measures the proportional change in output as all (both) inputs are varied in fixed proportion, in other words, as we move along a *factor beam* (ray line). A factor beam is a straight line through the origin in factor–factor space (see Figure 2.16). Note that as one moves out from the origin along a factor beam, the factors x_1 and x_2 are held in fixed proportion to one another. The choice of a particular factor beam is arbitrary. At any point on the production surface, ϵ measures the percent change in output *if* x_1 and x_2 were varied along the particular factor beam passing through that point.

As was mentioned earlier, it is useful to think in terms of two general classes of production functions—those that exhibit *variable proportional returns* and those exhibiting *constant proportional returns* (homogeneous functions). If ϵ is *not* everywhere the same on the production surface [i.e., $\epsilon = f(x_1,x_2)$], the function exhibits *variable proportional returns.* On the other hand, if ϵ is everywhere the same on the surface [i.e., $\epsilon \neq f(x_1,x_2)$, or rather, $\epsilon = k$ where k is a constant] the function exhibits *constant proportional returns.* This latter class

---

[8]In the concluding section of this chapter, we extend the ideas of the function coefficient and returns to scale to *n* factors and introduce a third elasticity concept, that of a quasi-function coefficient as a measure of proportional variation of a subset (two or more) of *s*-variable factors.

of production functions is referred to as homogeneous functions. Such functions are *not* like that represented in Figure 2.15—not the classical three-stage textbook function with respect to proportional factor variation as well as single-factor variation.

Before considering the special case of homogeneous functions, let us consider the more general case of variable proportional return functions. Generally,

> *if we move outward along an arbitrary* rising *curve in the factor diagram (that is to say, a curve where all factor quantities* simultaneously *increase, or more generally no factor quantity diminishes and at least one rises when we move along the curve), the passus coefficient [Frisch's terminology for the function coefficient] will* diminish *steadily from values in excess of 1 to values less than zero. (Frisch, 1965, p. 120)*

This idea is presented geometrically in Figure 2.17. The arbitrary rising curve referred to in the Frisch quotation, is the one with arrows, 0Z. For a variable proportional return production function, we would expect to encounter, as we move out from the origin, first an area where the function coefficient is "large" (greater than unity) prior to point A. At some point, say A, we find a function coefficient value of unity. *Note*, however, at point A, the function coefficient measures the proportional change in output we would get *if* x_1 and x_2 were expanded, not along the arbitrary rising curve, 0Z, but rather

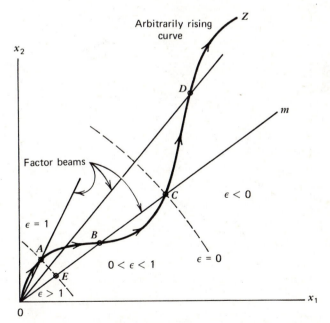

Figure 2.17. Geometric interpretation of the function coefficient for the variable proportional return case.

along the factor beam passing through point A. If we continue along $0Z$ past A, we encounter ϵ values less than unity and getting ever smaller until we reach point C where $\epsilon = 0$ (again, the proportional change being measured along the factor beam passing through B and C). Continued increased usage of x_1 and x_2 past point C implies a function coefficient value that is negative. That is, in the most general case (Frisch's regular ultrapassum law), as we move up along the production surface from the origin (e.g., along an isocline) we would find areas where $\epsilon > 1$, $\epsilon = 1$, $0 < \epsilon < 1$, $\epsilon = 0$, and $\epsilon < 0$.

Another way of conceptualizing this textbook function is to consider the concept of a *scale input* represented by, for example, the factor beam passing through $0EBC$ in Figure 2.17. Let us call this new (scale) input, m, where m is represented by a particular proportional combination of x_1 and x_2. In Figure 2.18, m is plotted against output; m_0, m_E, m_B, and m_C correspond to that level of the scale input comprised of x_1 and x_2 levels at point 0, E, B, and C, respectively, in Figure 2.17. Finally, in Figure 2.19, the traditional three-stage textbook production function given in Figure 2.15 is reproduced in terms of isopartial *and* isofunction coefficient curves. The logic of the location of the particular isopartial curves noted in Figure 2.19 was developed in the discussion pertaining to Figure 2.15. Since $\epsilon = E_1 + E_2$, the isofunction coefficient curve $\epsilon = 1$ in Figure 2.19 must pass through the points ($E_1 = 0, E_2 = 1$, and $E_1 = 1, E_2 = 0$) and the curve $\epsilon = 0$ must pass through ($E_1 = 0, E_2 = 0$).

Although it is conceptually possible for a given production function to exhibit function coefficient values from $\epsilon > 1$ to $\epsilon < 0$, every production func-

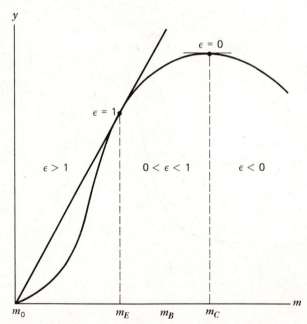

Figure 2.18. Response surface for scale input—three-stage variable proportional return case.

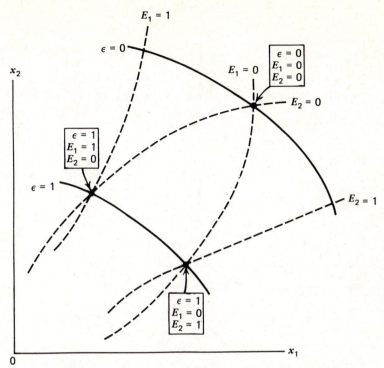

Figure 2.19. A traditional three-stage textbook production function depicted in terms of isoelasticity contours.

tion need not show every range; for example, ϵ for a Cobb–Douglas type production function is everywhere constant. As was noted earlier, such functions are referred to as *constant proportional return* or *homogeneous* functions.[9] For such functions, a plot of output against the scale input, m, will look like one of the three possibilities shown in Figure 2.20. In Figure 2.20a, output (total product with respect to scale, TPP_m) increases at an increasing rate everywhere on the surface in response to a proportional increase in all inputs; ϵ is constant and equal to some number in excess of unity, $\epsilon = k > 1$. Figure 2.20b represents the decreasing (diminishing) proportional returns case; Figure 2.20c gives the constant proportional returns case. Yet all three are possibilities for a constant proportional return production function *because* ϵ is constant. Only the case where ϵ is constant and equal to unity do we have TPP_m linear.

Perhaps we can rise above this jargon crisis by focusing our thinking in terms of the more familiar idea of *returns to scale*. Again, since the concept of the function coefficient requires a proportional change in *all* inputs, it is useful in considering returns to scale. In order to distinguish between average and

---

[9]It will be shown in the next section that homogeneous functions are constant proportional returns functions.

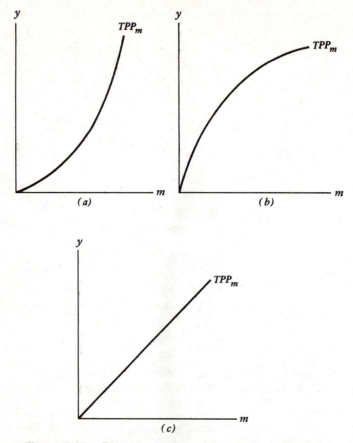

Figure 2.20. Response surface for constant proportional return production function—three possible cases. (a) Constant ϵ—increasing returns ($\epsilon = k > 1$). (b) Constant ϵ—decreasing returns ($\epsilon = k < 1$). (c) Constant ϵ—constant returns ($\epsilon = k = 1$). *Note:* Only case c represents "constant" returns to scale.

marginal returns to scale, consider the production function, $y = f(x_1,x_2)$. Recall that we suggested that when x_1 and x_2 are combined in fixed proportion, we can express the production function in terms of a single (scale) input, m. For example, we can let $m = x_1$. Since x_1 and x_2 are combined in fixed proportions, we have $x_2 = kx_1 = km$. Thus, by substituting m for x_1 and km for x_2 in the production function, we may express output as a function of the scale input:

$$y = f(x_1,x_2) = f(m,km) = \bar{f}(m) \qquad (2.90)$$

Note that $y = \bar{f}(m)$ does not give the complete production surface; rather, it gives output for all points on a particular factor beam. It should be obvious that an infinite number of scale inputs could be defined simply by changing k in $x_2 = kx_1$.

Using (2.90), we can mathematically define *marginal returns to scale* (i.e., marginal physical productivity of *a* scale input) as

$$MPP_m \equiv \frac{dy}{dm} \equiv \frac{d\bar{f}(m)}{dm} \tag{2.91}$$

which shows the change in output as we make an infinitesimal movement along a factor beam. Another scale concept is *average returns to scale*, (i.e., average physical product of *a* scale input) defined as

$$APP_m \equiv \frac{y}{\bar{m}} \equiv \frac{\bar{f}(m)}{\bar{m}} \tag{2.92}$$

For the most general textbook case we observe the following (see Figure 2.21):

1. When $\epsilon > 1$, APP_m is increasing, MPP_m can be increasing or decreasing, and $MPP_m > APP_m$.
2. When $\epsilon = 1$, APP_m is maximum, MPP_m is decreasing, and $APP_m = MPP_m$.
3. When $\epsilon < 1$, APP_m is decreasing, MPP_m is decreasing, and $APP_m > MPP_m$.
4. When $\epsilon = 0$, APP_m is decreasing, MPP_m is zero, and $APP_m > MPP_m$.
5. When $\epsilon < 0$, APP_m is decreasing, MPP_m is negative and decreasing, and $APP_m > MPP_m$.

Thus, ϵ is an indicator of the nature of average returns with respect to scale in Stage I, of both average and marginal scale returns in Stage II, and of marginal scale returns in Stage III. Thus, when using the term *return to scale*, it is just as important to insert the appropriate qualifying adjective (*marginal* or *average*) as when referring to the nature of single-factor productivity (response). Unfortunately, this careful use of language is often not adhered to in economics literature. For example, many times references will be made simply to increasing returns to scale whenever $\epsilon > 1$. Yet we see in Figure 2.21 that marginal returns to scale can be diminishing in this area.

Perhaps this common untidiness in our use of economic terms has to do with our invalid tendency to ascribe properties that hold for special cases to more general situations. Indeed, there exists a class of production functions for which it is unnecessary (although still sloppy) to distinguish between marginal and average returns to scale, just as it is unnecessary (although sloppy) to distinguish between marginal and average productivity of an input for certain discussions. For *some* production functions it is not inaccurate to say the function exhibits diminishing returns (to an individual factor or with respect to scale)—the reason being that the behavior of the average and marginal curves is everywhere the same. That is, for some functions, both average and marginal returns *everywhere* increase, or *everywhere* decrease, or *everywhere* remain constant. When the returns concept is that of scale, such functions are said to exhibit *constant proportional returns*. They are *homogeneous*.

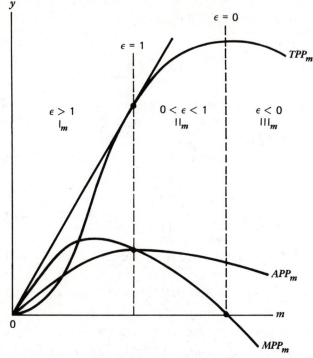

Figure 2.21. Scale stages of production for the traditional three-stage textbook production function.

2.2.i Homogeneous Production Functions

When a production function exhibits constant proportional returns, $\epsilon = k$ (i.e., it is homogeneous), then the three possibilities presented in Figure 2.22 exist:

1. If $\epsilon > 1$, the function exhibits increasing returns to scale (*both* average and marginal) throughout (Figure 2.22*a*).
2. If $\epsilon = 1$, the function exhibits constant returns to scale (*both* average and marginal) throughout (Figure 2.22*b*).
3. If $0 < \epsilon < 1$, the function exhibits decreasing returns to scale (*both* average and marginal) throughout (Figure 2.22*c*).

Clearly the possibility of $\epsilon \leq 0$ is irrelevant for the constant proportional returns case since negative marginal returns everywhere would require negative total product everywhere.

A production function, or for that matter any function, is *homogeneous of degree k* if the function can be expressed as

$$f[(tx_1),(tx_2)] = t^k f(x_1,x_2) \tag{2.93}$$

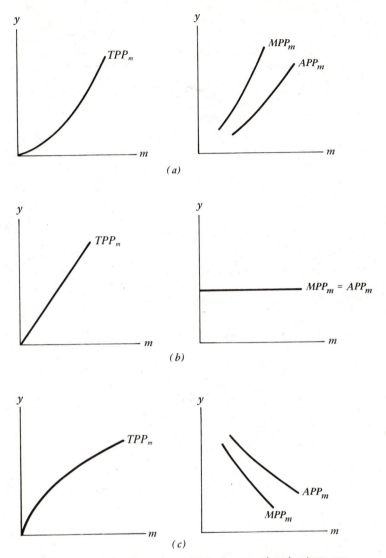

Figure 2.22. Alternative constant proportional return production function shapes with respect to marginal and average returns to scale. (*a*) Increasing marginal and average returns to scale. (*b*) Constant marginal and average returns to scale. (*c*) Decreasing marginal and average returns to scale.

where k is a constant and t is any positive real number. If a function is homogeneous, the degree of homogeneity, k, indicates the returns to scale (marginal and average) that the function exhibits. It should be obvious then that a homogeneous production function exhibits constant proportional returns; that is, $\epsilon = k$ everywhere on the surface.

Functions that are homogeneous of degree one are sometimes called *linearly homogeneous* or *linear and homogeneous*. The second statement is misleading because the function need *not* be linear in an algebraic sense. As an illustration, consider the next two examples.

Example 2.9 Suppose

$$y = b_1 x_1 + b_2 x_2 \tag{2.94}$$

Then

$$
\begin{aligned}
f(tx_1, tx_2) &= b_1 tx_1 + b_2 tx_2 \\
&= t(b_1 x_1 + b_2 x_2) \\
&= tf(x_1, x_2)
\end{aligned}
\tag{2.95}
$$

Hence, (2.94) is homogeneous of degree 1 (the exponent of t is one). This function is linearly homogeneous and is linear in an algebraic sense.

Example 2.10 Consider the generalized Cobb–Douglas production function:

$$y = A x_1^{b_1} x_2^{b_2} \tag{2.96}$$

where $0 < b_1 < 1$ and $0 < b_2 < 1$. Then

$$
\begin{aligned}
f(tx_1, tx_2) &= A (tx_1)^{b_1} (tx_2)^{b_2} \\
&= A t^{b_1} x_1^{b_1} t^{b_2} x_2^{b_2} \\
&= t^{b_1 + b_2} A x_1^{b_1} x_2^{b_2} \\
&= t^{b_1 + b_2} f(x_1, x_2)
\end{aligned}
\tag{2.97}
$$

Thus, the generalized Cobb–Douglas function is homogeneous of degree $b_1 + b_2$. If $b_1 + b_2 = 1$, the function is linearly homogeneous, but the function itself is not linear.

Example 2.11 Consider the function:

$$Z = 14 v_1^2 + 13 v_1 v_2 + 12 v_2^2 \tag{2.98}$$

Thus,

$$
\begin{aligned}
f(tv_1, tv_2) &= 14(tv_1)^2 + 13(tv_1)(tv_2) + 12(tv_2)^2 \\
&= 14 t^2 v_1^2 + 13 t^2 v_1 v_2 + 12 t^2 v_2^2 \\
&= t^2 (14 v_1^2 + 13 v_1 v_2 + 12 v_2^2)
\end{aligned}
\tag{2.99}
$$

and the function is homogeneous of degree 2.

Example 2.12   Suppose that the function is

$$y = \frac{a_1x_1 + b_1x_2}{a_2x_1 + b_2x_2} \tag{2.100}$$

Then

$$\begin{aligned}
f(tx_1, tx_2) &= \frac{a_1(tx_1) + b_1(tx_2)}{a_2(tx_1) + b_2(tx_2)} \\
&= \frac{t(a_1x_1 + b_1x_2)}{t(a_2x_1 + b_2x_2)} \\
&= \frac{a_1x_1 + b_1x_2}{a_2x_1 + b_2x_2} = t^0 f(x_1, x_2)
\end{aligned} \tag{2.101}$$

and we conclude that the function is homogeneous of degree 0, since $t^0 = 1$.

2.2.j Properties of Homogeneous Functions

Homogeneous functions have a number of mathematical properties that are notable. We will find in later chapters that these properties, when embodied in a production function, simplify many of the economic derivations we will be making.

Property 1 *The first derivatives of a function homogeneous of degree k are homogeneous of degree k − 1.*

The proof of this property follows directly from our definition of homogeneity. Recall that $f(x_1, x_2)$ is said to be homogeneous of degree k if $f(tx_1, tx_2) = t^k f(x_1, x_2)$. Taking the derivative of both sides of this expression with respect to, say x_1, gives $tf_1(tx_1, tx_2) = t^k f_1(x_1, x_2)$. Dividing through by t we get $f_1(tx_1, tx_2) = t^{k-1} f_1(x_1, x_2)$, which by definition implies that f_1 is homogeneous of degree $k − 1$. Thus, the marginal productivities of a homogeneous production function are homogeneous of one degree less than that of the production function.

Property 2 *Isoclines for homogeneous functions are ray lines (factor beams).*

This property follows directly from Property 1. Recall that along an isocline f_1/f_2 is constant. If both f_1 and f_2 are homogeneous of degree $k − 1$, then f_1/f_2 is homogeneous of degree zero: $t^{k-1}f_1/t^{k-1}f_2 = t^0 f_1/f_2$. Thus, if we multiply both factor levels by t, then $RTS_{12} = f_1/f_2$ does not change. It follows immediately that isoclines are ray lines (factor beams) since slope is unchanged (see Figure 2.23).

We will see later that Property 2 implies that the input expansion path for a perfectly competitive firm (in factor markets) with a homogeneous production function is a ray line. This is especially handy in deriving factor demand, cost curves and product supply functions from homogeneous production functions.

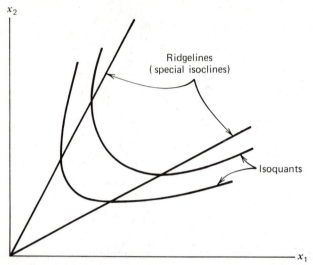

Figure 2.23. Isoquants and ridgelines for a homogeneous production function that exhibits three stages of production under single-factor variation.

Property 3 *For homogeneous functions $ky = f_1x_1 + f_2x_2$.*

To establish this property, recall that the degree of homogeneity, k, is the return to scale exhibited by the function. Thus,

$$k = \epsilon = E_1 + E_2 = MPP_1/APP_1 + MPP_2/APP_2 = f_1\,x_1/y + f_2\,x_2/y.$$

Multiplying by y gives $ky = f_1x_1 + f_2x_2$.

This property is known as *Euler's Theorem*. It says that if a production function is homogeneous of degree one ($k = 1$) and if each factor was paid in accordance with its marginal productivity then output would be exactly exhausted. Similarly, if $k < 1$ (>1) then a similar payment scheme to factors would underexhaust (overexhaust) output.[10]

2.2.k Returns to Size

Because the notion of returns to size, unlike returns to scale, is not exclusively a technical issue, considering it at this point is somewhat premature. However, we consider it here because of its frequent confusion with the notion of returns to scale. As we have seen, return to scale has to do with expansion of output in response to an expansion of all factors in fixed proportion—a movement along a factor beam. Returns to size has to do with a proportional change in output as factors are expanded in least-cost or expansion path proportions (see Chapter 3). The expansion path, as will be seen later, may or may not

---

[10]The reader is cautioned that there are many erroneous assertions in the literature that have been suggested as following from Euler's Theorem. See Chiang (1974, p. 407) and Henderson and Quandt (1980, pp. 109, 148–149) for discussion of the kinds of misinformation and wrong implications that have been derived from Euler's Theorem.

be a factor beam. In fact, only for the special case of a constant proportional returns production function and constant factor prices will the expansion path be a factor beam. Since combinations of factors in least-cost proportion are assumed in deriving the cost functions of the firm (see Chapter 4), it is actually this concept rather than that of returns to scale that is most important in the theory of firm growth or optimum firm size. Return to size has to do with the economic notion of what is happening (decreasing, constant, or increasing) to costs (average variable cost and marginal cost) as *output* is expanded. Unfortunately, the distinction between returns to scale and size is not always made clear and, in fact, the terminology is sometimes inappropriately used interchangeably.

2.2.l Isoquant Patterns Revisited

In Section 2.2.c we looked briefly at isoquant patterns. However, our discussion was limited to considering the shape of individual isoquants. We did not consider isoquant spacing. We looked at the RTS_{12}, which is $-dx_2/dx_1$, and rate of change of the slope (d^2x_2/dx_1^2) in order to establish isoquant slope and convexity, concavity, or lack thereof. We shall now complete our discussion of isoquant patterns by looking at the spacing of isoquants. For this purpose the concept of *marginal return to scale* is useful.

When MPP_m is increasing (increasing marginal returns to scale) successively numbered isoquants get ever closer together. When MPP_m is decreasing successively numbered isoquants get ever farther apart (Figure 2.24). Again, this is what we generally expect under Frisch's regular ultra-passum law—that is, three stages of production with respect to scale as well as single-factor

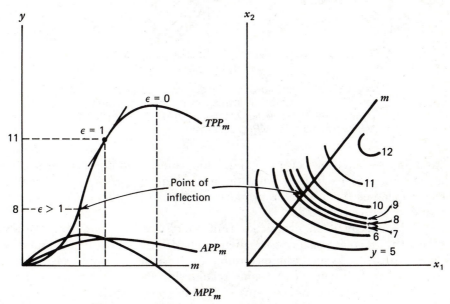

Figure 2.24. Relationship of isoquant spacing to ϵ for a three-stage (with respect to scale) variable proportional return production function.

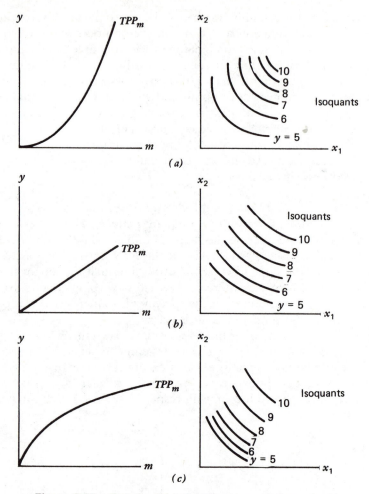

Figure 2.25. Relationship of isoquant spacing to ϵ for alternative single-stage (with respect to scale) constant proportional return production functions. (a) MPP_m increasing. (b) MPP_m constant. (c) MPP_m decreasing.

variation. As noted by Levenson and Solon, contrary to popular belief $\epsilon > 1$ is *not* associated exclusively with the area where the isoquants are getting closer together for a variable proportional return production function like that depicted in Figure 2.24.

Alternatively, if the production function of interest is homogeneous (exhibits *constant proportional returns*), then when MPP_m is increasing, constant, or decreasing, APP_m is increasing, constant, or decreasing, respectively. That is, APP_m and MPP_m maintain the same relationship to each other (both always increasing, decreasing, or constant) everywhere on the surface. Thus, in such special cases, the degree of homogeneity or function coefficient, ϵ, tells us how the isoquants are spaced. That is, $\epsilon > 1$ implies that the isoquants get closer together as output increases; $\epsilon = 1$ implies equal spacing; and $\epsilon < 1$ implies that the isoquants get farther apart as output increases *everywhere* on the surface (Figure 2.25). It is likely that this property of homogeneous functions led some authors to presume incorrectly that the magnitude of ϵ revealed the nature of isoquant spacing in general.

2.2.m Symmetry of Stages of Production

One of the properties of linearly-homogeneous production functions is *symmetry of production stages*; that is, I_1 (Stage I for factor 1) corresponds to III_2 (Stage III for factor 2) and vice versa. It also follows that II_1 and II_2 comprise the same area in the factor–factor diagram for such functions. By way of contrast, in our discussion of Figure 2.15, the traditional three-stage textbook (*nonhomogeneous*) production function, it was suggested that the area enclosed by the ridgelines is not *generally* exclusively Stage II in the factor–factor diagram, contrary to the assertion of several leading intermediate theory textbooks. That is, several authors curiously and mistakenly have argued that the ridgelines always enclose exclusively and solely Stage II even for nonhomogeneous functions.

Because of this common misunderstanding and the tendency to inappropriately generalize properties of special cases, we develop and discuss the notation of symmetry *and* asymmetry of production stages at some length in this section—in fact, out-of-proportion to its importance. (We are tempted to argue that symmetry of production stages is nothing more than a mere theoretical nicety of limited practical importance.)

As a point of departure, recall the following definition: For factor x_1, I_1 is defined simply as that area over which APP_1 is increasing, II_1 is defined as that area over which APP_1 is declining and MPP_1 is positive, and III_1 is defined as that area over which MPP_1 is negative. Stages for factor two are defined similarly. Thus, stages for each factor are defined with regard to the nature of the APP and MPP of that factor "independent" of the other factor.[11]

Let us begin the geometric interpretation of the *asymmetry* of production stages by considering the most general case, that being a production function that exhibits variable proportional returns (nonhomogeneous) and that gives rise to the traditional three-stage textbook diagram whether passing across the factor–factor space vertically, horizontally, or diagonally (along a factor beam)—see Figures 2.15, 2.19, and 2.21 in Sections 2.2.g and 2.2.h. That is, if output is expanded by moving along an arbitrarily chosen factor beam or

---

[11] It should be noted that our definition of production stages is different from that used by Mundlak (1958). Mundlak holds that for Stage I the APP of the variable factor is increasing *and* the MPP of the "fixed" factor is negative; for Stage II, the MPPs and APPs of *both* factors are positive and declining; and for Stage III, the MPP of the variable factor is negative *and* the APP of the "fixed" factor is increasing. This definition is very restrictive in that it is strictly relevant only for a homogeneous function of the first degree. It unduly binds us in attempts to generalize the discussion of production stages and "economic and uneconomic" regions to variable proportional returns production functions. Our definition is consistent with definitions in most intermediate theory texts, for example, Gould and Ferguson (1980, pp. 138–139), and most of the agricultural economics literature.

by increasing x_1 while holding x_2 constant or vice versa, we observe the three-stage phenomenon. A production surface is depicted for which the function coefficient varies from $\epsilon > 1$ to $\epsilon < 0$ as we move out any factor beam (scale line) from the origin. Similarly, as we move horizontally (vertically) across the surface, the partial elasticity of production for x_1, E_1 (and for x_2, E_2) monotonically decreases for some value greater than unity to negative.

The important thing to remember about Figures 2.15 and 2.19 is that the isoelasticity lines denote loci of points that are of special interest in specifying stages of production. Since, by definition, $E_i = MPP_i/APP_i$, it follows that the lines $E_1 = 0$ and $E_2 = 0$ locate the points where the respective factor marginal productivities are zero. These are the familiar ridgelines that separate Stages II and III for x_1 and x_2, respectively. Similarly, the lines $E_1 = 1$ and $E_2 = 1$ represent loci of points where the respective average products are maximum since $MPP_i = APP_i$ at these points; they represent the extensive margins and separate Stages I and II for the respective factors (see Figure 2.15).

From Figure 2.15, *asymmetry* of stages for this traditional textbook case is readily apparent. That is, it is not true for *all* possible combinations of x_1 and x_2 that I_1 corresponds to III_2, I_2 corresponds to III_1, and II_1 corresponds to II_2; therefore, the stages are asymmetric. For example, if we follow a straight line parallel to the x_1 axis that passes above the global maximum (where $E_1, E_2 = 0$), we observe that while we are continuously in Stage III for x_2 we pass through all three stages for x_1. A similar asymmetric pattern is observed for any other path we might consider.

The variable proportional returns case discussed above is instructive because it vividly demonstrates the rather special circumstances that must occur for symmetry of stages to exist. Again returning to Figure 2.15, if for all points in the factor–factor space we are to observe that I_1 corresponds to III_2, and I_2 corresponds to III_1, and II_1 to II_2, then it must be that the line $E_1 = 0$ must be the same as for $E_2 = 1$ and that $E_2 = 0$ be the same locus of points as for $E_1 = 1$. Obviously a rather special situation. For this to occur requires that $\epsilon = 1$ for all (x_1, x_2) rather than $\epsilon = f(x_1, x_2)$ as in Figure 2.15. That is, not only does symmetry require a constant proportional return (homogeneous) production function, but specifically one for which the proportional return is unity (a function homogeneous of degree one).

Such a situation is depicted in Figure 2.26. That is, for symmetry to hold, the ridgeline for $x_1(x_2)$ must correspond to the locus of maximum APPs for $x_2(x_1)$—implying linear ridgelines emanating from the origin.[12] Note that as x_1 is increased holding x_2 constant, APP_1 is premaximal when MPP_2 is negative, is maximal when MPP_2 is zero, and is postmaximal when MPP_2 is positive for all x_2. Similarly, as x_2 is increased holding x_1 constant, APP_2 is premaximal, maximal, and postmaximal when MPP_1 is negative, zero, and positive, respectively. Thus, above the uppermost ridgeline, x_1 is in Stage I and x_2 is in

---

[12]Recall, Section 2.2.j established that homogeneous functions have isoclines (and thus ridgelines) that are straight lines passing through the origin (factor beams).

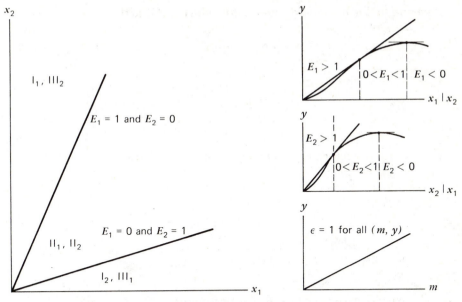

Figure 2.26. Isoelasticity curves and stages of production for a production function homogeneous of degree one ($\epsilon = 1$).

Stage III; below the lower ridgeline x_1 is in Stage III and x_2 is in Stage I; in between both are in Stage II—implying symmetry.

As a final note, the fact that the ridgelines of a homogeneous function must be factor beams is frequently overlooked in textbook treatments of symmetry and the economic region of production. It therefore merits special attention. As noted earlier, many authors in reference to a diagram with curved ridgelines will argue that the area within the ridgelines is *exclusively Stage II for both factors*. As we have seen, such statements are only true if the ridgelines are factor beams. Otherwise, Figure 2.15 prevails in which case it is clear that the area bounded by the ridgelines can include portions of Stage I for x_1 and/or x_2. That area within the ridgelines that constitutes the economic region of production is discussed in Chapter 3.

2.3 ONE PRODUCT, s-VARIABLE FACTORS

This section extends ideas developed in Section 2.2 to the *s*-variable factor case. For the most part we merely present the expanded equations for the concepts developed earlier. One exception is that of the quasi-function coefficient, a new idea introduced in this section.

A production process with a single output and *s*-variable factors of production is represented by the production function,

$$y = f(x_1, \ldots, x_s | x_{s+1}, \ldots, x_n) \tag{2.102}$$

with associated average and marginal productivity functions

$$APP_i \equiv y/x_i \qquad \text{for } i = 1, \ldots, s \tag{2.103}$$

and

$$MPP_i \equiv \partial y/\partial x_i \qquad \text{for } i = 1, \ldots, s \tag{2.104}$$

In the s-variable factor case, isoquants are production surfaces in s dimensions with y held constant.

Definitions of other technical concepts for the s-variable factor case are analogous to the two-factor case. Hence

$$\sigma_{il} = \frac{f_i f_l (x_i f_i + x_l f_l)}{x_i x_l (2 f_{il} f_i f_l - f_{ii} f_l^2 - f_{ll} f_i^2)} \qquad \text{for } i,l = 1, \ldots, s \text{ and } i \neq l \tag{2.105}$$

are the partial elasticities of factor substitution;

$$E_i \equiv \partial y/\partial x_i \cdot x_i/y = MPP_i/APP_i \qquad i = 1, \ldots, s \tag{2.106}$$

are the partial elasticities of production; and the function coefficient is

$$\epsilon \equiv (dy/y)/(dx_k/x_k) = dy/dx_k \cdot x_k/y \tag{2.107}$$

where $dx_1/x_1 = dx_2/x_2 = \cdots = dx_n/x_n$ and k is any factor. Again,

$$\epsilon = \sum_{i=1}^{n} E_i \tag{2.108}$$

In the case of production functions with three or more factors an additional production elasticity concept is useful. We call this elasticity, for lack of a better term, the *quasi-function coefficient.* The quasi-function coefficient is like the function coefficient in that it is a measure of percentage change in output in response to a given proportional percentage change in input. However, for the quasi-function coefficient only a *subset* of the factors must be varied proportionally whereas the function coefficient requires proportional variation of *all* factors—fixed and variable. Let the quasi-function coefficient be denoted ξ (the Greek letter, xi, pronounced as zī). Then

$$\xi \equiv (dy/y)/(dx_k/x_k) = dy/dx_k \cdot x_k/y \tag{2.109}$$

where $dx_1/x_1 = dx_2/x_2 = \cdots = dx_m/x_m$ and k is any factor $1, \ldots, m$ and $2 \le m \le n - 1$. Like for the function coefficient,

$$\xi = \sum_{i=1}^{m} E_i \tag{2.110}$$

Thus, the quasi-function coefficient, of which there are many, measures percentage change in output for a proportional percentage change in whatever subset of factors one may wish to consider variable. We will find this concept useful in Chapters 3 and 4 when we are considering factor demand functions and product supply functions for alternative lengths of run.

2.4 GEOMETRIC INTERPRETATION OF CONCAVITY AND QUASI-CONCAVITY

In previous sections of this chapter, we have used the terms concave and convex to describe the shape of production functions and isoquants. We digress from technical aspects of production in this section to give formal definition and geometric interpretation to these and related mathematical terms. Specifically, we will distinguish between concavity, weak concavity, strict concavity and quasi-concavity. Similar convexity terminology will also be defined. The student should fully understand these concepts before moving on to other chapters, as these concepts are directly tied to the second-order conditions for economic optimization.

2.4.a Functions of a Single Variable

First consider the case of a function $s(x)$ that has a single argument, x. For any two points x^0 and x^1, a strictly concave function is a function that lies above the straight line connecting $s(x^0)$ and $s(x^1)$. Formally, if x^m is a point between x^0 and x^1 (i.e., $x^0 < x^m < x^1$) given by

 strictly concave

$$x^m = \lambda x^0 + (1 - \lambda)x^1 \quad \text{with } 0 < \lambda < 1 \tag{2.110}$$

then $s(x)$ is *strictly concave* if it satisfies the *strict inequality*,

$$s(x^m) > \lambda s(x^0) + (1 - \lambda)\,s(x^1) \tag{2.111}$$

The variable, λ, in (2.110) and (2.111) is used in the definition to indicate that the inequality in (2.111) must hold for *all* values of x (and all values of λ between zero and one) between the arbitrary points x^0 and x^1. The right-hand side of the inequality (2.111) is the height of a straight line between $s(x^0)$ and $s(x^1)$ evaluated at the point x^m; that is, it is a linear interpolation between $s(x^0)$ and $s(x^1)$ evaluated at x^m. A strictly concave function is illustrated in panel (*a*) of Figure 2.27. Point A is the left-hand side of (2.111), $s(x^m)$,

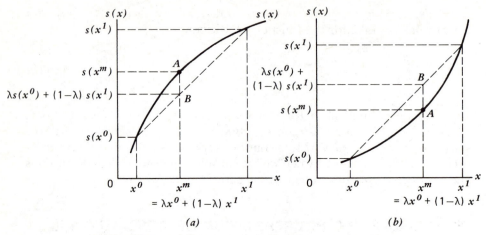

Figure 2.27. A two-dimensional geometric interpretation of concavity and convexity. (*a*) A concave function. (*b*) A convex function.

whereas point B is the right-hand side of (2.111). Since $A > B$ for all values of x between x^0 and x^1, the function is strictly concave.

A *strictly convex* function is defined by reversing the strict inequality in (2.111); that is,

$$s(x^m) < \lambda s(x^0) + (1 - \lambda) s(x^1) \tag{2.112}$$

A strictly convex function is shown in panel (b) of Figure 2.27.

A *weakly concave* or simply *concave* function is defined as a function that satisfies the inequality,

$$s(x^m) \geq \lambda s(x^0) + (1 - \lambda) s(x^1) \tag{2.113}$$

whereas a *weakly convex* or *convex* function satisfies

$$s(x^m) \leq \lambda s(x^0) + (1 - \lambda) s(x^1) \tag{2.114}$$

Note that (2.113) differs from (2.111) and (2.114) differs from (2.112) only in that > is replaced by ≥ and < is replaced by ≤, respectively. If the equality in (2.113) or (2.114) is satisfied for all λ, then the segment of the function between x^0 and x^1 is linear. A function that is both weakly concave and weakly convex is linear. Finally, a function can be strictly concave for some values of x and strictly convex for other values of x.

The notion of quasi-concavity is less restrictive than concavity. Formally, a *quasi-concave* function is one that satisfies

$$s[\lambda x^0 + (1 - \lambda)x^1] \geq \min[s(x^0), s(x^1)] \quad \text{with } 0 < \lambda < 1 \tag{2.115}$$

Using our definition of x^m, it can be seen that the left-hand side of (2.115) is $s(x)$ evaluated at x^m. The function is *strictly quasi-concave* if a strict inequality holds for (2.115), and *weakly quasi-concave* if the inequality *or* equality of (2.115) holds.

Figure 2.28a illustrates a function that is strictly quasi-concave. Note that the function, which has the shape of a traditional three-stage production function, is strictly convex for some values of x and strictly concave for other values. Thus, a quasi-concavity condition is less restrictive than a concavity condition.

A quasi-convex function is defined as one satisfying

$$s[\lambda x^0 + (1 - \lambda)x^1] \leq max[s(x^0), s(x^1)] \tag{2.116}$$

Moreover, the function is *strictly quasi-convex* if (2.116) holds with strict inequality and *weakly quasi-convex* if (2.116) holds with inequality or equality. Figure 2.28b illustrates a function that is strictly quasi-convex for values of x between 0 and the x value associated with the maximum point (x^2), but quasi-concave for values of x to the right of that associated with the minimum point (x^m). Thus, we see that quasi-concavity and quasi-convexity may overlap.

2.4.b Functions of More Than One Variable

Formal definition of the above curvature terminology is the same for a function of n variables, $s(x_1, \ldots, x_n)$, as for the single variable case, except that x^0, x^m, and x^1 should be thought of as points in n-dimension space. That is, let $x^0 = (x_1^0, \ldots, x_n^0)$, $x^1 = (x_1^1, \ldots, x_n^1)$, and $x^m = (x_1^m, \ldots, x_n^m)$. Consequently, we will not repeat formal statements of the preceding curvature definitions. How-

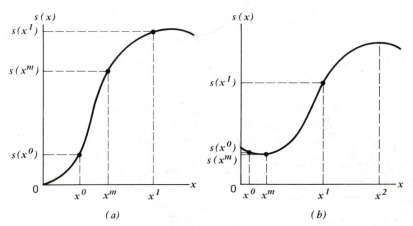

Figure 2.28. A two-dimensional geometric interpretation of quasi-concavity and quasi-convexity. (a) A strictly quasi-concave function. (b) A function that is not quasi-concave over its whole domain.

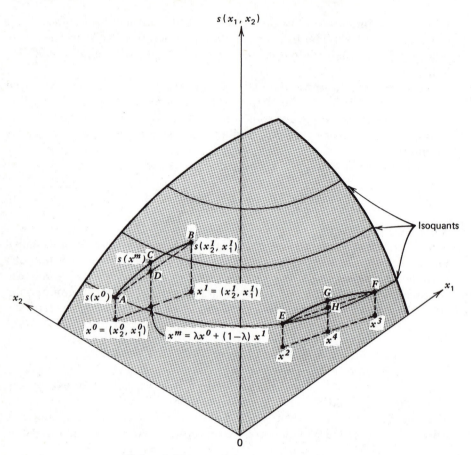

Figure 2.29. A strictly concave function.

ever, we will graphically illustrate their meaning in the two-independent variables case.[13] To add relevance, our illustration will be in terms of a production surface.

Figure 2.29 illustrates a strictly concave production surface for two variable factors, x_1 and x_2; x^0 represents the point (x_1^0, x_2^0) and x^1 represents the point (x_1^1, x_2^1). The point x^m is on a line between x^0 and x^1 in the (x_1, x_2) space. Point A is the height of the function $s(x_1, x_2)$ evaluated at x^0, while point B is the height of function at x^1. The heavy curve connecting points A and B traces out the production surface associated with points along the dashed line between x^0 and x^1. Point C is the height of the surface evaluated at x^m, and point D is a linear interpolation between A and B at x^m. Since C is higher than D, the surface is strictly concave by definition (2.111).

[13]Our graphical presentation closely follows Chiang (1974).

To illustrate that a strictly concave function has convex isoquants, consider the points x^2 and x^3 in Figure 2.29. The height of the production surface at these points, E and F, respectively, is drawn to be the same; thus E and F lie on a single isoquant. The heavy curve between E and F traces out the production surface associated with factor combinations on a line between x^2 and x^3. As drawn, the point G, which is associated with a point x^4 between x^2 and x^3, exceeds the linear interpolation point H. Thus, the surface is strictly concave in this region. But carefully note that this can occur *only* if isoquants are convex to the origin. If isoquants are concave to the origin, the heavy line that would trace out the production surface between E and F would sag down rather than bulge up, implying that the production surface was convex, not concave. The fact that a strictly concave production function implies convex isoquants is critical, so the student should carefully study Figure 2.29 until this fact becomes clear.

Differences between concavity and quasi-concavity are more subtle in the n-variable case than in the single variable case; these differences are extremely important in the context of production economics theory. To illustrate similarities and differences in these concepts, consider Figure 2.30. The heavy line between A and B traces out the production surface for factor combinations on a line between x^0 and x^1. Since any point on this line, say C, is greater than A (the minimum of A and B), the production function is strictly quasi-concave in this region. Note, however, that the function in Figure 2.30 is not concave in this region.

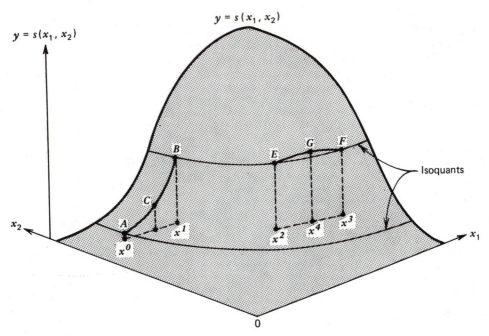

Figure 2.30. A strictly quasi-concave function.

Now consider points E and F in Figure 2.30. E and F are on an isoquant and the production surface associated with factor combinations on a line between x^2 and x^3 bulges up. Since any point between E and F, say G, is greater than E or F, the production function is strictly quasi-concave in this region. Again, note that the only way the curve EF can bulge up (thus, implying strict quasi-concavity) is for isoquants to be convex to the origin.

Now compare Figures 2.29 and 2.30. Both concave and quasi-concave functions imply isoquants that are convex to the origin. However, a quasi-concave function can exhibit all three stages of production, while a concave production function cannot exhibit Stage I. Thus concavity is a more restrictive condition than quasi-concavity. Worded another way, concavity implies quasi-concavity, but quasi-concavity does not necessarily imply concavity.

The student is encouraged to draw three-dimensional graphs that illustrate convex and quasi-convex functions, and to graph functions that do not satisfy any of these conditions for all values of the variables.

As a final note, we should point out that the interpolation formulae used to define curvature concepts are not very useful for mechanically checking the curvature of particular functions. Rather, for functions of a single variable, curvature is typically checked by applying the second derivative test, whereas curvature of functions of two or more variables is typically determined by algebraically or numerically checking the signs of the determinants of principal minors of Hessian or bordered Hessian matrices. In chapters which follow, we will state second-order conditions for economic optimization in terms of both curvature of the objective function and in terms of the appropriate Hessian (for unconstrained optimization) or bordered Hessian (for constrained optimization). Readers who have an intuitive understanding of curvature concepts will be clearly advantaged in understanding second-order conditions, even though algebraic methods of determining curvature are essential in empirical studies and for examining the theoretical properties of particular functions. The reader is referred to Chapters 9, 11, and 12 of Chiang (1974) for further discussion.

2.5 NOTES ON FUNCTIONAL FORMS AND EMPIRICAL STUDIES

Only a few mathematical forms of production functions are commonly used (i.e., those that are easy to analytically manipulate) in textbook and classroom problems. We trust that the student, when faced with an empirical problem, will be more creative, imaginative and thorough in selecting a functional form than professors or authors of textbooks. Ideally, the empirical analyst should first appeal to technical (biological, chemical, nutritional, etc.) theory for specification of the functional form for modeling the particular production process in question. Given a functional form, the analyst can proceed directly to the problem of parameter estimation. Typically, however, technical theory does not provide much guidance in terms of selecting a particular mathematical form.[14] This being the case, the analyst should statistically compare the fit of different functional forms or use an extremely flexible form to avoid forcing certain technical attributes on the data—attributes that are not justified a priori. Unfortunately, general functional forms are usually difficult to manipulate mathematically (often not amenable to analytic solutions) and pose statistical problems. Nevertheless, the mathematical and statistical difficulties posed by general forms are quite often justified by the increased precision allowed by the general forms. The fact that numerical search techniques and sophisticated econometric estimation procedures are readily available to most analysts these days, relegates analytical solution and model simplicity to a lower order of importance in empirical work than in the past.

It is beyond the scope of this book to address estimation considerations, but we do provide a summary of several common textbook production functions (Table 2.1) and some less widely used functional forms (Table 2.2) that should be considered for empirical problems. Some technical properties of the functions are also given in these tables.

The functions given in Table 2.1 have certain desirable properties but also force certain technical attributes on the data. For example, the Cobb–Douglas function has convex isoquants, but it has unitary elasticity of substitution; it does not allow for technically independent or competitive factors, nor does it allow for Stages I and III along with Stage II. That is, MPP_i and APP_i are monotonically decreasing functions for all x_i—the entire factor–factor space is Stage II—given $0 < b_i < 1$, which is the usual case. However, the Cobb–Douglas may be a good approximation for production processes for which factors are imperfect substitutes over the entire range of x_1, x_2 values. Also, the Cobb–Douglas is relatively easy to estimate because in logarithmic form it is linear in parameters; also, it is parsimonious in parameters.

The quadratic production function (Table 2.1) is appealing because it gives a second-order local (Taylor's series) approximation to any function. (An nth-order approximation to a function means that the first n derivatives of that function, as well as the height of the function, are approximated about a particular point.) A cubic specification (not shown) is even more appealing because it gives a third-order approximation to any function. Both the quadratic and cubic functions are relatively easy to statistically estimate but are messy to mathematically manipulate.[15] Consequently, polynomials are quite often used in empirical studies but are less frequently used for textbook derivations.

Most classroom instructors and writers of production textbooks have another bad habit in that they tend to draw production functions that show maximum TPP as a single point on the production surface. With many agricultural production processes, especially crop yield response to plant nutrients, it is much more common to find an extended yield plateau before

---

[14]For a discussion of this issue in the context of the response of crops to plant nutrients, see Swanson (1963) and the National Academy of Sciences report (1961).

[15]To provide an incentive to touch up on matrix algebra, we note that economic calculations based on the quadratic function are much more easily done in matrix form.

Table 2.1 Forms and Properties of Some Commonly Used Production Functions

Production Function		Restrictions	
		Strict Concavity	Strict Quasi-concavity
Generalized Cobb–Douglas	$y = Ax_1^{b_1}x_2^{b_2}$	$0 < b_1 < 1$ $0 < b_2 < 1$ $0 < (b_1 + b_2) < 1$ $A > 0$	$b_1 > 0$ $b_2 > 0$ $A > 0$
Quadratic[a]	$y = a_0 + a_1x_1 + a_2x_2$ $\quad + \frac{1}{2}b_1x_1^2 + \frac{1}{2}b_2x_2^2$ $\quad + b_3x_1x_2$	$b_1b_2 > b_3^2$ $b_1 < 0$ $b_2 < 0$ $a_1 > 0$ $a_2 > 0$	Without strict concavity, the quadratic function may be quasi-concave in local, but not global regions
Generalized constant elasticity of substitution (CES)	$y = A[bx_1^{-g} + (1 - b)x_2^{-g}]^{-v/g}$	$A > 0$ $0 < b < 1$ $0 < v \le 1$ $g > -1$	$A > 0$ $0 < b < 1$ $v > 0$ $g > -1$
Transcendental	$y = Ax_1^{a_1}e^{b_1x_1}x_2^{a_2}e^{b_2x_2}$	Strictly concave globally if $b_i < 0$, $A > 0$ and $0 < a_i \le 1$; may be satisfied locally for other parameter values	Strictly quasi-concave globally if $A > 0$ and $a_i > 0$; may be satisfied locally for other parameter values

Homogeneity	Factor Elasticity	Function Coefficient
Homogeneous of degree $(b_1 + b_2)$	$E_1 = b_1, E_2 = b_2$	$\epsilon = b_1 + b_2$
Not homogeneous	$E_i = \dfrac{a_i x_i + b_i x_i^2 + b_3 x_i x_l}{a_0 + a_1 x_1 + a_2 x_2 + \frac{1}{2}b_1 x_i^2 + \frac{1}{2}b_2 x_2^2 + b_3 x_1 x_2}$ for $i,l = 1, 2$	$\epsilon = E_1 + E_2$
Homogeneous of degree v	$E_1 = vb[bx_1^{-g} + (1 - b)x_2^{-g}]^{-1}x_1^{-g}$ $E_2 = v(1 - b)[bx_1^{-g} + (1 - b)x_2^{-g}]^{-1}x_2^{-g}$	$\epsilon = v$
Not homogeneous unless $b_1 = b_2 = 0$ in which case it reduces to the Generalized Cobb–Douglas function	$E_1 = b_1 x_1 + a_1$ $E_2 = b_2 x_2 + a_2$	$\epsilon = a_1 + a_2$ $+ b_1 x_1 + b_2 x_2$

Table 2.1 (Continued)

Production Function	Elasticity of Substitution	Technical Interdependence	Ridgeline Pattern
Generalized Cobb–Douglas	$\sigma = 1$	Complementary factors only $K \gtreqless 0$ $A > 0$ $b_1 > 0$ $b_2 > 0$	No ridgelines
Quadratic[a]	Messy equation; σ is not a constant	$b_3 < 0$: Competitive factors $b_3 = 0$: Independent factors $b_3 > 0$: Complementary factors	a. Ridgelines are positively sloped if factors are complementary b. Ridgelines are negatively sloped if factors are competitive c. Ridgelines are rectangular if factors are independent
Generalized constant elasticity of substitution (CES)	$\sigma = \dfrac{1}{1 + g}$	$v + g < 0$: Competitive factors $v + g = 0$: Independent factors $v + g > 0$: Complementary factors	No ridgelines
Transcendental[b]	Messy equation; σ is not a constant except for the Cobb–Douglas case	Complementary factors in regions of negatively sloped isoquants; independent factors on the ridgelines; and competitive factors in regions of positively sloped isoquants	Rectangular ridgelines

Isoquant			
Slope	*Convexity*	*Spacing*	*Stages of Production*
Negative	Convex to origin	$b_1 + b_2 > 1$: Isoquants converge $b_1 + b_2 = 1$: Isoquants equally spaced $b_1 + b_2 < 1$: Isoquants diverge	a. Exhibits Stage II only for each individual factor and with respect to scale given strict concavity b. Exhibits Stage I *or* II only for each individual factor and with respect to scale given strict quasi-concavity
Isoquants are elliptical; thus there are areas of both positive, negative, zero, and infinite slope	Convex to origin[c]	$a_i, b_i > 0$: Isoquants converge $b_i < 0$: Isoquants diverge for $i = 1,2$	a. Exhibits Stages II and III for each individual factor and with respect to scale given strict concavity b. Exhibits Stage I only or II and III with respect to each individual factor and scale given strict quasi-concavity
Negative	Convex to origin	$v > 1$: Isoquants converge $v = 1$: Isoquants equally spaced $v < 1$: Isoquants diverge	a. Exhibits Stage II only for each individual factor and with respect to scale given strict concavity b. Exhibits Stage I *or* II only with respect to scale given strict quasi-concavity
Areas of positive and areas of negative slope	Convex to origin[c]	Isoquants converge, then diverge with strict quasi-concavity	a. Exhibits Stages I, II, and III with respect to each factor and scale given quasi-concavity restrictions b. Exhibits Stages II and III for each individual factor and with respect to scale given strict concavity

[a]The parameters b_1 and b_2 are multiplied by $\frac{1}{2}$ to simplify terms of the derivations based on this function. The quadratic function serves as a second-order local approximation to any function (Taylor's series).

[b]The transcendental function is more versatile than the Cobb–Douglas, but it is more difficult to analytically manipulate. For additional discussion of the transcendental function, see Halter, Carter and Hocking.

[c]Within the ridgelines and given the appropriate parameter restrictions.

Table 2.2 Forms and Properties of Uncommon and Flexible Production Functions

Production Function		Curvature	Properties	Notes
Liebig	$y = \min[y_m, (a_1 + b_1 x_1),$ $(a_2 + b_2 x_2)]$	Weakly concave if $b_1, b_2 \geq 0$	a. Factors x_1 and x_2 are technically independent if neither is limiting, but technically complementary at the kink in the production function attributal to the other factor being limiting b. y_m is maximum yield when neither x_1 nor x_2 is limiting	a. The function is a mathematical formulation of Justus von Liebig's (a mid 19th century soil scientist) "law of the minimum" of plant growth; according to this law, plants linearly respond to a particular nutrient (x_1) until another nutrient (x_2) becomes limiting; with x_2 limiting, y does not change as x_1 is increased, thus exhibiting a yield plateau b. Most present day plant and soil scientists subscribe (perhaps loosely) to this concept of plant growth; however, there is no definitive evidence that this should be regarded as a "law" in the strict sense nor any definitive evidence that a discontinuity exists in production functions for plant growth

Name	Equation	Concavity	Properties	Notes
Mitscherlich–Baule	$y = \beta_1(1 - e^{-\beta_3(\beta_4 + x_1)}) \cdot (1 - e^{-\beta_5(\beta_6 + x_2)})$	Strictly concave if $\beta_1, \beta_3, \beta_5 > 0$	a. Exhibits Stage II only b. Has an asymptotic yield plateau c. Allows only for technically complementary factors	a. Another one of the so-called laws of plant growth; this concept followed Liebig's law b. The parameters β_4 and β_6 can be thought of as levels of x_1 and x_2, respectively, that are inherent in the production system; for example, if x_1 is applied nitrogen, then β_4 can be thought of as nitrogen provided to the plant by native fertility of the soil
Generalized Mitscherlich–Baule	$y = \beta_1(1 - e^{-\beta_3(\beta_4 + x_1)^{\beta_7}}) \cdot (1 - e^{-\beta_5(\beta_6 + x_2)^{\beta_8}})$	Strictly quasi-concave if $\beta_1, \beta_3, \beta_5, \beta_7, \beta_8 > 0$	Same as above, except that it exhibits Stages I and II for x_1 if $0 < \beta_7 < 1$ and Stages I and II for x_2 if $0 < \beta_8 < 1$	Same as for Mitscherlich–Baule
Hyperbolic for technically complementary factors	$y = [\beta_1 \coth(\beta_2 + \beta_3 x_1) + \beta_4 \coth(\beta_5 + \beta_6 x_2)]^{-1}$	Strictly quasi-concave if $\beta_i > 0$ for all i	a. Exhibits Stages I and II or Stage II only b. Has an asymptotic yield plateau c. Allows only for technically complementary factors	a. Coth u is the hyperbolic cotangent of u b. A flexible function except that it allows only for technically complementary factors
Hyperbolic for technically independent factors	$y = \beta_1 \tanh(\beta_2 + \beta_3 x_1) + \beta_4 \tanh(\beta_5 + \beta_6 x_2)$	Strictly quasi-concave if $\beta_1, \beta_3, \beta_4,$ and $\beta_6 > 0$	a. Exhibits Stage I and II or Stage II only b. Has an asymptotic yield plateau c. Allows only for technically independent factors	a. Tanh u is the hyperbolic tangent of u. In comparing this function with the hyperbolic/complementary factor function, note that tanh = 1/coth u

Table 2.2 (Continued)

Production Function	Curvature	Properties	Notes
Liebig (x_1)/Mitscherlich (x_2, x_3)	$y = \min[\beta_1(1 - e^{-\beta_3(\beta_4 + x_2)}), (1 - e^{-\beta_5(\beta_6 + x_3)})(\beta_7 + \beta_8 x_1)]$ Weakly concave if $\beta_1, \beta_3, \beta_5, \beta_8 > 0$		a. Some soil scientists have argued that mobile plant nutrients (e.g., nitrogen) obey Liebig's law, while immobile nutrients (e.g., phosphorus and potassium) obey the Mitscherlich–Baule concept of plant growth. This function mathematically combines these concepts
Spillman	$y = (\beta_1 - \beta_2\beta_3^{x_1}) \cdot (\beta_4 - \beta_5\beta_6^{x_2})$ Strictly concave if $\beta_2, \beta_3, \beta_5, \beta_6 > 0$	a. Similar to Mitscherlich–Baule function	
Cobb–Douglas with intercept	$y = \beta_1 + \beta_2 x_1^{\beta_3} x_2^{\beta_4}$ Strictly concave if $\beta_2 > 0$; $0 < \beta_3 < 1$; $0 < \beta_4 < 1$	a. Same as conventional Cobb–Douglas	a. A generalization of the Cobb–Douglas curvature to allow for a nonzero intercept
Square root	$y = \beta_1 + \beta_2 x_1 + \beta_3 x_2 + \beta_4\sqrt{x_1} + \beta_5\sqrt{x_2} + \beta_6\sqrt{x_1 x_2}$ Strictly concave if $\beta_4, \beta_5, \beta_6 > 0$; may be strictly concave locally if $\beta_6 < 0$ and $\beta_4, \beta_5 > 0$	a. Similar to quadratic	a. Loosely speaking, the square root allows for sharper curvature near maximum TPP and a less rapid decrease of TPP in Stage III than does the conventional quadratic

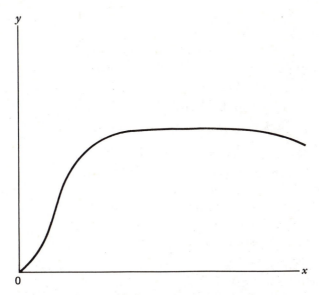

Figure 2.31.   An illustration of the yield plateau concept.

Stage III is encountered. This yield plateau concept is graphically illustrated for the single-factor case in Figure 2.31; several of the functions in Table 2.2 allow for this general shape without the Stage III component.

In this chapter, we discussed certain attributes of particular production functions, such as whether they were homogeneous or exhibited constant elasticity of substitution. However, *there is nothing sacred about such properties unless technical theory or empirical data indicate these properties.* Nevertheless, we must be aware of the properties of alternative production function specifications in order to know the technical and economic implications of a particular functional form.

As a final note, the production functions and results presented in Tables 2.1 and 2.2 can be extended in a straightforward way to the *n*-factor case.

2.6 PROBLEMS

2-1. Given the single-variable factor production function $y = 16x^2 - 4x^3$, find the input levels that form the boundaries of Stage II. Sketch *TPP*, *APP*, and *MPP* on a common set of axes, and show the locations of the stages of production. Remember to check second-order conditions.

2-2. Given the production function $y = Ax_1^{b_1}x_2^{b_2}$, find the equation of the isocline defined by $RTS = 1$.

2-3. Distinguish between factor substitution and factor interdependence. Define and show geometrically the three cases possible for each.

2-4. Show that the production function $y = 10x_1^2 + 11x_1x_2 + 19x_2^2$ exhibits increasing returns to scale.

2-5. For each of the two-variable production functions listed below, deduce the sign and magnitude that each parameter must have in order to assure that the function exhibits diminishing marginal productivity. Then, sketch *TPP*, *APP*, and *MPP* for factor x_1 for each function.

(a) $y = b_1x_1 + b_2x_2$ (linear).

(b) $y = Ax_1^{b_1}x_2^{b_2}$ (Cobb–Douglas).

(c) $y = b_1x_1 + b_2x_2 + \frac{1}{2}b_3x_1^2 + \frac{1}{2}b_4x_2^2 + b_5x_1x_2$ (quadratic).

(d) $y = Ax_1^{a_1}e^{b_1x_1}x_2^{a_2}e^{b_2x_2}$ (transcendental).

2-6. For each of the functions in Problem 2-5, determine the nature of the isoquant pattern (slope and convexity) for the appropriate parameter signs and ranges. In addition, determine the ridgeline equations for each function. Finally, sketch the isoquants.

2-7. Draw a strictly quasi-concave function, $y = s(x)$, that is

(a) Strictly concave.

(b) Strictly convex.

(c) Strictly concave for some values of x and strictly convex for the other values of x.

(d) Linear.

2.7 SELECTED BIBLIOGRAPHY

Carlson, S. *A Study on the Pure Theory of Production.* New York: Sentry Press, 1965, Chapter 2.

Chiang, A. C. *Fundamental Methods of Mathematical Economics.* New York: McGraw-Hill, 1974.

Dillon, J. L. *The Analysis of Response in Crop and Livestock Production.* Oxford: Pergammon Press, 1968, Chapter 1.

Ferguson, C. E. *The Neoclassical Theory of Production and Distribution.* Cambridge: Cambridge University Press, 1969, Chapters 4 and 5. This book is a comprehensive treatment of production economics. The level of difficulty is mixed. Numerous citations of appropriate literature make this book a valuable reference for the serious student of production economics.

Frisch, R. *Theory of Production.* Chicago: Rand McNally, 1965, Chapters 5–8. Like Carlson, this book is a classic in production economics theory. Unfortunately, it is out of print. Chapters 5–8, dealing with technical matters, are excellent. The notation and terminology used in the book will seem foreign to U.S. students. The book is an advanced treatment of production theory.

Gould, J. P., and C. E. Ferguson. *Microeconomic Theory.* Homewood, IL: Irwin, 1980, Chapters 5–6. This is a good intermediate microeconomic theory textbook with more than the usual attention to theory of the firm.

Halter, A. N., H. O. Carter, and J. G. Hocking. "A Note on the Transcendental Production Function," *J. Farm Econ.*, Vol. 39 (1957): pp. 966–974.

Heady, E. O. *Economics of Agricultural Production and Resource Use.* New York: Prentice-Hall, 1952, Chapters 2, 3, and 5.

Heady, E. O., and J. L. Dillon. *Agricultural Production Functions.* Ames: Iowa State University Press, 1961, Chapter 3.

Henderson, J. M., and R. E. Quandt. *Microeconomic Theory: A Mathematical Approach.* 3rd ed. New York: McGraw-Hill, 1980, Chapters 4 and 5.

Levenson, A. M., and B. S. Solon. "Returns to Scale and the Spacing of Isoquants," *Amer. Econ. Rev.,* Vol. 56 (1966): pp. 501–505.

Mundlak, Y. "A Note on the Symmetry of Homogeneous Production Functions and the Three Stages of Production," *J. Farm Econ.,* Vol. 40 (1958): pp. 756–761.

National Academy of Sciences–National Research Council. *Status and Methods of Research in Economic and Agronomic Aspects of Fertilizer Response and Use.* Washington, D.C.: NAS Publication 918, 1961.

Swanson, E. R. "The Static Theory of the Firm and the Three Laws of Plant Growth," *Soil Sci.,* Vol. 88 (1963): pp. 338–343.

CHAPTER 3

ECONOMIC ASPECTS OF PRODUCTION: THE INPUT PERSPECTIVE

Technical concepts discussed in the previous chapter are related to economic concepts in this and succeeding chapters. The focus in this chapter is on the economics of the firm as viewed from the "input side" as contrasted with the "output side" perspective, which is the thrust of Chapter 4. That is, in this chapter mathematical relationships and economic ideas related thereto are expressed with inputs as the independent variables, whereas in the next chapter output will be treated as the independent variable. We begin with the case of a single product and one-variable factor of production.

3.1 ONE-PRODUCT, ONE-VARIABLE FACTOR

Corresponding to the set of physical productivity functions is a set of value productivity functions; namely, the total, average, and marginal value productivity functions. *Total value product* is the value of output and is given by the price of the product times the quantity produced. To generalize the concepts for firms operating in imperfectly competitive markets, we assume that price can be a function of the quantity sold:

$$p = g(y) \tag{3.1}$$

Given this price (inverse product demand) function, total value product (TVP) is given by

$$TVP \equiv py \equiv p\,TPP = g(y)\,f(x) = g[f(x)]\,f(x) \tag{3.2}$$

Traditionally, when price times output is expressed as a function of input usage it is referred to as total value product, and when it is expressed as a function of output, it is referred to as total revenue (see Chapter 4).

Example 3.1 Let the production function be

$$y = 6x^2 - x^3 \tag{3.3}$$

and the price function be

$$p = y^{-1/2} \tag{3.4}$$

Then

$$TVP = y^{-1/2}(6x^2 - x^3)$$
$$= \frac{6x^2 - x^3}{(6x^2 - x^3)^{1/2}}$$
$$= (6x^2 - x^3)^{1/2} \tag{3.5}$$

If we assume perfect competition in the product market, which implies that a firm's output does not influence product price, then

$$TVP = p\, f(x) \tag{3.6}$$

The *average value product* (*AVP*) function is defined in general as

$$AVP \equiv \frac{TVP}{x} = \frac{g[f(x)]\, f(x)}{x} \tag{3.7}$$

and with perfect competition in the product market, we have

$$AVP = \frac{p\, f(x)}{x} \tag{3.8}$$

Marginal value productivity (*MVP*) of x, which is sometimes called marginal revenue product, is the exact rate of change of total value product resulting from an infinitesimal change in x. Thus,

$$MVP \equiv \frac{d(TVP)}{dx} = \frac{d\{g[f(x)]\, f(x)\}}{dx} \tag{3.9}$$

With a perfectly competitive product market, *MVP* is given simply as

$$MVP = \frac{d[p\, f(x)]}{dx} = p\, \frac{df(x)}{dx} = p\, MPP \tag{3.10}$$

Let us return to the previous example and derive *AVP* and *MVP* from the *TVP* function.

Example 3.2 Given

$$TVP = (6x^2 - x^3)^{1/2} \tag{3.11}$$

we have

$$AVP \equiv \frac{TVP}{x} = \frac{(6x^2 - x^3)^{1/2}}{x} = (6 - x)^{1/2} \tag{3.12}$$

and

$$MVP \equiv \frac{d(TVP)}{dx} = \frac{d[(6x^2 - x^3)^{1/2}]}{dx}$$

$$= \tfrac{1}{2}(6x^2 - x^3)^{-1/2}(12x - 3x^2) \qquad (3.13)$$

Closer investigation and interpretation of *MVP* is in order. Recall from (3.9) that

$$MVP = \frac{d\{g[f(x)]\ f(x)\}}{dx} \qquad (3.14)$$

Using the product rule for derivatives, (3.14) is

$$MVP = g[f(x)]\frac{d[f(x)]}{dx} + f(x)\frac{d\{g[f(x)]\}}{dx} \qquad (3.15)$$

Therefore,

$$MVP = p\ MPP + TPP\frac{dp}{dx} \qquad (3.16)$$

The first term on the right-hand side of (3.16), *p MPP*, represents the *value of the marginal physical productivity* (*VMP*) evaluated at a particular price. The last term, *TPP* (*dp/dx*), represents the change in *TVP*, which stems from the change in the price of *y* due to the increase in *x*, multiplied by the total output produced.[1] Hence,

$$MVP = VMP + \text{the change in total value product due}$$
$$\text{to the change in product price} \qquad (3.17)$$

The relationship shown in (3.17) is graphically illustrated in Figure 3.1. Note that in a perfectly competitive product market *MVP = VMP* since the price effect is zero.

We can further investigate the price effect in (3.17) for a firm in an imperfectly competitive product market by noting that (from the chain rule)

$$\frac{dp}{dx} = \frac{dp}{dy}\frac{dy}{dx} \qquad (3.18)$$

---

[1]Price, *p*, is a differentiable function of *x* because *p* = *g(y)* is a differentiable function of *y* and *y* = *f(x)* is a differentiable function of *x*; thus it makes sense to consider *dp/dx*.

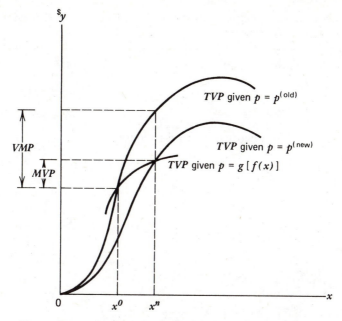

Figure 3.1. Graphic interpretation of relationship between *TVP*, *MVP*, and *VMP* when $dp/dx < 0$ (i.e., for downward sloping product demand).

Substituting (3.18) into (3.16) for dp/dx yields

$$MVP = p\ MPP + TPP\ \frac{dp}{dy}\left(\frac{dy}{dx}\right)$$

$$= p\ MPP + y\ \frac{dp}{dy}\ MPP$$

$$= p\ MPP + y\ \frac{p}{p}\frac{dp}{dy}\ MPP$$

$$= p\ MPP\left(1 + \frac{y}{p}\frac{dp}{dy}\right)$$

$$= VMP(1 + \lambda_p) = VMP\left(1 + \frac{1}{E_p}\right) \qquad (3.19)$$

where λ_p is the *price flexibility of demand* and E_p is the *price elasticity of demand.* From (3.19), note that if $\lambda_p < 0$, then *MVP* lies below *VMP*; if $\lambda_p = 0$, then *MVP* = *VMP*; and if $\lambda_p > 0$, then *MVP* lies above *VMP*. Of course, $\lambda_p > 0$ implies an upward sloping demand curve which only occurs with a Giffen good. Also note that *MVP* = 0 when *VMP* = 0 (i.e., *MPP* = 0) or when $\lambda_p = -1$ (i.e., the point of unitary elasticity of demand).

Let us consider a specific example of the relationship between MVP and VMP for $\lambda_p < 0$.

Example 3.3 Assume the quadratic production function,

$$y = 6x - \tfrac{1}{2}x^2 \tag{3.20}$$

and the linear inverse-product-demand function,

$$p = 16 - \tfrac{1}{2}y \tag{3.21}$$

Then

$$TPP = 6x - \tfrac{1}{2}x^2 \tag{3.22}$$

$$APP \equiv \frac{TPP}{x} = 6 - \tfrac{1}{2}x \tag{3.23}$$

$$MPP \equiv \frac{d(TPP)}{dx} = 6 - x \tag{3.24}$$

and

$$TVP \equiv p\,TPP = [16 - 3x + \tfrac{1}{4}x^2][6x - \tfrac{1}{2}x^2]$$
$$= 96x - 26x^2 + 3x^3 - \tfrac{1}{8}x^4 \tag{3.25}$$

$$MVP \equiv \frac{d(TVP)}{dx} = 96 - 52x + 9x^2 - \tfrac{1}{2}x^3 \tag{3.26}$$

$$VMP \equiv p\,MPP = [16 - 3x + \tfrac{1}{4}x^2](6 - x)$$
$$= 96 - 34x + 4.5x^2 - \tfrac{1}{4}x^3 \tag{3.27}$$

Equations 3.21 through 3.27 are plotted in Figure 3.2. Note that $MVP < VMP$ when $VMP > 0$ and that $MVP = 0$ at $x = 4$ and $VMP = 0$ at $x = 6$. As a special exercise we challenge the reader to explain why the TVP and MVP curves in Figure 3.2c behave strangely as x gets large. *Hint*: Consider the implication of (3.19) and related discussion as well as the fact that the maximum attainable output for this firm is 18 units.

3.1.a Factor Costs

Total factor cost is defined as factor price, r, which in general may be a function of the amount of the factor used, times the quantity of the factor employed, x, plus fixed costs, b. For the monopsonist firm (imperfect competition in the factor market),

$$r = h(x) \tag{3.28}$$

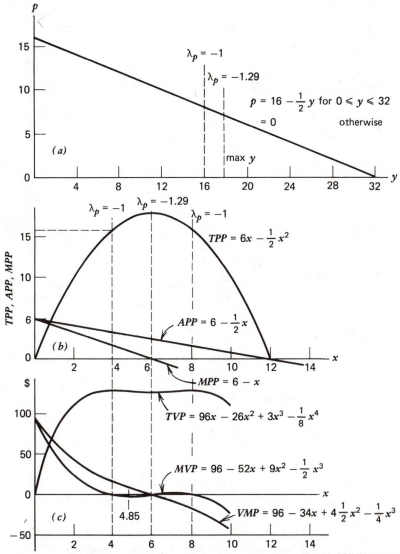

Figure 3.2. Relationship between *TVP*, *MVP*, *VMP*, *TPP*, and *MPP* for a quadratic production function and linear product demand function with $\lambda_p < 0$. (a) Product demand function. (b) Productivity functions. (c) Value productivity functions.

Equation 3.28 represents the firm's average factor cost or factor supply function. It relates the factor price to the quantity used and is typically assumed to be positively sloped.

In general, then, total factor cost, C, is given by

$$C \equiv r\,x + b = h(x)\,x + b \tag{3.29}$$

and for the perfectly competitive (factor market) firm

$$C \equiv r\,x + b \tag{3.30}$$

Finally, *variable factor cost* is given merely by dropping the fixed cost component from (3.29) or (3.30). For the perfectly competitive case, variable factor cost, c, is

$$c \equiv r\,x \tag{3.31}$$

Consistent with the distinction between *TVP* and total revenue (*TR*), in this chapter we use the terminology total *factor* cost (*C*) and variable *factor* cost (*c*) where these costs are expressed in terms of input usage. In Chapter 4 we will use the traditional terminology, total cost (*TC*) and variable cost (*VC*) when costs are expressed as a function of output.

Using equation 3.29, we can define *marginal factor cost (MFC)* as

$$MFC \equiv \frac{dC}{dx} = \frac{d[h(x)x + b]}{dx} \tag{3.32}$$

Expanding the derivative in (3.32) gives

$$MFC = h(x) + x\,\frac{d[h(x)]}{dx} + 0 \tag{3.33}$$

or

$$
\begin{aligned}
MFC &= r + x\,\frac{dr}{dx} \\
&= r\!\left(1 + \frac{x}{r}\frac{dr}{dx}\right) \\
&= r(1 + \lambda_r)
\end{aligned}
\tag{3.34}
$$

where λ_r is *factor price flexibility*. If we assume perfect competition in the factor market ($\lambda_r = 0$), it follows from (3.34) that $MFC = r$. So, as in the case of *VMP* versus *MVP*, we see that *MFC* is the general case and a constant factor price is merely a special case.

3.1.b Profit and Maximum Profit

Given the previous definition of total factor costs, *C*, and total value product, *TVP*, we can define the *profit* (π) equation as

$$\pi \equiv TVP - C \tag{3.35}$$

or, using our general notation for the production function and product and factor price relationships,

$$\pi = g[f(x)] \, f(x) - [h(x)x + b] \tag{3.36}$$

If we assume perfect competition in both the product and factor markets, (3.36) reduces to

$$\pi = p \, f(x) - r \, x - b \tag{3.37}$$

Referring back to profit equation 3.36, we should ask ourselves: What is the slope of the equation when profit is maximum? The obvious answer is that the slope is zero, which suggests that the *first-order condition for unconstrained profit maximization* is

$$d\pi/dx = 0 \tag{3.38}$$

To gain insight into what the first-order condition for maximum profit (3.38) implies, we take the derivative of the general profit equation 3.36 with respect to x and set the result equal to zero. This gives

$$\frac{d\pi}{dx} = g[f(x)] \frac{df(x)}{dx} + f(x) \frac{dg[f(x)]}{dx}$$

$$- h(x) - x \frac{dh(x)}{dx} = 0 \tag{3.39}$$

which implies

$$g[f(x)] \frac{df(x)}{dx} + f(x) \frac{dg[f(x)]}{dx} = h(x) + x \frac{dh(x)}{dx} \tag{3.40}$$

or that

$$MVP = MFC \tag{3.41}$$

Notice that if we assume perfect competition in both product and factor markets, we obtain

$$\frac{d\pi}{dx} = p \frac{df(x)}{dx} - r = 0 \tag{3.42}$$

which implies

$$p \, MPP = r \tag{3.43}$$

Condition (3.43) simply says that the profit-maximizing level of x is obtained by equating *VMP* with factor price. Or, it can be expressed as equating *MPP* with the ratio of factor price to product price:

$$MPP = r/p \tag{3.44}$$

We know, of course, that *MVP* and *MFC* in (3.41) and *MPP* in (3.43) or (3.44) are in general functions of the variable input, *x*. Thus, solving any of these expressions for *x* yields the input level where the first-order condition is satisfied. Consider the following example for the perfectly competitive case.

Example 3.4 Suppose that a firm, operating in perfectly competitive product and factor markets, faces the production function,

$$y = a \ln x \qquad \text{with } a > 0 \tag{3.45}$$

and desires to maximize profit, which is

$$\begin{aligned} \pi &= p\,y - r\,x - b \\ &= p\,a \ln x - r\,x - b \end{aligned} \tag{3.46}$$

The first-order condition for maximum profit is

$$\frac{d\pi}{dx} = \frac{p\,a}{x} - r = 0 \tag{3.47}$$

Solving (3.47) for *x*, we get

$$x^* = \frac{p\,a}{r} \tag{3.48}$$

which is the optimal factor level as a function of product and factor prices and the production function parameter, *a*. The exponent, *, is used throughout to denote an optimal level of a variable.

From the example as well as from equation 3.40 or 3.42, we see that the general statement of the first-order condition and/or the optimal input level is independent of the level of fixed cost in the profit equation, 3.36, 3.37, or 3.46. That is, the first-order condition for profit maximization is unaffected by the level of fixed cost.

With any particular theoretical or applied problem, we have no a priori assurance that the profit equation is concave or convex or whether it has only one peak. Thus, the first-order condition, (3.38), is only a necessary condition and is not sufficient for maximum profit (see Figure 3.3). The *second-order*

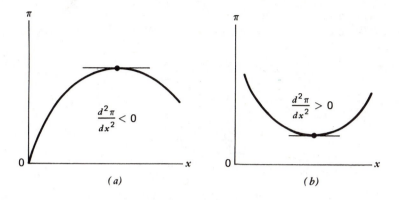

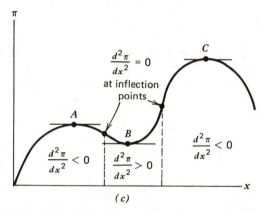

Figure 3.3. Various types of profit functions and interpretation of first- and second-order conditions. (a) The solution to $d\pi/dx = 0$ gives maximum profit. (b) The solution to $d\pi/dx = 0$ gives minimum profit. (c) Three solutions to $d\pi/dx = 0$: Solution A is a local maximum; B is a minimum; and C is the global maximum.

condition for maximum profit requires that[2]

$$d^2\pi/dx^2 < 0 \qquad\qquad (3.49)$$

That is, the profit function must be strictly concave in the neighborhood of the solution to the first-order condition.

It is instructive for this single-variable factor case to interpret the second-order condition in terms of the relationship between *MVP* and *MFC* in the

[2]Note the exception to this second derivative test that is stated in footnote 1 of Chapter 1.

neighborhood of the point where the first-order condition is satisfied (i.e., where *MVP* and *MFC* intersect). Equation 3.49 may be expressed as

$$\frac{d^2\pi}{dx^2} = \frac{d(MVP - MFC)}{dx} = \frac{d\,MVP}{dx} - \frac{d\,MFC}{dx} < 0 \qquad (3.50)$$

which implies that

$$\frac{d\,MVP}{dx} < \frac{d\,MFC}{dx} \qquad (3.51)$$

That is, the second-order condition requires in general that the rate of change of *MFC* must exceed the rate of change of *MVP*. Or, stated another way, *MFC must intersect MVP from below.*

To verify the above assertion consider Figure 3.4, where all possible configurations of intersecting *MVP* and *MFC* curves are presented. Panels *a*, *b*, and *c* represent cases where the intersection occurs in a region of declining *MVP*. If *MFC* is positively sloped, as in panel *a*, then clearly profit is positive and *MFC* intersects *MVP* from below. In panels *b* and *c* *MFC* as well as *MVP* is negatively sloped; in panel *b* the rate of change of *MFC* exceeds that of

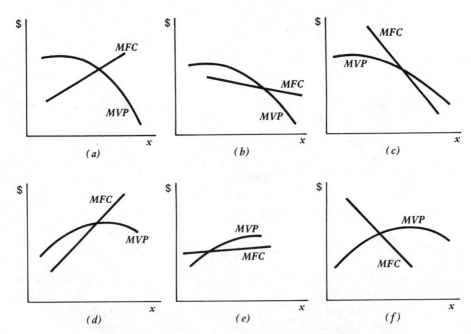

Figure 3.4. Possible configurations of MVP and MFC when first- and second-order conditions for profit maximization are satisfied and not satisfied. (*a*) Maximum. (*b*) Maximum. (*c*) Minimum. (*d*) Maximum. (*e*) Minimum. (*f*) Minimum.

MVP (*MFC* has *less* negative slope) suggesting a maximum, whereas in panel *c* the opposite is true. The reader can make analogous interpretations for the case of positively sloped *MVP* in panels *d*, *e*, and *f* to verify that the second-order condition for profit maximization requires that *MFC* intersect *MVP* from below.

Thus we can conclude that the first- and second-order conditions, taken together, are *sufficient* for profit maximization. Unfortunately, satisfaction of these two conditions does not necessarily imply that the profit-maximizing entrepreneur will choose that input level. Why? There is yet a third condition that must be taken into account. The local profit maximum implied by the first- and second-order conditions, (3.38) and (3.49), may occur at an input level where total value product is less than variable factor costs. That is, there is a *total condition* that must be satisfied as well; namely, the profit-maximizing level of x must be associated with $TVP \geq c$ lest the entrepreneur will find it advantageous to choose not to produce at all in the short run.

In Figure 3.5, two possibilities are presented assuming perfect competition in the factor market, that is, one case where $MFC = r^0$ and one case where $MFC = r^1$ and $r^0 < r^1$. Notice that first- and second-order conditions for profit maximization are satisfied at x^0 for the case where $MFC = r^0$ and at x^1 for $MFC = r^1$; that is, in both cases $MVP = MFC$ and MFC intersects *MVP* from below. But what do we know about the difference between total value product and variable factor cost for these two situations? In the second case ($MFC = r^1$), we observe that the function $TVP - c$ has a local maximum at x^1, *but* that local maximum does not lie above the horizontal axis. Rather, $TVP < c$ for this case. That is, one might say that "profit" (exclusive of fixed

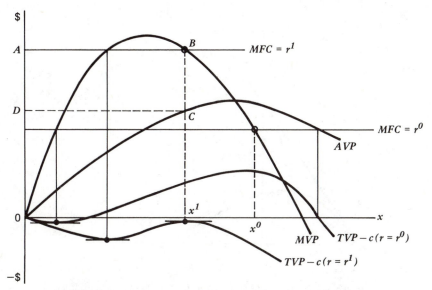

Figure 3.5. Profit maximization versus optimal input usage.

cost) is negative (area $0AB\,x^1$ > area $0DC\,x^1$), so for this short-run situation the entrepreneur will choose a zero input level rather than x^1. Notice that the curve labeled $TVP - c$ ($r = r^1$) in Figure 3.5 lies everywhere below the horizontal axis except at $x = 0$, where its function value is zero. Since returns above variable factor costs are everywhere less than or equal to zero, the point of maximum profit cannot be optimal in this case.

Accordingly, while satisfaction of first- and second-order conditions are sufficient for maximum profit, we see that this does not guarantee an optimal solution. Thus we must check yet a third condition, namely, the total condition, to ensure that the optimal input level has been determined. Necessary and sufficient conditions for *optimal input usage* are summarized as follows:

1. First-order condition: $MVP = MFC$
2. Second-order condition: $d^2\pi/dx^2 < 0 \Rightarrow MFC$ must intersect MVP from below
3. Total condition: $TVP \geq c$ at the maximum profit point.

All three of the above conditions are necessary for optimal input usage, and taken together are sufficient.

3.1.c Economic Region of Production

The production surface is traditionally divided into three regions (stages) as depicted in Figure 3.6. Recall that Stage I is defined as that region over which

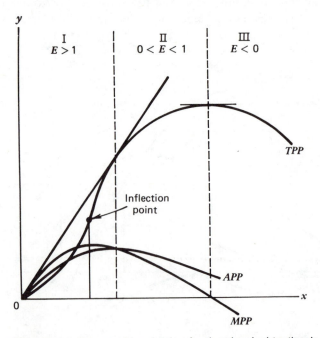

Figure 3.6. Stages of production for the classical textbook production function.

APP is rising (i.e., $E > 1$); Stage II is that region where *APP* is declining and *MPP* is positive (i.e., $0 < E < 1$); and Stage III is that region where *MPP* is negative (i.e., $E < 0$).

Interest in stages of production has to do with the purported correspondence of Stage II with the so-called economic region of production (that region in which the optimal solution must occur). The conventional wisdom, as reported in most economic theory textbooks, holds that the profit-maximizing firm facing positive prices will operate only in Stage II; that is, the profit-maximizing solution is uniquely associated with Stage II.

The purpose of this section is to examine the validity of that assertion. In so doing we will consider all possible profit-maximizing outcomes that satisfy the first-order, second-order, and total conditions for maximum profit both with and without a budget constraint and for cases of flexible, as well as inflexible, product and factor prices. We contend that the economic region of production is uniquely associated with Stage II only for the case when product and factor price flexibilities are zero, the firm has unlimited funds (budget) for the purchase of the variable factor, and with nonnegative prices. Our criteria for deducing the economic, or rational, stage of production with unlimited funds are that profit be maximum, which implies that *MVP* = *MFC* with *MFC* intersecting *MVP* from below, and that *TVP* $\geq c$.

Now let us deduce the economic region of production for each of the following cases:

Case I Suppose that the firm has *unlimited funds and faces perfectly competitive product and factor markets with nonnegative prices.* Given the assumption of perfect competition in the product market, the factor levels delimiting the production stages in Figure 3.6 also mark the locus of points of maximum *AVP* and *TVP*, respectively, as well as maximum *APP* and *TPP*. This will not be the case for $\lambda_p \neq 0$ (Case II). Now we ask the question: Is Stage III economic? The answer is no, since *MVP* is negative in Stage III; thus the factor level for which *MVP* = *MFC* cannot be in this stage because of the restriction that $r > 0$. For example, in Figure 3.7 the factor-level x^0 is inadmissible because $r < 0$, although first- and second-order conditions are satisfied.

Next: Is Stage I economic? With a three-stage production function, we can have two points for which *MVP* = *MFC* for a given factor price, say $r = r^1$, one of which is in Stage II (x^1 in Figure 3.7) and one of which is in Stage I (x^4 in Figure 3.7). However, the point x^4 in Stage I occurs where *MFC* intersects *MVP* from *above*, which violates the second-order condition. Now consider *MFC* = r^2 in Figure 3.7. At x^2 first- and second-order conditions are satisfied, but according to our earlier discussion of Figure 3.5, we know that *TVP* $< c$ at x^2, which violates the total condition. Only for r values between 0 and r^3 can all three conditions for optimal input usage be satisfied. Note that r^3 in Figure 3.7 corresponds to maximum *AVP* and

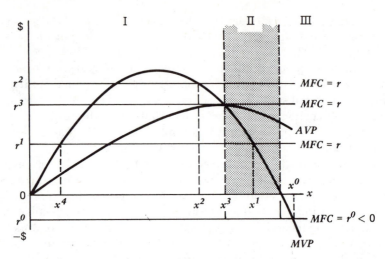

Figure 3.7. Economic region of production for case I—$r > 0$, $\lambda_p = 0$, $\lambda_r = 0$, and unlimited funds.

that $r = r^3$ is the maximum factor price for which the total condition can be satisfied at the critical x value. That is, at x^3, we observed that $MFC = MVP$, MFC intersects MVP from below *and* the value of the product produced is just equal to the variable costs of the factor ($TVP = c$). Thus the factor level where AVP is maximum represents the lower bound on the amount of factor that a profit-maximizing firm will employ rather than choosing not to produce. Since the x level where AVP is maximum is the same as that where APP is maximum for the perfectly competitive product market case, it then follows that production in Stage I is uneconomic. Accordingly, we see that all three optimality conditions can be satisfied only in Stage II for this case.

Case II   Assume that the firm faces an *imperfectly competitive product market, a perfectly competitive factor market, nonnegative prices, and has unlimited funds.* In this case, Stage III is uneconomic for the same reason as in Case I. However, portions of Stage I may be economic if maximum AVP occurs before maximum APP. Similarly, part of Stage II may be uneconomic if maximum AVP occurs after maximum APP. Let us consider this more closely, beginning with Stage I. The total condition that $TVP \geq c$ implies that if a firm produces at all it will use a factor level at least as great as the x level for which AVP is maximum, as discussed in Case I. Thus, to show that part of Stage I may be in the economic region, all we need to determine is if it is possible for maximum AVP to occur at a lower level of x than maximum APP. In other words, we need to determine the slope of AVP at the x level where APP is maximum.

This is not as difficult as it might seem, as we know the general relationship between AVP and APP. That is, $AVP = p \cdot APP$ where

$p = g(y)$ and $y = f(x)$. The slope of AVP as a function of x is

$$dAVP/dx = p(dAPP/dx) + APP(dp/dx) \qquad (3.52)$$

using the product and chain rules of differentiation. At maximum APP, $dAPP/dx = 0$, so (3.52) simplifies to

$$dAVP/dx = APP(dp/dx) \qquad (3.53)$$

Since $APP > 0$, the slope of AVP at the x level where APP is maximum is determined by $dp/dx = (dp/dy)(dy/dx)$. But at maximum APP we know that $MPP \equiv dy/dx$ is positive, so the slope of AVP at maximum APP is determined by the slope of the product demand curve, dp/dy. If $dp/dy = 0$, as in Case I, the factor level where APP and AVP are maximum correspond, since both slopes are zero. However, if $dp/dy < 0$, as in this case (imperfect competition in the product market), the AVP function will be negatively sloped when APP is maximum, which suggests that maximum AVP occurs at an x level prior to that where APP is maximum, in other words, *at an x level in Stage I*. Thus, it would be possible to satisfy first-order, second-order, *and* the total condition in Stage I—admittedly that portion of Stage I in the proximity of Stage II, but Stage I nevertheless.

In the rare case of a Giffen good, we have $(dp/dy) > 0$, which implies that AVP is increasing at the point of maximum APP. Hence, the initial part of Stage II would be uneconomic in that case.

Case III Assume *a perfectly competitive product market, an imperfectly competitive factor market, unlimited funds and nonnegative prices.* Under these assumptions, Stage III is uneconomic because $MVP < 0$. Part of Stage I is economic if MFC is an increasing function ($\lambda_r > 0$) in Stage I. This case is depicted in Figure 3.8. It can be seen that at x^0, $MVP = MFC$, MFC intersects MVP from below, and $TVP - c =$ (area $0ABx^0 -$ area $0DCx^0) > 0$. Thus, production at x^0, which is in Stage I, satisfies the first-order, second-order and total conditions for optimal input usage.

Case IV Assume *perfectly competitive product and factor markets, unlimited funds, a positive product price, but a negative factor price.* A negative factor price may seem illogical, but it can exist in certain situations. For example, suppose that the factor is sewage sludge that is used by an agricultural firm as fertilizer. Because municipalities must dispose of sludge, they may be willing to pay firms to dispose of it on their cropland. So, from the firm's standpoint, the factor has a negative price.[3] Even with a negative price, the first-order condition for maximum profit is that $MVP = r$, which implies that the firm should

---

[3]This particular problem can also be analyzed with a multiproduct framework (Chapter 5), with one product being the crop produced and the other product defined as waste disposal.

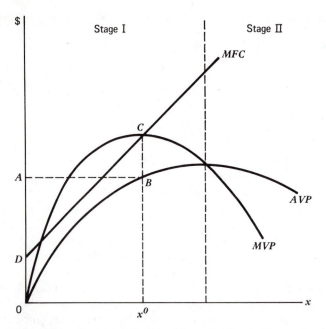

Figure 3.8.   Example of economic production in Stage I for Case III—$\lambda_r > 0$.

operate where $MVP < 0$, that is, at x^0, where $MFC = r^0 < 0$ in Figure 3.7. Thus, only Stage III is the economic region of production in this case.

Criteria for deducing the economic region of production for a firm with limited funds for purchasing variable factors are that $MVP \geq MFC$ and that $TVP \geq c$.

Case V   For this case, we assume *perfectly competitive product and factor markets, positive prices,* but *limited funds for purchase of the variable factor.* Again, Stage III can be dismissed as uneconomic for the same reason as given in the first three cases. Stage II is economic as it was in Case I; but is Stage I economic? The answer is that it may be economic. As an illustration of this case, consider Figure 3.9. Suppose the firm's budget constraint is such that the most x that it can purchase is x^0. For the situation depicted, $MVP > MFC$ and $TVP > c$. Thus, production at x^0 gives positive marginal and total profit (exclusive of fixed cost) and we have economic production occurring in Stage I because of the constraint (limited ability to purchase the input).

The five cases presented above do not exhaust all possibilities, but they do illustrate that in certain situations, production in Stage I or Stage III may be economic in addition to Stage II. Also it was noted that part of Stage II may be uneconomic for the monopolist producer of a Giffen good. The bottom line is that the uniqueness of Stage II as the sole area of optimal input usage

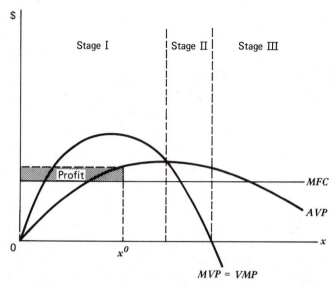

Figure 3.9. Example of economic production in Stage I for a budget constraint that limits factor purchases to x^0.

holds only for perfect competition in the product and factor market, with positive product and factor prices, and with unlimited funds for the purchase of the variable factor—an important but, nevertheless, special case.

3.1.d Factor Demand

The *demand for a factor of production*, like the demand for all goods and services, is a relationship between the quantity of the factor used and prices. That is, the demand for x represents the quantity of x demanded as a function of its own price, r, and product price, p.[4] Throughout this book we are concerned with factor demand relationships for a profit-maximizing firm. We should note, however, that demand relationships may be associated with other objective functions (behavioral postulates) and, for that matter, with apparently irrational or nonoptimizing behavior.

We will denote the factor demand function for a profit-maximizing firm by x^*, which is a function of p and r. Because of the maximization assumption, the inverse of the function x^* shows the maximum amount (the maximum r) that a firm is willing to pay for a specified amount of x given the product price, p.

The factor demand function is obtained from the first-order condition for maximum profit, which in the case of perfect competition is

$$r = p \cdot MPP \tag{3.54}$$

[4]We will see later that factor demand does not depend on product price for the case of the monopolist firm.

Solving (3.54) for x as a function of p and r gives

$$x^* = x^*(p,r) \tag{3.55}$$

Derivation of the demand for x is not yet complete, however. Recall that the firm with unlimited funds cannot maximize profit when $x < x^0$, where x^0 is that level of x for which AVP is maximum. Since a demand function reflects maximum willingness to pay, it is disjointed (truncated) at the value of r corresponding to x^0, say r^0.[5] Therefore,

$$x^* = \begin{cases} x^*(p,r) & \text{for } r \leq r^0 \\ 0 & \text{for } r > r^0 \end{cases} \tag{3.56}$$

The factor demand function is graphically illustrated in Figure 3.10. Note that the factor demand function for the single factor case is given by the inverse of the MVP function from maximum AVP to the right. It should also be noted from (3.56) that the demand for an input is a *derived demand* since it depends upon the price of the product and is thus derived indirectly from the demand for the product. This fact is acknowledged in Figure 3.10 by setting p in $x^* = x^*(p,r)$ equal to p^0, which indicates that the demand curve shown presumes that price is held constant at p^0. By changing the level of p, additional two-space factor demand curves could be represented in Figure

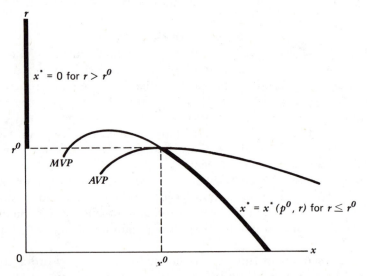

Figure 3.10.   Factor demand for single-variable factor case for traditional three-stage production function.

[5]In previous sections we treated prices p and r as constants; henceforth we treat prices as parameters rather than constants. That is, prices will be treated like *exogenous variables*. Superscripts will be used to denote particular values of p and r.

3.10. The truth is that, like most economic concepts, factor demand is *not* a two-dimensional concept. However, it is often convenient geometrically to reduce equations like (3.56) to two dimensions by fixing one or the other of the independent variables.

One other curiosity of Figure 3.10 is worthy of special attention. The more mathematically inclined reader may be troubled by the fact that the geometric representation of the demand curve seems to be inconsistent with the mathematical specification in (3.56). That is, there appears to be confusion here regarding the dependent variable. Ideally we economists should draw our pictures consistent with the economic logic we profess. Equation 3.56 suggests that the firm chooses its optimal level of input x^* *depending on* (given) the level of product and factor prices—x^* is the dependent variable. Yet in Figure 3.10 one might logically presume that r was the dependent variable since it is on the vertical axis; that is, Figure 3.10 suggests that r depends on x (x causes r, if you will) rather than x depending on r. The implied order of causation is reversed in the figure. Accordingly, we were tempted to present all geometric interpretations of demand and supply curves "right-side-up," or to refer to the conventional geometric representation (like Figure 3.10) of demand curves and supply curves as inverse curves. However, we ultimately resisted the temptation—inertia and convention are strong forces to reckon with.

Now let us consider a specific example of the derivation of a factor demand function.

Example 3.5   Assume that the production function is

$$y = 6x^2 - x^3 \tag{3.57}$$

then

$$\pi = p(6x^2 - x^3) - rx - b \tag{3.58}$$

with first-order condition,

$$\frac{d\pi}{dx} = p(12x - 3x^2) - r = 0 \tag{3.59}$$

Using the quadratic formula to solve (3.59) for x yields the inverse of $MVP = r$:

$$x^* = \frac{-12 \pm \sqrt{144 - 12r/p}}{-6} \tag{3.60}$$

Now we must set the limits on r. AVP is maximum when $(dAVP/dx) = 0$ and $(d^2AVP/dx^2) < 0$. Thus,

$$\frac{dAVP}{dx} = \frac{d[p(6x - x^2)]}{dx} \tag{3.61}$$

Setting (3.61) equal to zero and solving for x we find that $dAVP/dx = 0$ when $x = 3$. Taking the second derivative of AVP, we find

$$\frac{d^2AVP}{dx^2} = -2p \tag{3.62}$$

Since (3.62) is negative for all x, AVP is maximum at $x = 3$, and the profit-maximizing entrepreneur will use at least 3 units of x, or choose not to produce at all. Now we must determine the value of r that corresponds to x^0. This value is given by AVP evaluated at x^0; that is,

$$AVP^0 = p[6x^0 - (x^0)^2] = 9p \tag{3.63}$$

We now have all the information needed for complete specification of the demand function:

$$x^* = \begin{cases} \dfrac{-12 - \sqrt{144 - 12r/p}}{-6} & \text{for } 0 \le r \le 9p \\ \\ 0 & \text{for } r > 9p \end{cases} \tag{3.64}$$

Note that the positive square root in (3.60) was dropped in (3.64) because the associated x values do not satisfy the second-order condition for maximum profit; that is, the associated x values were in the range of increasing MVP. Factor demand equation 3.64 is graphically illustrated in Figure 3.11 for product prices of one and two. Note that an increase in product price results in an upward shift in the factor demand equation, but does not change the x value at which the discontinuity occurs. (The locus of maximum AVP does not change when product price is increased in the case of perfect competition in the product market.)

Both the theoretical discussion and the above example of the derivation of factor demand was for a firm operating in competitive factor and product markets. Let us now address the issue of deriving factor demand functions for a firm that operates in an imperfectly competitive factor or product market. First consider the case of an imperfectly competitive factor market and a perfectly competitive product market. In this case we have

$$\pi = p\,f(x) - h(x)\,x \tag{3.65}$$

and, as was shown previously, the first-order condition is

$$\frac{d\pi}{dx} = p\,f'(x) - r(1 + \lambda_r) \tag{3.66}$$

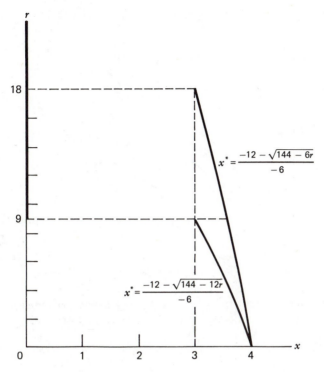

Figure 3.11. Factor demand for the production function, $y = -x^3 + 6x^2$, and $p = 1,2$.

which implies that $MVP = MFC$. Factor price r is given by the firm's factor supply function, which represents its average factor cost, AFC, rather than its MFC. Thus, except in special cases, $MFC \neq r$. Factor price in this monopsonistic case is endogenous to (determined by) the firm. So, the problem of considering factor demand in this instance is that the firm equates MVP with MFC and MFC is *not* factor price. Since r is endogenous we are no longer able to shock r to see what happens to the quantity of x used. That is, given $r = h(x)$, $p = p^0$ or $p = g[f(x)]$ and $y = f(x)$, x is uniquely determined as a single point (see Figure 3.12). A factor demand function for a monopsonist does not exist although a *demand point* exists.

Is the factor demand function for a firm operating in a competitive factor market but an imperfectly competitive product market also a single point? The general answer to this question is no, because factor price is exogenous to the firm and we have $MVP = MFC = r$; therefore, we can solve for x^* as a function of r. Note, however, that the factor demand function for this case does not depend on p because p is endogenous to the firm.

3.2 ONE-PRODUCT, TWO-VARIABLE FACTORS

Value productivity functions for two factors are related to one-factor value productivity functions in the same way as the physical productivity equations

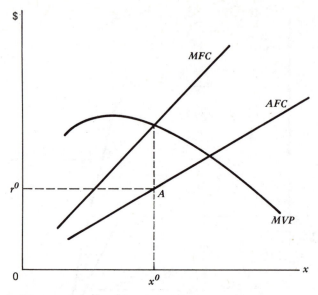

Figure 3.12. Nonexistence of firm's factor demand curve when $\lambda_r \neq 0$; demand is given by the single point, *A*.

are related in the two cases. So, we define *total value product* (*TVP*) as

$$TVP \equiv p\,y = g(y)\,y = g[f(x_1,x_2)]\,f(x_1,x_2) \tag{3.67}$$

where $p = g(y)$ and $f(x_1,x_2)$ is shorthand for $f(x_1,x_2|x_3,\ldots,x_n)$. If we assume perfect competition in the product market, then

$$TVP = p\,f(x_1,x_2) \tag{3.68}$$

Average value product functions are defined as

$$AVP_1 \equiv \frac{TVP}{x_1} = \frac{g[f(x_1,x_2)]\,f(x_1,x_2)}{x_1} \tag{3.69}$$

and

$$AVP_2 \equiv \frac{TVP}{x_2} = \frac{g[f(x_1,x_2)]\,f(x_1,x_2)}{x_2} \tag{3.70}$$

Marginal value productivity of a factor is the exact rate of change of total value product resulting from an infinitesimal change in that factor, *holding all other factors constant.* So

$$MVP_1 \equiv \frac{\partial TVP}{\partial x_1} = \frac{\partial\{g[f(x_1,x_2)]\,f(x_1,x_2)\}}{\partial x_1}$$

$$= g[f(x_1,x_2)]f_1 + f(x_1,x_2)g_1 \tag{3.71}$$

and

$$MVP_2 \equiv \frac{\partial TVP}{\partial x_2} = \frac{\partial\{g[f(x_1,x_2)]\ f(x_1,x_2)\}}{\partial x_2}$$

$$= g[f(x_1,x_2)]f_2 + f(x_1,x_2)g_2 \qquad (3.72)$$

Again, if perfect competition is assumed,

$$MVP_1 = p\ f_1(x_1,x_2) \qquad (3.73)$$

and

$$MVP_2 = p\ f_2(x_1,x_2) \qquad (3.74)$$

Total factor cost, C, is defined as

$$C \equiv r_1 x_1 + r_2 x_2 + b \qquad (3.75)$$

where b represents fixed costs. In the general case, assuming $r_1 = h^1(x_1)$ and $r_2 = h^2(x_2)$, total factor cost is

$$C = h^1(x_1)x_1 + h^2(x_2)x_2 + b \qquad (3.76)$$

Variable factor cost, c, is given by deleting the fixed cost, b, from (3.75) and (3.76) for the perfectly competitive and imperfectly competitive factor market cases, respectively.

Marginal factor cost for the first factor is defined as the change in total or variable factor cost resulting from an infinitesimal change in factor one, holding all other factors constant; that is,

$$MFC_1 \equiv \frac{\partial C}{\partial x_1} = \frac{\partial[h^1(x_1)x_1 + h^2(x_2)x_2 + b]}{\partial x_1}$$

$$= h^1(x_1) + x_1 h_1^1 = r_1 + x_1 \left(\frac{r_1}{r_1}\right)h_1^1$$

$$= r_1(1 + \lambda_{r_1}) \qquad (3.77)$$

Similarly, for factor two,

$$MFC_2 \equiv \frac{\partial C}{\partial x_2} = \frac{\partial[h^1(x_1)x_1 + h^2(x_2)x_2 + b]}{\partial x_2}$$

$$= h^2(x_2) + x_2 h_2^2$$

$$= r_2(1 + \lambda_{r_2}) \qquad (3.78)$$

The notation here is admittedly messy—h_1^1 in (3.77) is shorthand for $\partial h^1(x_1)/\partial x_1$, that is, the derivative of the price of x_1 (expressed in terms of x_1)

with respect to x_1. In (3.78), h_2^2 is interpreted similarly. Notice that with perfect competition in both factor markets (3.77) and (3.78) reduce to $MFC_1 = r_1$ and $MFC_2 = r_2$, respectively.

3.2.a Least-Cost Combination of Inputs and the Expansion Path

In the single-factor case, there was a one-to-one mapping between the factor and the product; hence, there was only one factor usage level that would result in a specified output level. However, in the two-factor case there are an infinite number of input combinations for producing a specified amount of the product (recall the technical concept of an isoquant), so it is instructive to consider the least-cost combination of the two factors. Whatever output level the entrepreneur chooses, it seems intuitive that the given output would be produced at lowest possible cost if the associated profit is maximum for that output level. An equation that shows the least-cost combination of inputs for all given levels of output is called the *expansion path*, which we now derive.

The least-cost bundle of factors for producing a prescribed level of output can be found by solving the following constrained cost-minimization problem:

$$\min_{x_1, x_2} \quad r_1 x_1 + r_2 x_2 + b \qquad (3.79)$$

$$\text{subject to} \quad y^0 - f(x_1, x_2) = 0 \qquad (3.80)$$

Notice that minimization of cost is subject to an equality, as opposed to an inequality, constraint. It is convenient to convert such constrained problems into the format of an unconstrained optimization problem for purposes of deducing the first-order conditions.

To accomplish this we can form a Lagrangean function, which is the original cost function augmented by the constraint:

$$
\begin{aligned}
LC &= r_1 x_1 + r_2 x_2 + b + \lambda [y^0 - f(x_1, x_2)] \\
   &= h^1(x_1) x_1 + h^2(x_2) x_2 + b + \lambda [y^0 - f(x_1, x_2)] \qquad (3.81)
\end{aligned}
$$

where λ is called a *Lagrangean multiplier*. The Lagrangean function, (3.81) is simply the factor cost function (3.79) augmented by the production function (3.80). Note that the term in brackets in (3.81) will vanish if the production function is satisfied, no matter what value λ takes. Thus, if the production function is satisfied, (3.81) reduces to the cost function (3.79). This suggests that we can treat λ as a variable and apply the first-order conditions for unconstrained minimization, namely,

$$\frac{\partial LC}{\partial \lambda} = y^0 - f(x_1, x_2) = 0$$

$$\frac{\partial LC}{\partial x_1} = h^1(x_1) + x_1 h_1^1 + \lambda(-f_1) = 0 \qquad (3.82)$$

$$\frac{\partial LC}{\partial x_2} = h^2(x_2) + x_2 h_2^2 + \lambda(-f_2) = 0$$

Notice that satisfying the first equation in (3.82) will automatically insure satisfaction of the production function relationship for given y.

The Lagrangean multiplier, λ, can be given an economic interpretation by noting that

$$\frac{\partial LC}{\partial y} = \lambda \qquad (3.83)$$

In Section 4.1.c (Chapter 4) it is shown that with the first-order conditions satisfied, $LC = c = $ *variable cost* (as a function of output), so the Lagrangean multiplier is the change in least total or variable factor cost for an infinitesimal change in output. In other words, λ is simply the marginal cost of producing y. Marginal cost is further discussed in Chapter 4 and in Chapter 6 in the context of a product supply equation.

Solving each of the last two conditions for λ in (3.82) results in

$$\lambda = \frac{h^1(x_1) + x_1 h_1^1}{f_1} \qquad (3.84)$$

and

$$\lambda = \frac{h^2(x_2) + x_2 h_2^2}{f_2} \qquad (3.85)$$

Equating (3.84) and (3.85) to eliminate λ gives

$$\frac{h^1(x_1) + x_1 h_1^1}{f_1} = \frac{h^2(x_2) + x_2 h_2^2}{f_2} \qquad (3.86)$$

Rearranging terms of (3.86) we get

$$\frac{f_1}{f_2} = \frac{h^1(x_1) + x_1 h_1^1}{h^2(x_2) + x_2 h_2^2} \qquad (3.87)$$

which is

$$\frac{MPP_1}{MPP_2} = \frac{MFC_1}{MFC_2} \qquad (3.88)$$

Hence, to minimize the cost of producing a prescribed amount of product, we must equate the ratio of marginal physical productivities to the ratio of marginal factor costs for that level of output. The expansion path is obtained by solving (3.87) for x_2 in terms of x_1 or vice versa. If we assume perfect competition in both factor markets, (3.87) reduces to

$$\frac{f_1}{f_2} = \frac{r_1}{r_2} \qquad (3.89)$$

or

$$\frac{MPP_1}{MPP_2} = \frac{r_1}{r_2} \tag{3.90}$$

The expansion path concept is graphically illustrated in Figure 3.13 for a firm that faces fixed factor prices. This figure shows the projection of the expansion path on the production surface as well as on the (x_1, x_2) plane. The latter projection is the most commonly used because it reduces a three-dimensional graph to two dimensions (see Figure 3.14). Returning to Figure 3.13, the straight lines projected on the (x_1, x_2) plane represent factor combinations that can be purchased for various cost outlays. These lines are also called budget constraints. For example, consider the line associated with a factor cost outlay of c^1 in Figure 3.14b. If all of c^1 is used to purchase x, then c^1/r_1 units of x_1 and no x_2 can be purchased; similarly, c^1/r_2 units of x_2 can be purchased if no x_1 is purchased. Under the assumption of constant factor prices, a straight line between these extreme points indicates the combinations of x_1 and x_2 that can be purchased for c^1. The slope of this factor cost line is $-r_1/r_2$. Since the slope of an isoquant is $-MPP_1/MPP_2$, it can be seen that the tangents between factor cost lines and isoquants trace out the expansion path. Panel b in Figure 3.14 is the usual illustration of an expansion path in two dimensions. Panel a illustrates the expansion path for a case where the

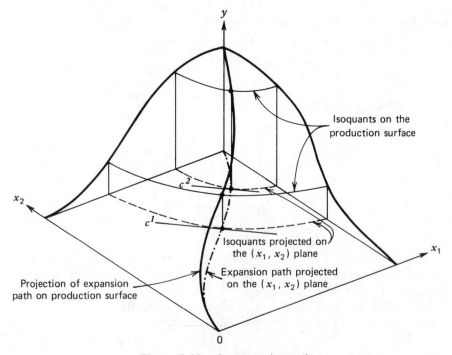

Figure 3.13.   An expansion path.

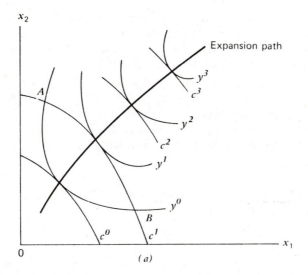

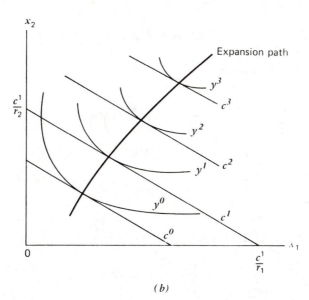

Figure 3.14. Expansion paths for $\lambda_{r_i} > 0$ and $\lambda_{r_i} = 0$. (*a*) Monopsonistic case (i.e., $\lambda_{r_i} > 0$). (*b*) Perfect competition (i.e., $\lambda_{r_i} = 0$).

firm does not face constant factor prices; consequently, the factor cost outlay lines are curved rather than straight as in the previous case.

Figure 3.14*a* can be used to get a geometric feel for what is involved in the mathematical derivation of the constrained cost minimization problem, namely, equations 3.79 through 3.88. Consider a fixed output level such as y^0. In a graphical sense, the Lagrangean technique is used to search for the factor cost outlay curve that allows y^0 to be produced at least cost. Now consider c^1 in panel a; given this cost outlay, observe that y^0 can be obtained at either point A or B. However, notice that y^0 can also be achieved by moving to a lower outlay curve. By moving to lower and lower outlay curves, the cost-minimization solution (point) for y^0 is obtained at an outlay of c^0, where there is tangency between the y^0 isoquant and the c^0 outlay curve. By choosing different levels of y, this process maps out the entire set of cost-minimizing points and thus maps out the expansion path.

As an illustration of the derivation of the expansion path, consider the following example.

Example 3.6   Assume perfect competition in both factor markets and the generalized Cobb–Douglas production function,

$$y = Ax_1^{b_1} x_2^{b_2} \tag{3.91}$$

Forming the Lagrangean function, we have

$$LC = r_1x_1 + r_2x_2 + b + \lambda[y^0 - Ax_1^{b_1}x_2^{b_2}] \tag{3.92}$$

with first-order conditions,

$$\frac{\partial LC}{\partial \lambda} = y^0 - Ax_1^{b_1}x_2^{b_2} = 0 \tag{3.93}$$

$$\frac{\partial LC}{\partial x_1} = r_1 - \lambda Ab_1x_1^{b_1-1}x_2^{b_2} = 0 \tag{3.94}$$

$$\frac{\partial LC}{\partial x_2} = r_2 - \lambda Ab_2x_1^{b_1}x_2^{b_2-1} = 0 \tag{3.95}$$

Solving (3.94) and (3.95) for λ gives, respectively,

$$\lambda = \frac{r_1}{Ab_1x_1^{b_1-1}x_2^{b_2}} \tag{3.96}$$

and

$$\lambda = \frac{r_2}{Ab_2x_1^{b_1}x_2^{b_2-1}} \tag{3.97}$$

Equating (3.96) and (3.97) gives

$$\frac{r_1}{Ab_1x_1^{b_1-1}x_2^{b_2}} = \frac{r_2}{Ab_2x_1^{b_1}x_2^{b_2-1}} \tag{3.98}$$

Rearranging terms in (3.98) yields

$$\frac{r_1}{r_2} = \frac{b_1 x_2}{b_2 x_1} \tag{3.99}$$

or

$$x_2 = \frac{b_2 r_1}{b_1 r_2} x_1 \tag{3.100}$$

which is the equation of the expansion path for a firm with a Cobb–Douglas technology that faces constant factor prices.[6]

The second-order condition for minimization of cost subject to an output constraint can be formulated in terms of the Lagrangean function. The easiest mathematical technique that can be used to check the second-order condition for two or more variables is to determine the sign of a "bordered Hessian determinent," which must be negative (see Chiang, 1974, Chap. 12). In the context of the Lagrangean function, (3.81), the bordered Hessian determinant is

$$|H| = \begin{vmatrix} \dfrac{\partial^2 LC}{\partial \lambda^2} & \dfrac{\partial^2 LC}{\partial \lambda \partial x_1} & \dfrac{\partial^2 LC}{\partial \lambda \partial x_2} \\[2ex] \dfrac{\partial^2 LC}{\partial \lambda \partial x_1} & \dfrac{\partial^2 LC}{\partial x_1^2} & \dfrac{\partial^2 LC}{\partial x_1 \partial x_2} \\[2ex] \dfrac{\partial^2 LC}{\partial \lambda \partial x_2} & \dfrac{\partial^2 LC}{\partial x_1 \partial x_2} & \dfrac{\partial^2 LC}{\partial x_2^2} \end{vmatrix} \tag{3.101}$$

which can also be expressed as

$$|H| = \begin{vmatrix} 0 & -f_1 & -f_2 \\ -f_1 & (2h_1' + x_1 h_{11}' - \lambda f_{11}) & -\lambda f_{12} \\ -f_2 & -\lambda f_{21} & (2h_2^2 + x_2 h_{22}^2 - \lambda f_{22}) \end{vmatrix} \tag{3.102}$$

Evaluating the determinant in (3.102) by a Laplace expansion (see Chiang, 1974, pp. 103–105) of the first row of the matrix H gives

$$\begin{aligned} |H| = &-(-f_1)[(-f_1)(2h_2^2 + x_2 h_{22}^2 - \lambda f_{22}) - (-f_2)(-\lambda f_{12})] \\ &+ (-f_2)[(-f_1)(-\lambda f_{21}) - (-f_2)(2h_1' + x_1 h_{11}' - \lambda f_{11})] \end{aligned} \tag{3.103}$$

---

[6]Recall in Section 2.2.j that one of the properties of homogeneous functions was ray-line isoclines. Sure enough, we find for the Cobb–Douglas function that the expansion path, which is an isocline when r_1 and r_2 are constants, is a ray-line.

Obviously, determining whether the second-order condition is satisfied can get quite messy in the general case. However, note that for perfect competition in both factor markets, (3.103) simplifies to

$$|H| = \lambda(f_1^2 f_{22} - 2f_1 f_2 f_{12} + f_2^2 f_{11}) \qquad (3.104)$$

Since $\lambda > 0$ (marginal cost is positive), (3.104) will be negative if the production function is strictly quasiconcave.

In the general case of imperfect competition, there are circumstances for which the second-order condition for constrained cost minimization will be satisfied with a production function that is not quasiconcave. Although unlikely, there are cases for which the second-order condition will be satisfied with concave isoquants. However, the concave curvature of the isoquants must be less than the concave curvature of the isocost curves for the solution to the first-order conditions to give a minimum solution.

Let us check the second-order condition for the previous example.

Example 3.7 Referring back to the first-order conditions in Example 3.6, it follows that the appropriate bordered Hessian determinant is

$$
|H| = \begin{vmatrix}
0 & -Ab_1 x_1^{b_1-1} x_2^{b_2} & -Ab_2 x_1^{b_1} x_2^{b_2-1} \\
-Ab_1 x_1^{b_1-1} x_2^{b_2} & -\lambda Ab_1(b_1-1)x_1^{b_1-2}x_2^{b_2} & -\lambda Ab_1 b_2 x_1^{b_1-1}x_2^{b_2-1} \\
-Ab_2 x_1^{b_1} x_2^{b_2-1} & -\lambda Ab_1 b_2 x_1^{b_1-1}x_2^{b_2-1} & -\lambda Ab_2(b_2-1)x_1^{b_1}x_2^{b_2-2}
\end{vmatrix}
$$

$$
= \lambda A^3[(b_1 x_1^{b_1-1}x_2^{b_2})^2 b_2(b_2-1)x_1^{b_1}x_2^{b_2-2}
$$
$$
- 2b_1^2 b_2^2 x_1^{b_1} x_2^{b_2} x_1^{2b_1-2} x_2^{2b_2-2}
$$
$$
+ (b_2 x_1^{b_1}x_2^{b_2-1})^2 b_1(b_1-1)x_1^{b_1-2}x_2^{b_2}]
$$

$$
= \lambda A^3 x_1^{3b_1-2} x_2^{3b_2-2}[b_1^2 b_2(b_2-1) - 2b_1^2 b_2^2 + b_2^2 b_1(b_1-1)]
$$

$$
= \lambda A^3 x_1^{3b_1-2} x_2^{3b_2-2}[-b_1^2 b_2 - b_2^2 b_1] \qquad (3.105)
$$

Since $\lambda > 0$ and $x_1, x_2 > 0$, (3.105) is negative and the second-order condition is satisfied if A, b_1, and $b_2 > 0$, which is traditionally the case for a Cobb–Douglas production function. Note that restrictions on b_1 and b_2 imply that $b_1 + b_2 > 0$, so strict quasi-concavity allows for increasing, constant, or decreasing returns to scale; contrastingly, strict concavity of the Cobb–Douglas function requires that $0 < b_1 + b_2 < 1$. Also note that isoquants for the Cobb–Douglas function are convex to the origin if strict quasi-concavity (or concavity) requirements are met.

In theoretical derivations that are given in the remainder of this book, we will appropriately assume that the second-order conditions are satisfied unless we state otherwise. We suggest that the student check to see if second-order conditions are met in all examples we give where such is appropriate. At the same time, we caution the student to not get so bogged down in the mathematics of checking these conditions that important economic principles are overlooked. For empirical applications that involve several variables, the second-order conditions can be checked *numerically* rather than algebraically, using common computer programs for evaluating determinants.

3.2.b Constrained Output Maximization

In this section we demonstrate an important duality[7] relationship; namely, that the optimal factor combination (expansion path) is the same whether based on minimizing the cost of producing a given level of output or on maximizing the output attainable for a given factor cost outlay.

To maximize output subject to a factor-cost constraint, we form a Lagrangean output function that is analogous to the previously discussed Lagrangean cost function, namely,

$$Ly = f(x_1, x_2) + \mu[c^0 - h^1(x_1)x_1 - h^2(x_2)x_2 - b] \qquad (3.106)$$

where μ is a Lagrangean multiplier and c^0 is the level at which cost is fixed. First-order conditions for maximization of (3.106) are

$$\frac{\partial Ly}{\partial \mu} = c^0 - h^1(x_1)x_1 - h^2(x_2)x_2 - b = 0$$

$$\frac{\partial Ly}{\partial x_1} = f_1 + \mu[-h^1(x_1) - x_1 h_1'] = 0$$

$$\frac{\partial Ly}{\partial x_2} = f_2 + \mu[-h^2(x_2) - x_2 h_2^2] = 0 \qquad (3.107)$$

Solving each of the last two equations in (3.107) for μ and equating the results, we obtain

$$\frac{f_1}{f_2} = \frac{h^1(x_1) + x_1 h_1'}{h^2(x_2) + x_2 h_2^2} \qquad (3.108)$$

or

$$\frac{MPP_1}{MPP_2} = \frac{MFC_1}{MFC_2} \qquad (3.109)$$

which is the same condition found for the constrained cost-minimization problem presented in the previous section. The special case of (3.109) for perfect competition in the factor markets is left for the reader to verify.

---

[7]Be forewarned that this concept of duality differs from "duality theory" covered in Chapter 6.

Second-order conditions require that the bordered Hessian determinant,

$$|H| = \begin{vmatrix} \dfrac{\partial^2 Ly}{\partial \mu^2} & \dfrac{\partial^2 Ly}{\partial \mu \partial x_1} & \dfrac{\partial^2 Ly}{\partial \mu \partial x_2} \\[2ex] \dfrac{\partial^2 Ly}{\partial \mu \partial x_1} & \dfrac{\partial^2 Ly}{\partial x_1^2} & \dfrac{\partial^2 Ly}{\partial x_1 \partial x_2} \\[2ex] \dfrac{\partial^2 Ly}{\partial \mu \partial x_2} & \dfrac{\partial^2 Ly}{\partial x_2 \partial x_1} & \dfrac{\partial^2 Ly}{\partial x_2^2} \end{vmatrix} \qquad (3.110)$$

be positive (Chiang, 1974, Chap. 12). With perfect competition in factor markets, the second-order condition is satisfied if the production function is strictly quasi-concave. We leave verification of this assertion, as well as examination of the general case, to the student. First-order conditions (3.107) taken together with the second-order condition (3.110) are sufficient for solution (3.109) to give a constrained maximum.

3.2.c Profit Maximization

From a mathematical standpoint, there are three different but equivalent approaches to determining factor levels and associated output that maximize profit as given by

$$\begin{aligned} \pi \equiv p\,y - c &= p\,y - r_1 x_1 - r_2 x_2 - b \\ &= g(y)y - h^1(x_1)x_1 - h^2(x_2)x_2 - b \end{aligned} \qquad (3.111)$$

subject to the production function, $y = f(x_1, x_2)$. One approach is to set up (3.111) as an unconstrained maximization problem simply by substituting the production function (constraint) for y in (3.111), then maximizing the resulting function with respect to x_1 and x_2. Substituting the production function for y automatically satisfies the constraint, so the maximization over x_1 and x_2 can be done in an unconstrained manner. This is the method developed here—the focus being on optimal factor levels.

An alternative unconstrained approach, which is developed in Chapter 4, is to set up an "output side" optimization problem. That is, one can form a minimum cost function, $\tilde{c}(y)$, which is exclusively a function of output,[8] and then maximize the profit function,

$$\pi = g(y)y - \tilde{c}(y) - b \qquad (3.112)$$

with respect to y. This is the familiar total revenue minus total cost setup that results in the first-order condition that the profit maximizing *output* level is found where marginal revenue equals marginal cost.

[8]With perfect competition in factor markets, the minimum cost function also depends on factor prices, that is, $\tilde{c}(y, r_1, r_2)$.

Yet a third approach, which is developed in Chapter 5, is to use a formal constrained optimization setup. That is, a Lagrangean profit function,

$$L\pi = g(y)y - h^1(x_1)x_1 - h^2(x_2)x_2 - b + \eta[y - f(x_1,x_2)] \quad (3.113)$$

is maximized with respect to x_1, x_2, y, and η, the Lagrangean multiplier.

Again, in this chapter, we use the first approach in order to focus on factor combinations that maximize profit. Substituting the production function for y in (3.111) gives

$$\pi = g[f(x_1,x_2)]f(x_1,x_2) - h^1(x_1)x_1 - h^2(x_2)x_2 - b \quad (3.114)$$

If perfect competition is assumed in both product and factor markets, then (3.114) is simply

$$\pi = p\, f(x_1,x_2) - r_1x_1 - r_2x_2 - b \quad (3.115)$$

First-order conditions for maximum profit in the general case of (3.114) are

$$\frac{\partial \pi}{\partial x_1} = g[f(x_1,x_2)]f_1 + f(x_1,x_2)g_1 - h^1(x_1) - x_1h_1^1 = 0$$

$$\frac{\partial \pi}{\partial x_2} = g[f(x_1,x_2)]f_2 + f(x_1,x_2)g_2 - h^2(x_2) - x_2h_2^2 = 0 \quad (3.116)$$

Rearranging terms in the first equation of (3.116) results in

$$g[f(x_1,x_2)]f_1 + f(x_1,x_2)g_1 = h^1(x_1) + x_1h_1^1 \quad (3.117)$$

or

$$MVP_1 = MFC_1 \quad (3.118)$$

Similarly, the second equation of (3.116) implies

$$MVP_2 = MFC_2 \quad (3.119)$$

Note that with perfect competition in all markets, the first-order conditions reduce to

$$VMP_1 = r_1 \quad (3.120)$$

and

$$VMP_2 = r_2 \quad (3.121)$$

Do the profit-maximizing conditions (3.118) and (3.119) satisfy the expansion path condition (the ratio of marginal physical productivities equals the ratio of marginal factor costs) that was derived in Section 3.2.a? To deduce the answer to this question, recall that for the ith factor, $MVP_i = p[1 + \lambda_p]MPP_i$. Thus, (3.118) and (3.119) can be respectively expressed as

$$p[1 + \lambda_p]MPP_1 = MFC_1 \tag{3.122}$$

and

$$p[1 + \lambda_p]MPP_2 = MFC_2 \tag{3.123}$$

Therefore,

$$p[1 + \lambda_p] = \frac{MFC_1}{MPP_1} \tag{3.124}$$

and

$$p[1 + \lambda_p] = \frac{MFC_2}{MPP_2} \tag{3.125}$$

Hence, equating (3.124) and (3.125):

$$\frac{MFC_1}{MPP_1} = \frac{MFC_2}{MPP_2} \tag{3.126}$$

or

$$\frac{MPP_1}{MPP_2} = \frac{MFC_1}{MFC_2} \tag{3.127}$$

Therefore, the profit maximizing conditions imply satisfaction of the expansion path condition.

That the profit-maximizing solution lies at some point on the expansion path makes intuitive sense. The profit-maximizing level of output should obviously be produced with an input combination that is least costly. Note further that it follows if one input is in profit-maximizing equilibrium and the inputs are in expansion path proportions then the other input must be in profit-maximizing equilibrium as well. Keep this idea in mind; it will be useful later when we consider factor demand and product supply for multiple-input cases.

Example 3.8 Assuming perfect competition in all markets and the production function used in Example 3.6, we can form the profit function,

$$\pi = p\,Ax_1^{b_1}x_2^{b_2} - r_1x_1 - r_2x_2 - b \tag{3.128}$$

First-order conditions for maximization of (3.128) are

$$\frac{\partial\pi}{\partial x_1} = p\,Ab_1x_1^{b_1-1}x_2^{b_2} - r_1 = 0$$

$$\frac{\partial\pi}{\partial x_2} = p\,Ab_2x_1^{b_1}x_2^{b_2-1} - r_2 = 0 \tag{3.129}$$

To obtain profit-maximizing factor levels the above two equations must be simultaneously solved for x_1 and x_2 as functions of prices. One way to do this is to solve one equation, say the second, for x_2 as a function of x_1 and prices, then substitute the result into the first equation. Solving the second equation for x_2 gives

$$x_2 = \left(\frac{r_2x_1^{-b_1}}{p\,Ab_2}\right)^{1/(b_2-1)} \tag{3.130}$$

Substituting (3.130) for x_2 in the first equation of (3.129) gives

$$p\,Ab_1x_1^{b_1-1}\left(\frac{r_2x_1^{-b_1}}{pAb_2}\right)^{b_2/(b_2-1)} = r_1 \tag{3.131}$$

which upon rearranging terms is

$$x_1^* = [(b_1p\,A)^{-1}b_2^{-b_2}(b_1r_2)^{b_2}r_1^{(1-b_2)}]^{1/(b_1+b_2-1)} \tag{3.132}$$

Substituting (3.132) for x_1 in (3.130) and again rearranging terms gives

$$x_2^* = [(b_2p\,A)^{-1}b_1^{-b_1}(b_2r_1)^{b_1}r_2^{(1-b_1)}]^{1/(b_1+b_2-1)} \tag{3.133}$$

By specifying values for the production function parameters and by specifying prices, (3.132) and (3.133) can be used to obtain numerical values for factor levels that maximize profit. The profit-maximizing output level can then be obtained by substituting (3.132) and (3.133) into the production function.

In equations 3.122 through 3.127 we established that the profit-maximizing level of the inputs occurred on the expansion path. Convince yourself that this is true by obtaining the results in (3.132) and (3.133) using each equation in (3.129) simultaneously with the expansion path equation 3.100 rather than the other first-order condition for profit maximization.

Second-order conditions for maximum profit require that the principal minors of the unbordered Hessian determinant alternate in sign, beginning with a negative sign. Thus, the second-order conditions are that

$$\frac{\partial^2 \pi}{\partial x_1^2} < 0$$

$$\frac{\partial^2 \pi}{\partial x_2^2} < 0 \tag{3.134}$$

$$\begin{vmatrix} \dfrac{\partial^2 \pi}{\partial x_1^2} & \dfrac{\partial^2 \pi}{\partial x_1 \partial x_2} \\[2mm] \dfrac{\partial^2 \pi}{\partial x_2 \partial x_1} & \dfrac{\partial^2 \pi}{\partial x_2^2} \end{vmatrix} > 0$$

evaluated at the values of x_1 and x_2 that satisfy (3.116). In the case of perfect competition in all markets, the second-order conditions, (3.134), are satisfied if isoquants are convex to the origin *and* if marginal physical productivities are declining; that is,

$$\frac{\partial^2 \pi}{\partial x_1^2} = p \, f_{11} < 0$$

$$\frac{\partial^2 \pi}{\partial x_2^2} = p \, f_{22} < 0 \tag{3.135}$$

$$\begin{vmatrix} p \, f_{11} & p \, f_{12} \\ p \, f_{21} & p \, f_{22} \end{vmatrix} = p^2 \begin{vmatrix} f_{11} & f_{12} \\ f_{21} & f_{22} \end{vmatrix} = p^2(f_{11}f_{22} - f_{12}f_{21}) > 0$$

This is equivalent to requiring that the production function be strictly concave in the neighborhood of the values of x_1 and x_2 that satisfy the first-order conditions.

First-order conditions (3.116) together with second-order conditions (3.134), and the condition that $TVP \geq c$, are sufficient for maximum positive profit (exclusive of fixed cost).

3.2.d Factor Demand Functions

As in the single variable factor case (Section 3.1.d), factor demand equations for a profit-maximizing firm can be derived from the first-order conditions. In the multiple input situation, the demand for a factor is a relationship between the factor and its price, prices of other variable factors, product price, and quantities of the fixed factors. Again, we note that factor demand is a derived demand—derived from the underlying demand for the product and the production function.

To highlight the difference between *short-run* and *long-run* demand functions, we reintroduce our production function notation which distinguished between fixed and variable factors,

$$y = f(x_1, x_2 | x_3, \ldots, x_n) \tag{3.136}$$

where x_3 through x_n are fixed for the production period of interest. To derive factor demand functions, it is necessary to assume perfect competition in markets for both variable factors;[9] otherwise, demand is a single point as in the case discussed in Section 3.1.d. For convenience, we also assume perfect competition in the product market.

To derive factor demand functions, we do not fix r_1 or r_2 because it is these prices that we intend to vary to determine corresponding quantities demanded of x_1 and x_2, respectively. Thus, prices are treated as parameters rather than constants. Intuitively, it can be seen that factor demand functions reflect satisfaction of first-order conditions for various price levels. So, we can mathematically derive factor demand functions from the first-order conditions which, for the above assumptions, are

$$p\, f_1(x_1, x_2 | x_3, \ldots, x_n) - r_1 = 0 \tag{3.137}$$

and

$$p\, f_2(x_1, x_2 | x_3, \ldots, x_n) - r_2 = 0 \tag{3.138}$$

Simultaneously solving (3.137) and (3.138) for x_1 and x_2, we obtain the short-run factor demand functions,

$$x_1^* = x_1^*(r_1, r_2, p | x_3, \ldots, x_n) \tag{3.139}$$

and

$$x_2^* = x_2^*(r_1, r_2, p | x_3, \ldots, x_n) \tag{3.140}$$

In this text, as in much of the literature, the fixed factors in the above functions are not always explicitly noted; in which case the factor demands are given by

$$x_1^* = x_1^*(r_1, r_2, p) \tag{3.141}$$

and

$$x_2^* = x_2^*(r_1, r_2, p) \tag{3.142}$$

[9]Perfect competition in both factor markets is assumed here because we want to derive demand functions for both x_1 and x_2. However, if we were interested in, say, only the demand for x_2, then perfect competition in the x_1 factor market would not be essential (see analogous discussion vis-a-vis product market assumptions in the last paragraph of Section 3.1.d).

It is critical to note that factor demand equations are derived by *simultaneously* solving the first-order conditions for x_1 and x_2, rather than individually solving the first-order conditions. For example, if we solve $MVP_1 = r_1$ for x_1 without considering $MVP_2 = r_2$, we get

$$x_1 = w^1(r_1, p, x_2 | x_3, \ldots, x_n) \tag{3.143}$$

Equation 3.143 is *not* the demand function for x_1 when both x_1 and x_2 are variable. Rather, (3.143) traces out a two-space (r_1, x_1) curve where the other input (x_2) must be held constant, just as the fixed factors and product price are held constant.

In the general two-variable factor case, usage of one factor, say x_2, changes when the price of the other factor changes. Note, however, that if we were dealing with a shorter production period in which only x_1 is variable, then (3.143) would be a short-run factor demand equation. [In effect, the vertical bar in (3.143) would come before rather than after x_2.] The relationship between the short-run demand function (x_1^*) for factor x_1 when both x_1 and x_2 are variable and the short-run demand function for x_1 when x_2 is fixed (MVP_1) is shown in Figure 3.15.

In Figure 3.15, suppose initially that $r_1 = r_1^0$ and the firm is in profit-maximizing equilibrium at $x_1 = x_1^0$ and $x_2 = x_2^0$. If x_2 is fixed at x_2^0 and r_1 falls from r_1^0 to r_1^1, then the firm responds (regains profit-maximizing equilibrium) by increasing the quantity demanded of x_1 from x_1^0 to x_1^1 (panel *a*). That is, when x_2 is fixed at x_2^0, $MVP_1 | x_2^0$ is the firm's short-run demand for x_1.

On the other hand, if x_2 is *not* fixed, then what happens if r_1 falls from r_1^0 to r_1^1? In this case the expansion path comes into play (panel *b*). If r_1 falls from r_1^0 to r_1^1, the budget constraint shifts (i.e., becomes less steeply sloped) and the firm adjusts *both* the level of x_1 and x_2 in order to keep on its expansion path (the expansion path shifts rightward in this case). In so doing, we see that the firm increases its usage of x_2 as well as x_1 causing MVP_1 in panel *a* to shift rightward. Thus when both x_1 and x_2 are variable, a drop in the price of r_1 from r_1^0 to r_1^1 gives rise to an increase in the quantity demanded of x_1, not from x_1^0 to x_1^1, but rather from x_1^0 to x_1^2. The more horizontal line in panel *a* is the short-run demand for x_1 in this case and we see that it has one common point with $MVP_1 | x_2^0$ and with $MVP_1 | x_2^1$, namely, (x_1^0, x_2^0) and (x_1^2, x_2^1), respectively. The case demonstrated in Figure 3.15, as we shall see in Section 3.2.k, is a consequence of the LeChatelier principle.

Also Figure 3.15 should suggest to you an alternative mathematical procedure for deriving the short-run demand functions, (3.139) and (3.140), when x_1 and x_2 are variable. Recall that equations 3.122 through 3.127 established that profit maximizing input levels satisfied the expansion path as in Figure 3.15. How might we get (3.139) a different way? You no doubt already know, but just in case the point was missed, return to the derivation leading up to (3.132) in Example 3.8; see if you can get (3.132) by introducing the expansion path equation, implicit in Example 3.8 (you will have to derive it), into the first equation of (3.129). In Example 3.9 we will note that (3.132) in

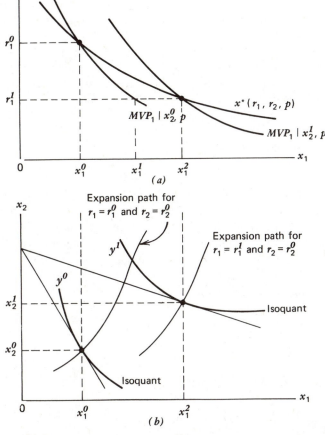

Figure 3.15. Relationship of *MVP*, factor demand, and the expansion path. (*a*) *MVP* versus factor demand. (*b*) Expansion path relationships.

Example 3.8 turns out to be the short-run demand function for x_1 for the Cobb–Douglas production function.

The *long-run* demand function for the *i*th factor is given by simultaneously solving the first-order conditions assuming *all* factors are variable. Thus, the long-run factor demand equations are expressed as

$$x_i^* = x_i^*(r_1, r_2, \ldots, r_n, p) \qquad \text{for } i = 1, 2, \ldots, n \qquad (3.144)$$

The reader should note that there are many possible short-run factor demand functions for a particular multifactor production function, but there is just one long-run demand function for each factor.

In addition to showing own-price effects, factor demand functions show the effects on quantity demanded of changes in other factor prices and changes in product price (assuming the firm is a perfect competitor in these markets as well). From a graphical standpoint, changes in other factor prices or product price are shown as shifts in the factor demand function, rather than a movement along a curve.

Example 3.9 In the previous example, we showed how to determine *levels* of x_1 and x_2 that maximized profit for given factor and product prices. However, as an intermediate step in determining factor levels, we simultaneously solved the first-order conditions, (3.129), for x_1 and x_2 as a function of prices and parameters of the Cobb–Douglas production function. Allowing prices to vary, the resulting functions, (3.132) and (3.133), we now know are short-run factor demand equations for x_1 and x_2, respectively.[10]

As noted at the end of Chapter 2, the quadratic production function is very popular for use in empirical studies. However, it is not often used for textbook problems because some longhand algebraic manipulations get quite onerous. The following example shows how matrix algebra can be used to easily obtain factor demand equations for the quadratic production function. Students not familiar with matrix algebra are encouraged to work through the problem using conventional algebra.[11]

Example 3.10 Consider the quadratic production function,

$$y = a_0 + a_1x_1 + a_2x_2 + \tfrac{1}{2}b_1x_1^2 + \tfrac{1}{2}b_2x_2^2 + b_3x_1x_2 \tag{3.145}$$

In matrix form (3.145) can be expressed as

$$y = a_0 + [a_1\ a_2]\begin{bmatrix}x_1\\x_2\end{bmatrix} + \tfrac{1}{2}[x_1\ x_2]\begin{bmatrix}b_1 & b_3\\b_3 & b_2\end{bmatrix}\begin{bmatrix}x_1\\x_2\end{bmatrix} \tag{3.146}$$

or

$$y = a_0 + A'X + \tfrac{1}{2}X'BX \tag{3.147}$$

where A and X are vectors, B is a matrix, and the prime indicates the transpose of a matrix.

Assume perfect competition in product and factor markets. Profit is given by

$$\pi = p\,y - r_1x_1 - r_2x_2 \tag{3.148}$$

---

[10] In Example 3.8, it was implicitly assumed that second-order conditions were satisfied. Note that satisfaction of second-order conditions, implying strict concavity, is tantamount to saying that the appropriate short-run representation of the Cobb–Douglas production function must exhibit decreasing returns to the quasiscale factor, that is, $\xi = b_1 + b_2 < 1$. If $\xi \geq 1$, the second-order conditions are violated, thus solutions to the first-order conditions (if they exist) cannot be interpreted as demand functions.

[11] If you attempt the problem using conventional algebra, remember the sage advice of Mark Twain: "When angry, count to four! When very angry, swear."

or, in matrix form,

$$\pi = p\,y - [r_1\ r_2]\begin{bmatrix} x_1 \\ x_2 \end{bmatrix} = p\,y - \mathbf{r}\,X \tag{3.149}$$

where $\mathbf{r}$ is a vector. Substituting (3.147) into (3.149) for y gives

$$\pi = p(a_0 + A'X + \tfrac{1}{2}X'BX) - \mathbf{r}\,X \tag{3.150}$$

One nicety of a quadratic function such as (3.150) is that derivatives (or the first-order conditions) can also be expressed in matrix form:

$$\frac{d\pi}{dX} = p(A + BX) - \mathbf{r}' = 0 \tag{3.151}$$

Note that $d(A'X)/dX = A$ and that $d(\tfrac{1}{2}X'BX)/dX = BX$. Showing the elements of the matrices, (3.151) is

$$\frac{d\pi}{dX} = p\begin{bmatrix} a_1 \\ a_2 \end{bmatrix} + \begin{bmatrix} b_1 & b_3 \\ b_3 & b_2 \end{bmatrix}\begin{bmatrix} x_1 \\ x_2 \end{bmatrix} - \begin{bmatrix} r_1 \\ r_2 \end{bmatrix} = \begin{bmatrix} 0 \\ 0 \end{bmatrix} \tag{3.152}$$

or, using conventional algebraic notation, (3.151) and (3.152) are equivalent to

$$\frac{d\pi}{dX} = \begin{cases} \partial\pi/\partial x_1 = pa_1 + pb_1x_1 + pb_3x_2 - r_1 = 0 \\ \partial\pi/\partial x_2 = pa_2 + pb_3x_1 + pb_2x_2 - r_2 = 0 \end{cases} \tag{3.153}$$

Returning to matrix notation, the first-order conditions, (3.151), can be written as

$$A + BX = \frac{1}{p}\mathbf{r}' \tag{3.154}$$

or

$$A + BX = R \tag{3.155}$$

where $R' = [r_1/p \quad r_2/p]$ is a vector of factor prices "normalized" by product price. Rearranging terms, we have

$$BX = R - A \tag{3.156}$$

Assuming that B is nonsingular, (3.156) can be solved for X by premultiplying both sides of the equation by B^{-1}:

$$X^* = B^{-1}BX = IX = B^{-1}(R - A) \tag{3.157}$$

where I is the identity matrix. Since B is symmetric, B^{-1} will be symmetric; thus, we let

$$B^{-1} = \begin{bmatrix} \beta_1 & \beta_3 \\ \beta_3 & \beta_2 \end{bmatrix}$$

Equation 3.157 can now be written in expanded form as

$$x_1^* = \begin{bmatrix} x_1^* \\ x_2^* \end{bmatrix} = \begin{bmatrix} \beta_1 & \beta_3 \\ \beta_3 & \beta_2 \end{bmatrix} \begin{bmatrix} r_1/p \\ r_2/p \end{bmatrix} - \begin{bmatrix} \beta_1 & \beta_3 \\ \beta_3 & \beta_2 \end{bmatrix} \begin{bmatrix} a_1 \\ a_2 \end{bmatrix}$$

$$= \begin{bmatrix} \beta_1\left(\dfrac{r_1}{p}\right) + \beta_3\left(\dfrac{r_2}{p}\right) \\ \beta_3\left(\dfrac{r_1}{p}\right) + \beta_2\left(\dfrac{r_2}{p}\right) \end{bmatrix} - \begin{bmatrix} \beta_1 a_1 + \beta_3 a_2 \\ \beta_3 a_1 + \beta_2 a_2 \end{bmatrix} \tag{3.158}$$

Thus, the factor demand equations are

$$x_1^* = -\beta_1 a_1 - \beta_3 a_2 + \beta_1\left(\frac{r_1}{p}\right) + \beta_3\left(\frac{r_2}{p}\right)$$

$$x_2^* = -\beta_3 a_1 - \beta_2 a_2 + \beta_3\left(\frac{r_1}{p}\right) + \beta_2\left(\frac{r_2}{p}\right) \tag{3.159}$$

Although our derivations have been long for expository purposes, the only essential steps other than definitions are

$$\frac{d\pi}{dX} = p(A + BX) - \mathbf{r}' = 0$$

$$\Rightarrow A + BX = R$$

$$\Rightarrow X^* = B^{-1}(R - A) \tag{3.160}$$

Finally, notice that B is nonsingular (required for B^{-1} to exist) if the second-order condition is satisfied; this condition is satisfied if the production function is strictly concave.

3.2.e Homogeneity of Factor Demand Functions

The concept of homogeneity of a function was introduced in Section 2.2.i in the context of a production function. We now consider homogeneity of factor demand functions in terms of prices. In Section 2.2.i we were concerned with the homogeneity of $y = f(x_1, x_2)$ *in terms of* x_1 *and* x_2, whereas we are now concerned with the homogeneity of $x_i^* = x_i^*(p, r_1, r_2)$ *in terms of* p, r_1 *and* r_2. Although we argued in Chapter 2 that there is no a priori reason to expect production functions to be homogeneous, we will see that factor demand functions obtained from the classical profit-maximization problem are *always* homogeneous of degree zero in all prices, even if the underlying production function is nonhomogeneous in the factors. We are concerned only with perfect competition in all markets, because factor demand functions (or points) do not depend on all (or perhaps even any) prices in the various imperfectly competitive cases; thus, it is meaningless to consider homogeneity in prices for imperfectly competitive cases.

Zero-degree homogeneity of factor demand functions has intuitive appeal. If we double all prices (factor and product), we would not expect optimal factor usage to change, although profit would double. That is, it makes intuitive sense for factor demand functions to be homogeneous of degree zero in prices and for the profit function to be homogeneous of degree one in prices.

To show the latter consider (assuming zero fixed cost)

$$\pi = p\, f(x_1, x_2) - r_1 x_1 - r_2 x_2 \tag{3.161}$$

If we increase all prices in profit equation 3.161 by a proportionality factor, t, then we obtain

$$\begin{aligned} \pi' &= (tp)f(x_1, x_2) - (tr_1)x_1 - (tr_2)x_2 \\ &= t^1[p\, f(x_1, x_2) - r_1 x_1 - r_2 x_2] \\ &= t\,\pi \end{aligned} \tag{3.162}$$

Therefore, the profit function is homogeneous of degree one.

The fact that increasing all prices by a proportionality factor, t, does not influence optimal factor usage (and thus demand) can be seen from the first-order conditions for maximization of (3.162):

$$\frac{\partial \pi'}{\partial x_1} = tp\, f_1 - tr_1 = 0 \Rightarrow p\, f_1 = r_1$$

$$\frac{\partial \pi'}{\partial x_2} = tp\, f_2 - tr_2 = 0 \Rightarrow p\, f_2 = r_2 \tag{3.163}$$

Since t cancels out of the first-order conditions, it does not influence the solution of the first-order conditions. Hence, t is not an argument in the factor demand functions [which we recall are obtained by solving (3.163) for x_i]; thus, $x_i^* = x_i^*(p, r_1, r_2)$ are homogeneous of degree zero in all prices. Careful examination of (3.163) will reveal that this conclusion is independent of whether or not $f(x_1, x_2)$ is homogeneous in x_i.

Zero-degree homogeneity of factor demand equations should not be ignored, although it often is, in empirical studies. For example, specification of

$$x_1 = a_0 + a_1 p + a_2 r_1 + a_3 r_2 \tag{3.164}$$

to represent a demand function must be regarded as suspect because it violates the fundamental homogeneity property. To estimate the parameters of (3.164) and conclude that one had a factor demand function would be folly. The "demand" model represented in (3.164) suffers from what econometricians call specification bias. Unfortunately, models like (3.164) are not uncommon in applied economic literature.

3.2.f Comparative Statics of the Profit-Maximization Model and Symmetry

In contemporary mathematical microeconomic theory, comparative static analysis involves determination of qualitative information (i.e., signs) of the partial derivatives in an economic model. In the case of the profit-maximization model we are interested, among other things, in how the optimal factor levels and output change in response to changes in product and factor prices. That is, the economist is interested in knowing the nature of $\partial x_i^*/\partial r_i$, $\partial x_i^*/\partial p$, $\partial y^*/\partial r_i$, and $\partial y^*/\partial p$, as related to properties of the production function. Comparative static analysis is important because it is a convenient way of (a) generating empirically testable hypotheses (see Silberberg, 1978, Chaps. 1 and 7) about the slopes of factor demand and product supply functions, (b) showing the relationship between the technical concept of factor interdependence and the economic concept of factor interdependence, and (c) showing that cross-price effects in certain optimization models are symmetric. Although we do not formally deal with the topic in this text, it may also be advantageous to examine the comparative static implications of changing technology (production function) parameters that are embedded in factor demand and product supply functions. In fact, the possibilities for comparative static analysis are many, and the analytical leverage afforded by the framework is considerable.

In this section we present the comparative static framework for deducing the signs of $\partial x_i^*/\partial r_i$ and $\partial x_i^*/\partial p$. That is, we will deduce the slopes of the demand functions for x_1 and x_2, the nature of the shift in factor demands in response to a change in the product price, and how factor demand shifts in response to a change in the price of an alternative factor; that is, the cross-price effect as opposed to the own-price effect. A complementary section in Chapter 4 presents the full comparative static framework for the profit-maximization model.

Given a particular set of factor demand functions, as in the Cobb–Douglas Examples 3.8 and 3.9, it is a relatively easy task to obtain $\partial x_1^*/\partial r_1$, $\partial x_1^*/\partial r_2$, $\partial x_1^*/\partial p$ and $\partial x_2^*/\partial r_2$, $\partial x_2^*/\partial r_1$, $\partial x_2^*/\partial p$ directly from (3.132) and (3.133). Indeed, both direction and magnitude of changes in factor usage given a change in various price parameters fall out immediately.

However, all that one might like to know about the nature of factor demand *in general* (e.g., a, b, and c above) must be deduced another way. (Note that the $\partial x_1^*/\partial r_1$ from (3.139) or (3.141), for example, reveals nothing.) To analyze the comparative statics of the profit-maximization model for the factor side, recall the first-order conditions for maximum profit,

$$\partial \pi/\partial x_1 = p\,f_1 - r_1 = 0$$

$$\partial \pi/\partial x_2 = p\,f_2 - r_2 = 0$$

(3.165)

As factor prices change, the firm adjusts factor levels and output in order to satisfy (3.165); in fact, the solution to the first-order conditions (x_1^* and x_2^*) reflect the firm's adjustments.

Thus, to determine how factor levels change in response to price changes, we take the total differential of the first-order conditions treating x_1, x_2, p, r_1 and r_2 as variables. That is,

$$pf_{11}\, dx_1^* + pf_{12}\, dx_2^* = dr_1 - f_1\, dp$$
$$pf_{21}\, dx_1^* + pf_{22}\, dx_2^* = dr_2 - f_2\, dp \qquad (3.166)$$

In (3.166), dx_1^* and dx_2^* are treated as variables whose values we wish to determine (endogenous), whereas dr_1, dr_2, and dp are treated as parameters (exogeneous variables). Since the total differentials in (3.166) are taken from the first-order conditions, (3.165), the solution to (3.166) for dx_1^* and dx_2^* require the firm to stay in a profit-maximizing configuration (i.e., adjust x_1 and x_2 in response to changes in p, r_1, and r_2, so that maximum profit is preserved). That is why the total differentials with respect to the factors are denoted dx_1^* and dx_2^* rather than dx_1 and dx_2.

To determine either dx_1^* or dx_2^* for factor price changes, dr_1 or dr_2, we must simultaneously solve (3.166). Solution of (3.166) is more easily accomplished using matrix algebra than with other methods, so we state these equations in matrix form as

$$\begin{bmatrix} pf_{11} & pf_{12} \\ pf_{21} & pf_{22} \end{bmatrix} \begin{bmatrix} dx_1^* \\ dx_2^* \end{bmatrix} = \begin{bmatrix} (dr_1 - f_1 dp) \\ (dr_2 - f_2 dp) \end{bmatrix} \qquad (3.167)$$

or

$$\begin{bmatrix} dx_1^* \\ dx_2^* \end{bmatrix} = \begin{bmatrix} pf_{11} & pf_{12} \\ pf_{21} & pf_{22} \end{bmatrix}^{-1} \begin{bmatrix} (dr_1 - f_1 dp) \\ (dr_2 - f_2 dp) \end{bmatrix} \qquad (3.168)$$

Note that while the set of partial derivatives f_{ij} are functions of x_1 and x_2, (3.168) is evaluated for given values of p, r_1, r_2, x_1^*, and x_2^*; thus, the 2×2 matrix of coefficients in (3.168) is a matrix of constants. Consequently, we can use linear algebra techniques to solve (3.166) for dx_1^* and dx_2^*.

By Cramer's rule,

$$dx_1^* = \frac{\begin{vmatrix} (dr_1 - f_1 dp) & pf_{12} \\ (dr_2 - f_2 dp) & pf_{22} \end{vmatrix}}{\begin{vmatrix} pf_{11} & pf_{12} \\ pf_{21} & pf_{22} \end{vmatrix}}$$

$$= \frac{pf_{22}(dr_1 - f_1 dp) - pf_{12}(dr_2 - f_2 dp)}{p^2(f_{11}f_{22} - f_{21}f_{12})} \qquad (3.169)$$

Assuming $dp = dr_2 = 0$, we have

$$\frac{dx_1^*}{dr_1} = \frac{\partial x_1^*}{\partial r_1} = \frac{f_{22}}{p(f_{11}f_{22} - f_{21}f_{12})} \tag{3.170}$$

By Young's theorem, a cross-partial derivative is invariant with respect to the order of differentiation, so $f_{21} = f_{12}$ and (3.170) can be stated as

$$\frac{dx_1^*}{dr_1} = \frac{\partial x_1^*}{\partial r_1} = \frac{f_{22}}{p(f_{11}f_{22} - f_{12}^2)} \tag{3.171}$$

What can be said about the sign of (3.171)? The second-order condition for profit maximization requires that the production function be strictly concave; for the two-factor case the production function has this curvature if $f_{22} < 0$ and $(f_{11}f_{22} - f_{12}^2) > 0$. Therefore, factor demand functions are *always* downward sloping assuming unconstrained profit maximization. This may come as no surprise to you, but be forewarned that demand functions derived from other types of models are not necessarily downward sloping. For example, Giffen goods in the theory of consumer behavior provide one example of positively sloping demand functions, whereas Problem 4-4 provides another example.

Letting $dp = dr_1 = 0$ and $dr_2 \neq 0$ in (3.169) gives

$$\frac{dx_1^*}{dr_2} = \frac{\partial x_1^*}{\partial r_2} = \frac{-f_{12}}{p(f_{11}f_{22} - f_{12}^2)} \tag{3.172}$$

Notice that we cannot deduce the sign of (3.172) from the second-order conditions, because even though $(f_{11}f_{22} - f_{12}^2) > 0$, f_{12} can be positive, negative, or zero.

Finally, with $dr_1 = dr_2 = 0$, we obtain

$$\frac{dx_1^*}{dp} = \frac{\partial x_1^*}{\partial p} = \frac{-f_1 f_{22} + f_2 f_{12}}{p(f_{11}f_{22} - f_{12}^2)} \tag{3.173}$$

which can be of either sign since f_{12} may be positive or negative.

Solving (3.168) for dx_2^* gives

$$dx_2^* = \frac{\begin{vmatrix} pf_{11} & (dr_1 - f_1 dp) \\ pf_{21} & (dr_2 - f_2 dp) \end{vmatrix}}{\begin{vmatrix} pf_{11} & pf_{12} \\ pf_{21} & pf_{22} \end{vmatrix}}$$

$$= \frac{pf_{11}(dr_2 - f_2 dp) - pf_{21}(dr_1 - f_1 dp)}{p^2(f_{11}f_{22} - f_{12}^2)} \tag{3.174}$$

Setting appropriate price differentials equal to zero in (3.174) gives

$$\frac{dx_2^*}{dr_2} = \frac{\partial x_2^*}{\partial r_2} = \frac{f_{11}}{p(f_{11}f_{22} - f_{12}^2)} \tag{3.175}$$

$$\frac{dx_2^*}{dr_1} = \frac{\partial x_2^*}{\partial r_1} = \frac{-f_{21}}{p(f_{11}f_{22} - f_{12}^2)} \tag{3.176}$$

and

$$\frac{dx_2^*}{dp} = \frac{\partial x_2^*}{\partial p} = \frac{-f_2 f_{11} + f_1 f_{12}}{p(f_{11}f_{22} - f_{12}^2)} \tag{3.177}$$

Symmetry of cross-price effects can be seen by comparing (3.172) and (3.176). Since $f_{12} = f_{21}$, it follows that $(\partial x_1^*/\partial r_2) = (\partial x_2^*/\partial r_1)$. Thus, the symmetry or reciprocity condition, as it is frequently referred to, requires not only that the cross-price effects be of the same sign, but also of the same magnitude—the comparative static results are *identical*. This important property of factor demand functions, like homogeneity of degree zero, is a consequence of the profit-maximization postulate and holds irrespective of the production technology. Also, like homogeneity, this property is frequently overlooked in applied problems. If profit maximization is presumed, then symmetry conditions should be imposed when estimating factor demand systems.

Although symmetry holds for the classical unconstrained profit-maximization model, it should be noted that cross-price effects are not symmetrical for all optimization models. Again, Problem 4-4 is an example of such a case. Finally, the reader is reminded that the symmetry condition is a phenomenon only of perfect competition; for example, $\partial x_1^*/\partial r_2$ is undefined if the firm is a monopsonist in the x_2 market. Additional symmetry conditions that must hold between the firm's factor demand functions and its product supply function(s) are introduced in Chapters 4 and 5 for the perfectly competitive, profit-maximization model.

3.2.g Economic Interdependence of Factors

In considering the interrelation of two factors in an economic sense, we are concerned with what happens to the quantity employed of a factor (quantity demanded) as the price of another factor changes. A factor of production x_1, is *economically* complementary to, independent of, or competitive with another factor, x_2, if an increase in r_2 decreases, does not affect, or increases the use of x_1. That is, if $(\partial x_1^*/\partial r_2) < 0$, then x_1 and x_2 are *economically complementary*; if $(\partial x_1^*/\partial r_2) = 0$, then x_1 and x_2 are *economically independent*; and if $(\partial x_1^*/\partial r_2) > 0$, then x_1 and x_2 are *economically competitive*. The classification is motivated by the presumption that an increase in r_2 results in a decrease in usage of x_2. If x_1 usage also falls, the term *complementary* seems appropriate; if x_1 usage increases (moves opposite x_2), then it seems appropriate to say that x_1 and x_2 are competitive or rival in demand.[12]

Referring back to (3.172) and (3.176), it can be seen that the sign of these cross-partial derivatives is determined by the sign of f_{12}. In Section 2.2.f, we defined technical interdependence on the basis of f_{12}. Therefore, in the case of perfect competition in all markets, economic interdependence and technical interdependence of factors are synonymous concepts: technical complementarity, independence, or competitiveness implies economic complementarity, independence, or competitiveness, respectively. The concepts differ in magnitude but not in sign.

Example 3.11   In Example 3.8 we derived

$$x_1^* = [(b_1 pA)^{-1} b_2^{-b_2} (b_1 r_2)^{b_2} r_1^{(1-b_2)}]^{1/(b_1+b_2-1)} \tag{3.178}$$

Thus,

$$\frac{\partial x_1^*}{\partial r_2} = [(b_1 pA)^{-1} b_2^{-b_2} b_1^{b_2} r_1^{(1-b_2)}]^{1/(b_1+b_2-1)} \left[\frac{b_2}{b_1+b_2-1} \right]$$
$$\cdot r_2^{(1-b_1)/(b_1+b_2-1)} \tag{3.179}$$

which is negative if $(b_1 + b_2) < 1$ and $0 < b_i < 1$. Therefore, the Cobb–Douglas production function imposes technical and economic complementarity for all values of x_1 and x_2.

If you compute $\partial x_2^*/\partial r_1$ from (3.133) in Example 3.8, you will find that $\partial x_1^*/\partial r_2$ from above equals $\partial x_2^*/\partial r_1$; that is, the symmetry conditions for this example are satisfied as proved earlier in the general case.

3.2.h Conditional Factor Demand Functions

In deriving factor demand functions for a profit-maximizing firm, we allowed the firm to adjust output as well as factor levels in response to price changes. Although seldom used, another type of demand function shows the *conditional demand for a factor*. Conditional factor demand is defined as the relationship

---

[12]Some authors, for example, R. G. D. Allen (1966, p. 611), refer to the case where $\partial x_i^*/\partial r_l > 0$ ($i \neq l$) as the factors being "substitutes in production." The terminology *substitutes* is tempting because in a very real sense the relatively lower-priced factor (ex post) is replacing (being substituted for) the higher-priced factor. However, we, like Ferguson (1969, p. 189), adopt the terms *competitive* or *rival in demand*, reserving the concept of factor substitution exclusively for cases of *conditional factor demand* (next section) where movement is constrained to that along an isoquant. The factor demand relationships under discussion here, as is most often the case, are those derived from unconstrained profit maximization. Therefore, change in factor usage in response to a change in a factor price involves more than just a movement along an isoquant, that is, output is *not* held constant for comparative statics under unconstrained profit maximization. Thus, just as in Chapter 2, where we carefully maintained a clear distinction between terminology for factor substitution (Section 2.2.c) and that for factor interdependence (Section 2.2.f), the same distinction is relevant for factor demand, lest we not know exactly what our fellow economists are talking about.

between the quantity of the factor used and factor prices, *holding output constant*. Thus, conditional factor demand reflects cost-minimizing movements along an isoquant as factor prices change. Since we wish to consider the change in factor usage in response to factor price changes, it should be clear that conditional factor demand functions, like their unconditional, profit-maximizing counterparts, are defined only by assuming perfect competition in the appropriate factor markets. We denote the conditional factor demand functions by

$$x_1^c = x_1^c(r_1, r_2, y) \qquad (3.180)$$

and

$$x_2^c = x_2^c(r_1, r_2, y) \qquad (3.181)$$

Again, since we are holding output constant, the relevant optimization framework for deriving conditional factor demands is constrained cost minimization as presented in Section 3.2.a. Using the Lagrangean cost-minimization framework, conditional factor demand equations are obtained by *simultaneously* solving the Lagrangean first-order conditions, perfectly competitive equivalents of (3.82), for x_1^c, x_2^c, and λ^c, each as a function of r_1, r_2, and y. This derivation is illustrated in the following example.

Example 3.12 Recall Example 3.6 where, assuming the Cobb–Douglas production function, we derived the following first-order conditions for minimization of cost subject to a specified output level:

$$\frac{\partial LC}{\partial \lambda} = y - Ax_1^{b_1}x_2^{b_2} = 0$$

$$\frac{\partial LC}{\partial x_1} = r_1 - \lambda Ab_1 x_1^{b_1-1}x_2^{b_2} = 0 \qquad (3.182)$$

$$\frac{\partial LC}{\partial x_2} = r_2 - \lambda Ab_2 x_1^{b_1}x_2^{b_2-1} = 0$$

Conditional factor demand functions must satisfy all of the above first-order conditions for alternative factor prices. So, we must simultaneously solve the equations in (3.182).

This can be accomplished in various ways. But let us take a short-cut since we have already simultaneously solved the last two equations to get

$$x_2 = \frac{b_2 r_1}{b_1 r_2} x_1 \qquad (3.183)$$

which the reader will recognize as the equation of the expansion path, something to which we will return shortly. Equation 3.183 condenses the information in the last two equations of (3.182) into a single equation.

Substituting the expansion path, (3.183), for x_2 in the production function and rearranging terms, gives

$$x_1^c = \left(\frac{y}{A}\right)^{1/(b_1+b_2)} \left(\frac{b_1 r_2}{b_2 r_1}\right)^{b_2/(b_1+b_2)} \tag{3.184}$$

which is the conditional factor demand equation for x_1. Similarly, we can solve (3.183) for x_1 as a function of x_2, which, when substituted into the production function, gives the conditional factor demand equation for x_2,

$$x_2^c = \left(\frac{y}{A}\right)^{1/(b_1+b_2)} \left(\frac{b_2 r_1}{b_1 r_2}\right)^{b_1/(b_1+b_2)} \tag{3.185}$$

Now, why did we use the expansion path to obtain demand functions for which output is held constant? The answer is that equation 3.183 can be used to show how the relationship of x_2 to x_1 (or vice versa) changes as we vary factor prices, as well as showing the expansion path for constant prices. Or, viewed in the former way, (3.183) shows how the expansion path shifts as factor prices change (recall Figure 3.15b). By substituting this relationship into the production function we simply forced (3.183) to move along an isoquant, thus holding output constant, but maintaining a certain (minimum cost) relationship between x_1 and x_2.

Since the second-order condition for constrained cost minimization is that the production function be strictly quasi-concave, conditional factor demands are defined even for a production process characterized by constant or increasing proportional returns. Thus, the second-order conditions for conditional factor demand are less restrictive than for factor demand under unconstrained profit maximization. Recall that the latter factor demand was defined only for regions where the production function exhibited decreasing returns to the appropriate quasi-scale factor.

The relationship between factor demand and conditional factor demand for a conventional factor is illustrated in Figure 3.16, in which it is assumed that y^0 is the profit maximizing output level for r_1^0, r_2^0, and p^0. If r_1 increases above r_1^0, relatively less will be demanded if the firm adjusts (lowers) output in response to the higher price. Thus, the conditional factor demand is above profit-maximizing factor demand at prices above r_1^0, and below profit-maximizing factor demand for lower prices.

3.2.i Homogeneity of Conditional Factor Demand Functions

Conditional factor demand equations, $x_i^c(r_1, r_2, y)$, like their unconditional counterparts, are *always homogeneous of degree zero in factor prices*. For example, if

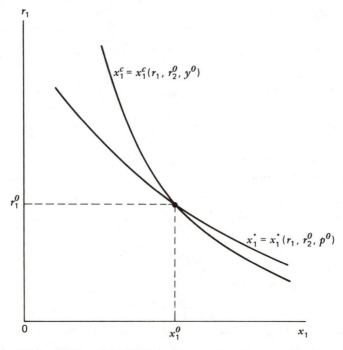

Figure 3.16. An illustration of the relationships between factor demand and conditional factor demand.

we double all factor prices (recall that output is held constant, so product price is not an argument in a conditional factor demand function), the optimal levels of the factors do not change, although variable factor costs would double.

Consider the variable factor cost function,

$$c \equiv r_1 x_1 + r_2 x_2 \tag{3.186}$$

If we increase both factor prices by a proportionality factor, t, then from (3.186) we get

$$
\begin{aligned}
c' &= (tr_1)x_1 + (tr_2)x_2 \\
&= t'[r_1 x_1 + r_2 x_2] \\
&= t \cdot c
\end{aligned}
\tag{3.187}
$$

Thus, the variable factor cost function is homogeneous of degree 1.

As in the unconditional factor demand case, increasing all prices by a proportionality factor, t, does not influence optimal factor usage (and thus demand) in the conditional case. This can be seen from the appropriate first-order conditions for the cost-minimization model. Minimization of (3.187) subject to a production function (output) constraint yields

$$\frac{\partial c'}{\partial \lambda} = y - f(x_1, x_2) = 0$$

$$\frac{\partial c'}{\partial x_1} = tr_1 + \lambda f_1 = 0 \tag{3.188}$$

$$\frac{\partial c'}{\partial x_2} = tr_2 + \lambda f_2 = 0$$

Solving each of the last two equations of (3.188) for λ and equating to eliminate λ gives

$$\frac{-tr_1}{f_1} = \frac{-tr_2}{f_2} \tag{3.189}$$

which implies that

$$f_1/f_2 = r_1/r_2 \tag{3.190}$$

Since t does not appear in (3.190), it does not influence the solution of the first-order conditions. Hence, t is not an argument in the conditional factor demand functions, which are obtained from a simultaneous solution of (3.190) and the production function, the first equation in (3.188). This result, as in the case of unconditional factor demand, is independent of whether or not $f(x_1, x_2)$ is homogeneous in x_i.

The zero-degree homogeneity property is demonstrated in Figure 3.17. Note that a proportional increase in *all* (both) factor prices has no effect on the slope, shape, or position of the isocost line. Also note that the intercepts on the x_1 and x_2 axes and the slope of the expenditure line in Figure 3.17 are the same before and after multiplying the factor prices by t. Consequently, the cost minimizing levels of factor usage, x_i^c (and thus conditional factor demands), are unaffected by the proportional change. True, costs will have increased by a factor of t, but the new isocost line, $t \cdot c$, will be identical (in a geometric sense) to the original isocost line, c.

Again, the zero-degree homogeneity property holds for isoquants derived from nonhomogeneous (in factor levels, x_i) as well as homogeneous production functions. However, if the production function is homogeneous of degree ξ *in variable factor levels*, the associated conditional factor demand equations will be homogeneous of degree $1/\xi$ *in output*, y. Proof of this assertion is more easily established by using duality theory than the methods of analysis presented so far (see Section 6.5.a).

3.2.j Comparative Statics of the Cost-Minimization Model

Just as we analyzed the comparative statics of the profit maximization model in Section 3.2.f, we can analyze the comparative statics of the cost-minimization model. For a firm operating in competitive markets, first-order conditions

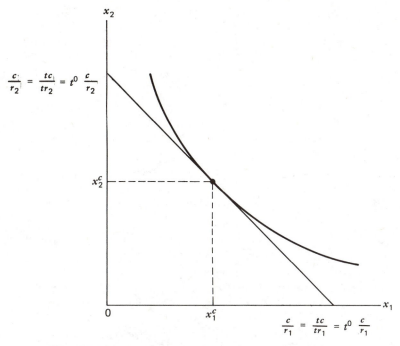

Figure 3.17. An illustration of the zero-degree homogeneity of x_i^c.

(3.82) simplify to

$$y - f(x_1, x_2) = 0$$
$$r_1 - \lambda f_1 = 0 \qquad (3.191)$$
$$r_2 - \lambda f_2 = 0$$

Treating x_1, x_2, and λ as variables, and r_1, r_2, and y as parameters, the total differentials of (3.191) are

$$\lambda^c f_{11} dx_1^c + \lambda^c f_{12} dx_2^c + f_1 d\lambda^c = dr_1$$
$$\lambda^c f_{21} dx_1^c + \lambda^c f_{22} dx_2^c + f_2 d\lambda^c = dr_2 \qquad (3.192)$$
$$f_1 dx_1^c + f_2 dx_2^c = dy$$

In matrix form, (3.192) can be expressed as

$$
\begin{bmatrix}
\lambda^c f_{11} & \lambda^c f_{12} & f_1 \\
\lambda^c f_{21} & \lambda^c f_{22} & f_2 \\
f_1 & f_2 & 0
\end{bmatrix}
\begin{bmatrix}
dx_1^c \\
dx_2^c \\
d\lambda^c
\end{bmatrix}
=
\begin{bmatrix}
dr_1 \\
dr_2 \\
dy
\end{bmatrix}
\qquad (3.193)
$$

Using Cramer's rule, (3.193) can be solved for dx_1^c:

$$
dx_1^c = \frac{\begin{vmatrix} dr_1 & \lambda^c f_{12} & f_1 \\ dr_2 & \lambda^c f_{22} & f_2 \\ dy & f_2 & 0 \end{vmatrix}}{\begin{vmatrix} \lambda^c f_{11} & \lambda^c f_{12} & f_1 \\ \lambda^c f_{21} & \lambda^c f_{22} & f_2 \\ f_1 & f_2 & 0 \end{vmatrix}} \tag{3.194}
$$

Expanding the determinants in (3.194) gives

$$
dx_1^c = \frac{f_1 f_2 dr_2 - f_2^2 dr_1 - \lambda^c f_1 f_{22} dy + \lambda^c f_2 f_{12} dy}{\lambda^c(-f_1^2 f_{22} - f_2^2 f_{11} + 2f_1 f_2 f_{12})} \tag{3.195}
$$

Now, setting $dr_2 = dy = 0$ gives

$$
\frac{dx_1^c}{dr_1} = \frac{\partial x_1^c}{\partial r_1} = \frac{-f_2^2}{\lambda^c(-f_1^2 f_{22} - f_2^2 f_{11} + 2f_1 f_2 f_{12})} \tag{3.196}
$$

Holding $dr_1 = dy = 0$ gives

$$
\frac{dx_1^c}{dr_2} = \frac{\partial x_1^c}{\partial r_2} = \frac{f_1 f_2}{\lambda^c(-f_1^2 f_{22} - f_2^2 f_{11} + 2f_1 f_2 f_{12})} \tag{3.197}
$$

Finally, holding $dr_1 = dr_2 = 0$ yields

$$
\frac{dx_1^c}{dy} = \frac{\partial x_1^c}{\partial y} = \frac{-f_1 f_{22} + f_2 f_{12}}{(-f_1^2 f_{22} - f_2^2 f_{11} + 2f_1 f_2 f_{12})} \tag{3.198}
$$

Similarly, solving (3.193) for dx_2^c and letting appropriate parameter changes equal zero gives the partial derivatives,

$$
\frac{dx_2^c}{dr_2} = \frac{\partial x_2^c}{\partial r_2} = \frac{-f_1^2}{\lambda^c(-f_1^2 f_{22} - f_2^2 f_{11} + 2f_1 f_2 f_{12})} \tag{3.199}
$$

$$
\frac{dx_2^c}{dr_1} = \frac{\partial x_2^c}{\partial r_1} = \frac{f_1 f_2}{\lambda^c(-f_1^2 f_{22} - f_2^2 f_{11} + 2f_1 f_2 f_{12})} \tag{3.200}
$$

$$
\frac{dx_2^c}{dy} = \frac{\partial x_2^c}{\partial y} = \frac{-f_2 f_{11} + f_1 f_{12}}{(-f_1^2 f_{22} - f_2^2 f_{11} + 2f_1 f_2 f_{12})} \tag{3.201}
$$

The set of simultaneous equations, (3.193), can also be solved for $d\lambda^c$, but since λ^c is marginal cost (as a function of output), we defer consideration of $d\lambda^c$ to Chapter 4.

Let us now examine the signs of (3.196) through (3.201). First notice that the sign of the term $(-f_1^2 f_{22} - f_2^2 f_{11} + 2f_1 f_2 f_{12})$ in the denominator of these equations indicates whether the production function is quasi-concave or quasi-convex; the function is quasi-concave if this term is positive. Since λ^c (marginal cost) is positive, the denominators of (3.196) through (3.201) are positive if the second-order condition for constrained cost minimization is satisfied. Now consider the numerator in (3.196). Even if f_2 (marginal productivity of x_2) is negative, the partial derivative (3.196) is negative; thus, conditional factor demand functions always slope downward.

It can be seen from (3.197) and (3.200) that cross-price effects are positive as long as marginal physical productivity is positive for both factors. Furthermore, since these two equations are identical, the symmetry condition for conditional factor demand functions is proven; that is, $(\partial x_1^c / \partial r_2) = (\partial x_2^c / \partial r_1)$ is a general consequence of the cost-minimization model.

Equations 3.198 and 3.201 show what happens to x_1 and x_2, respectively, when output is increased. Since $f_{ii} \gtreqless 0$ and $f_{ii} \gtreqless 0$ with the second-order condition satisfied, $\partial x_i^c / \partial y$ can be negative, zero, or positive. If $(\partial x_i^c / \partial y) > 0$, then x_i is said to be a *normal* factor, while a factor for which $(\partial x_i^c / \partial y) < 0$ is said to be an *inferior* factor.

3.2.k LeChatelier Principle and Factor Demand Functions

This section deals with a well-known, yet amazingly deceptive, property of demand functions—that longer-run demand functions are more elastic than their shorter-run counterparts. The concept is deceptive or tricky for two reasons. First, demand functions are negatively sloped and hence what appears to the eye to be the relatively more steeply sloped of two curves is actually less sloped, given that a *small negative number* (slope) is greater than a *large negative number* (slope). If that were not sufficiently confusing, the matter is made worse by the fact that we economists, as noted earlier, reverse the implied order of causation in our geometric representations of demand curves. Accordingly, the reader is advised to proceed cautiously.

If a factor, say x_1, is variable in the short run, then a longer-run demand function for that factor will have equal or less slope than a corresponding shorter-run function. For example,

$$\frac{\partial x_1^*(r_1, r_2, \ldots, r_n, p)}{\partial r_1} \leq \frac{\partial x_1^*(r_1, r_2, \ldots, r_{n-1}, p | x_n)}{\partial r_1} \leq \cdots$$
$$\leq \frac{\partial x_1^*(r_1, p | x_2, x_3, \ldots, x_n)}{\partial r_1} \qquad (3.202)$$

for the case of unconditional factor demand, and

$$\frac{\partial x_1^c(r_1, r_2, \ldots, r_n, y)}{\partial r_1} \leq \frac{\partial x_1^c(r_1, r_2, \ldots, r_{n-1}, y | x_n)}{\partial r_1} \leq \cdots$$
$$\leq \frac{\partial x_1^c(r_1, y | x_2, x_3, \ldots, x_n)}{\partial r_1} \qquad (3.203)$$

for the case of conditional factor demand. Longer-run factor demand functions have less slope than their shorter-run counterparts because in longer-run situations the firm can adjust factors that are fixed in the short run, to optimal levels in response to changes in the price of the factor that is variable in the short run. That is, the difference in the relative slopes of long-run versus short-run factor demand functions simply reflect the fact that a firm has more flexibility to adjust to price changes in longer-run cases.

The examples provided in (3.202) and (3.203) are special cases of the *LeChatelier principle*, which states that the slope of demand functions do not decrease (usually increase) *in absolute value* as constraints are added to the optimization problem. In this case the constraints amount to fixed factors of production.

The comparative static result showing the own-price effect for the two-variable factor model, (3.171), provides a convenient means of showing the impact of factor fixity on the slope of the demand function.[13] Given $dr_2 = dp = 0$,

$$\frac{dx_1^*}{dr_1} = \frac{\partial x_1^*}{\partial r_1} = \frac{f_{22}}{p(f_{11}f_{22} - f_{12}^2)} \tag{3.204}$$

Equation 3.204 is the slope of $x_1^*(r_1, r_2, p)$; that is, the slope of the long-run demand function for x_1 assuming a two-factor model.

In contrast, if *only* x_1 is variable in the production period of interest, we have the profit function,

$$\pi = pf(x_1, x_2^0) - r_1x_1 - r_2x_2^0 - b \tag{3.205}$$

where x_2 is fixed. The first-order condition (there is only one in this case) is

$$\frac{\partial \pi}{\partial x_1} = pf_1 - r_1 = 0 \tag{3.206}$$

Taking the total differential of (3.206), we have

$$f_1 dp + pf_{11}dx_1^s - dr_1 = 0 \tag{3.207}$$

where the superscript s denotes the optimal value of x_1 in the short run. Setting $dp = 0$, (3.207) simplifies to

$$\frac{dx_1^s}{dr_1} = \frac{\partial x_1^s}{\partial r_1} = \frac{1}{pf_{11}} \tag{3.208}$$

Assuming second-order conditions are satisfied, we need to compare (3.208), which is the slope of the demand function with x_2 fixed (i.e., the

[13]For a proof of the LeChatelier principle in the more general case, see Silberberg (1978, pp. 293–298).

short run), with the slope of the longer-run demand function, (3.204). That is, to demonstrate the LeChatelier principle we must establish that

$$\frac{f_{22}}{p(f_{11}f_{22} - f_{12}^2)} \le \frac{1}{pf_{11}} \tag{3.209}$$

First, if we multiply $1/pf_{11}$ by f_{22}/f_{22}, (3.209) may be rewritten as

$$\frac{f_{22}}{p(f_{11}f_{22} - f_{12}^2)} \le \frac{f_{22}}{pf_{11}f_{22}} \tag{3.210}$$

The left and right sides of (3.210) are the same except for $(f_{11}f_{22} - f_{12}^2)$ and $f_{11}f_{22}$, respectively, in the denominator of each side. Recall that $f_{11}, f_{22} < 0$ and $(f_{11}f_{22} - f_{12}^2) > 0$ for the second-order condition to be satisfied. Since $f_{11}f_{22} \ge (f_{11}f_{22} - f_{12}^2) > 0$, it follows that the left side of the inequality (the slope of the longer-run function) is a larger negative number than the right side of the inequality (the slope of the short-run function). Note that in comparing the left and right sides of (3.210) we are implicitly assuming that f_{11} and f_{22} are evaluated at the level of the fixed factor x_2, namely, x_2^*, which is the long-run optimal level; if f_{ii} were evaluated at any other level of x_2, then f_{ii} on the right side of (3.210) would not necessarily be equal to f_{ii} on the left side of (3.210). The practical implication of this is that we are comparing slopes at the point where the long- and short-run functions intercept (see Figure 3.18).

The LeChatelier principle is demonstrated in Figure 3.18 for the two-factor model. Again we caution the reader not to be fooled by the geometry, as the conventional labeling of the axes (as in Figure 3.18) is not consistent with the mathematical specification of factor demand.

3.2.l Economic Region of Production

In Chapter 2, Section 2.2.m, we discussed symmetry of production stages. We established in general that production stages are *not* symmetric, that is, I_1 does not correspond to III_2 and vice versa, except for linearly homogeneous production functions. Thus, it was argued that, contrary to conventional wisdom, the area within the ridgelines was not exclusively Stage II. We suggested the possibility that the entire area bounded by the ridgelines might not be economic; that is, all points within the ridgelines might not be admissible as potential profit-maximization points. It is the purpose of this section to demonstrate this point.

Recall from Section 3.1.c that we were able to establish for the single variable factor case that all of Stage II (and only Stage II) was potentially economic *if* the firm was a perfect competitor in its product and factor market and assuming no budget constraint impinging on the purchase of the variable factor. Further recall that relaxation of any of these critical assumptions (production determining forces) altered our conclusion that Stage II and only Stage II was economic. In this section we will show further that even for a

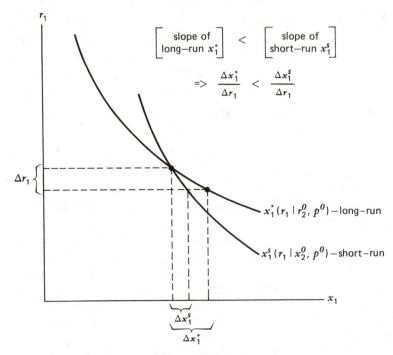

Figure 3.18. Comparison of relative slopes of long-run and short-run unconditional factor demand functions for x_1 in the two-factor model.

perfectly competitive firm with no budget constraints, only a portion of Stage II for both factors is economic.

Consider Figure 3.19, which is a repeat of Figure 2.15 with two additional isoelasticity contours noted, namely, $\xi = 0,1$. We assert that only the shaded area in Figure 3.19 is economic. Why?

First, it is clear that regions outside the ridgelines are uneconomic as discussed in Section 3.1.c because we cannot have profit maximization occurring in Stage III for either factor if factor prices are positive. Now what about the areas *within* the ridgeline where we are in Stage I with one or the other factor, that is, the areas denoted I_1, II_2 and II_1, I_2? Are these two small areas economic? Again appealing to the logic of Section 3.1.c, it seems intuitively plausible that these areas are uneconomic because the *AVP* for one or the other of the factors is rising in these regions. We let intuition suffice here because it is easier to show simply that the entire area southwest of (toward the origin from) the line $\xi = 1$ is uneconomic. That is, all regions where $\xi > 1$, whether or not both factors are in Stage II are uneconomic because the average return to the quasi-scale factor[14] is rising. If the average return to the quasi-

---

[14] In Section 2.3 we introduced the idea of the quasi-function coefficient. The "quasi-scale factor" for the case of proportional variation in a *subset* of factors is analogous to the scale factor, m, for proportional variation of *all* factors.

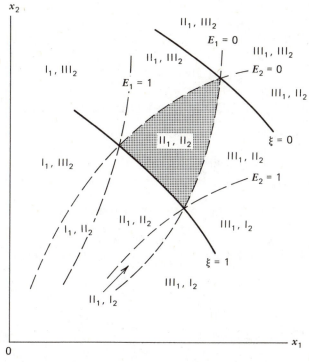

Figure 3.19. The economic region of production for an unconstrained perfectly competitive firm.

scale factor is rising (APP_m rising), then, by definition, we are in Stage I with respect to the quasi-scale factor. Again, our intuition suggests that we should expect production in such areas to not yield maximum profit for a perfectly competitive unconstrained firm. Our intuition is correct. In fact, if first- and second-order conditions are satisfied in this region ($\xi > 1$ in Figure 3.19), which they can be, profit (exclusive of fixed cost) will be locally maximum but negative! Why?

Unfortunately, the answer requires some ideas that have not yet been developed, but let us provide a swift preview of these ideas. In Chapter 4, we will show that there is an elasticity concept associated with cost curves that parallels (in fact is the reciprocal of) the quasi-function coefficient. We will show in Section 4.1.d that the flexibility of variable cost is one over the quasi-function coefficient and, analogous to the relationship between ϵ or ξ and APP_m (or E_i and APP_i). That is, when the flexibility of variable cost is less than unity, average variable cost is falling. What do we know about production in a region of declining average variable cost? If marginal revenue (product price for the perfectly competitive firm) intersects marginal cost at a point below minimum average variable cost, profit (exclusive of fixed cost) at this point will be negative. Again first- and second-order conditions may be satisfied but the total condition will not be. That is why we will see in Chapter

4 that the firm's short-run product supply function is truncated at minimum average value product (for the single-variable factor case). Thus, for the two-variable factor model, only in the shaded area of Figure 3.19 can first- and second-order *and* the total condition for maximum profit (exclusive of fixed cost) be satisfied for the perfectly competitive firm.

3.3 ONE-PRODUCT, *s*-VARIABLE FACTORS

The case of two-variable factors is easily generalized to any number, s, of variable factors. In the general case, we offer the following economic concepts.

Total value product, which is an $(s + 1)$-dimensional surface (in output and the variable factors), is given by

$$TVP \equiv py = g[f(\cdot)]f(\cdot) \qquad (3.211)$$

where $f(\cdot) = f(x_1, x_2, \ldots, x_s | x_{s+1}, \ldots, x_n)$ and $x_{s+1}, \ldots, x_n$ are fixed factors of production. Average value product for the ith factor is defined as

$$AVP_i \equiv \frac{TVP}{x_i} \qquad \text{for } i = 1, 2, \ldots, s \qquad (3.212)$$

and marginal value productivity is

$$MVP_i \equiv \frac{\partial TVP}{\partial x_i} \qquad \text{for } i = 1, 2, \ldots, s \qquad (3.213)$$

Variable factor cost is represented by

$$c \equiv \sum_{i=1}^{s} r_i x_i = \sum_{i=1}^{s} h^i(x_i) x_i \qquad (3.214)$$

and the marginal factor cost functions are given by

$$MFC_i \equiv \frac{\partial c}{\partial x_i} \qquad \text{for } i = 1, 2, \ldots, s \qquad (3.215)$$

Total factor cost is given by the addition of fixed costs, b, to (3.214). Using a Lagrangean formulation for the constrained cost-minimization problem, it can be shown that the expansion path conditions are given by $(s - 1)$ equations in factor space[15] that satisfy

$$\frac{MPP_i}{MPP_\ell} = \frac{MFC_i}{MFC_\ell} \qquad \text{for } i, \ell = 1, 2, \ldots, s \text{ and } i \neq \ell \qquad (3.216)$$

[15]For example, the expansion path conditions for the three-variable factor case include $f_1/f_2 = r_1/r_2$, $f_1/f_3 = r_1/r_3$, and $f_2/f_3 = r_2/r_3$ assuming perfect competition in the factor markets. However, from any pair of these equations one can derive the third. Thus, $s - 1 = 3 - 1 = 2$ of the expansion path equations are all that is needed.

The profit function in the general case is defined as

$$\pi \equiv TVP - C = g[f(\cdot)]f(\cdot) - \sum_{i=1}^{s} x_i h^i(x_i) - b \qquad (3.217)$$

First-order conditions for maximum profit require that

$$MVP_i = MFC_i \qquad \text{for } i = 1,2,\ldots,s \qquad (3.218)$$

Second-order conditions for maximum profit require that the naturally ordered principal minors of an $(s \times s)$ Hessian determinant alternate in sign. That is,

$$\frac{\partial^2 \pi}{\partial x_i^2} < 0 \qquad \text{for } i = 1,2,\ldots,s$$

$$\begin{vmatrix} \dfrac{\partial^2 \pi}{\partial x_1^2} & \dfrac{\partial^2 \pi}{\partial x_1 \partial x_2} \\[2mm] \dfrac{\partial^2 \pi}{\partial x_2 \partial x_1} & \dfrac{\partial^2 \pi}{\partial x_2^2} \end{vmatrix} > 0, \qquad \begin{vmatrix} \dfrac{\partial^2 \pi}{\partial x_1^2} & \dfrac{\partial^2 \pi}{\partial x_1 \partial x_2} & \dfrac{\partial^2 \pi}{\partial x_1 \partial x_3} \\[2mm] \dfrac{\partial^2 \pi}{\partial x_2 \partial x_1} & \dfrac{\partial^2 \pi}{\partial x_2^2} & \dfrac{\partial^2 \pi}{\partial x_2 \partial x_3} \\[2mm] \dfrac{\partial^2 \pi}{\partial x_3 \partial x_1} & \dfrac{\partial^2 \pi}{\partial x_3 \partial x_2} & \dfrac{\partial^2 \pi}{\partial x_3^2} \end{vmatrix} < 0,$$

$$\ldots,(-1)^s \begin{vmatrix} \dfrac{\partial^2 \pi}{\partial x_1^2} & \dfrac{\partial^2 \pi}{\partial x_1 \partial x_2} & \cdots & \dfrac{\partial^2 \pi}{\partial x_1 \partial x_s} \\[2mm] \vdots & \vdots & & \vdots \\[2mm] \dfrac{\partial^2 \pi}{\partial x_s \partial x_1} & \dfrac{\partial^2 \pi}{\partial x_s \partial x_2} & \cdots & \dfrac{\partial^2 \pi}{\partial x_s^2} \end{vmatrix} > 0 \qquad (3.219)$$

In the case of perfect competition in all markets, the second-order conditions imply that the production function must be strictly concave. Conditions (3.218) taken together with (3.219) and the requirement that $TVP \geq c$ are sufficient for maximum positive profit (exclusive of fixed cost).

Assuming the second-order conditions are satisfied, factor demand functions of the form

$$x_i^* = x_i^*(r_1, r_2, \ldots, r_s, p | x_{s+1}, \ldots, x_n) \qquad \text{for } i = 1,2,\ldots,s \qquad (3.220)$$

can be derived from the first-order conditions. If the second-order conditions for cost minimization are satisfied, conditional factor demand functions,

$$x_i^c = x_i^c(r_1, r_2, \ldots, r_s | y, x_{s+1}, \ldots, x_n) \qquad (3.221)$$

can be derived from the expansion path conditions combined with the production function. Note that both unconditional factor demand and conditional factor demand are functions of prices of those inputs that are variable and quantities of those inputs that are fixed. There are many possible short-run demand functions that might be specified (anywhere from 1 to n factors could be considered variable). There would be only one long-run demand function and one long-run conditional factor demand function, however; for the long-run case factor price arguments included in (3.220) and (3.221) would be $r_1, \ldots, r_n$ and there would be no fixed factor arguments.

Finally, two factors, x_i and x_ℓ, are economically interdependent if $(\partial x_i / \partial r_i) \neq 0$ for $i \neq \ell$ and $i, \ell = 1, 2, \ldots, s$. With logic demonstrated in the two-variable factor case, it can be shown that the symmetry conditions for factor demand,

$$\frac{\partial x_i^*}{\partial r_\ell} = \frac{\partial x_\ell^*}{\partial r_i} \qquad \text{for } i \neq \ell \text{ and } i, \ell = 1, 2, \ldots, s \qquad (3.222)$$

and homogeneity of degree zero in all prices must hold for a profit-maximizing firm.

3.4 CORNER SOLUTIONS

In all of the preceding optimality derivations we have implicitly assumed that there existed a mix of positive input levels that would satisfy the first-order conditions. There are, however, special cases for which the first-order conditions cannot be satisfied. These special cases, which are referred to as *corner solutions*, will be framed here in terms of the cost minimization model; the reader should note that corner solutions may also exist in the case of constrained output maximization and profit maximization.

One corner-solution case is for convex isoquants that intersect one or more of the axes, as illustrated in Figure 3.20. If factor prices are such that the cost equation is given by the line, c^0, then the first-order conditions as well as the second-order conditions for constrained cost minimization are satisfied at point B. However, if prices are such that the cost equation is c^1 (a relatively higher cost for x_1 or lower cost for x_2 than for c^0), the specified level of output, y^0, is produced by using all x_2 and no x_1 (point A). Note that at point A, the isoquant for y^0 is not tangent to the cost line. Therefore, the first-order condition is not satisfied and we cannot use calculus techniques to locate the optimum.

A second case for which a corner solution occurs is where isoquants are concave to the origin, as is illustrated in Figure 3.21. In this case, first-order conditions are satisfied at point A, but the second-order conditions (convex isoquants) are not satisfied. It can be seen that y^0 units can be produced at a lower cost ($c^0 < c^1$) by operating at point B in which case the firm uses x_1 and no x_2 to produce y^0. For the case illustrated in Figure 3.21, the cost-minimizing firm will operate at point B or D, depending on prices, but will never use a positive amount of both factors.

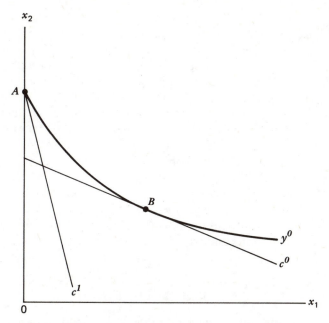

Figure 3.20. A corner solution for convex isoquants.

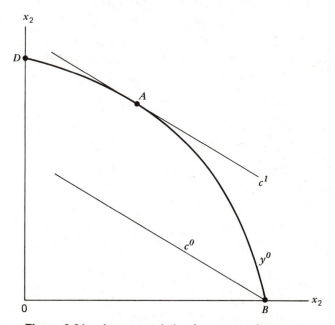

Figure 3.21. A corner solution for concave isoquants.

Both of the cases discussed above give rise to discontinuities in factor demand functions and in conditional factor demand functions. Either a first-order condition or a second-order condition was violated; moreover, traditional calculus techniques cannot be used to obtain an optimum. There are other situations, such as discontinuities in the production function or in a constraint, that prevent use of calculus for finding an optimum solution. However, the task of finding an optimum is not hopeless in such cases as a set of necessary and sufficient conditions which are more general than those discussed in this book exist. These conditions are referred to as the Kuhn–Tucker conditions, application of which is highly complicated for the *general* solution of problems with several variables. Nevertheless, the Kuhn–Tucker conditions lead to a reformulation of the optimization problem as a nonlinear programming problem for which *numerical* solutions can usually be obtained. Kuhn–Tucker conditions and nonlinear programming are beyond the scope of this book, but the interested reader should refer to Chiang (1974, Chap. 20) and Beightler, Phillips, and Wilde (1979, Chaps. 4–6).

3.5 FUNCTIONAL FORMS

The expansion path, conditional factor demand equations, and unconditional factor demand equations are given in Table 3.1 for four commonly used production functions. Technical properties of the production functions were given in Table 2.1.

3.6 PROBLEMS

3-1. Consider the single-factor, linear production function, $y = 8x$. Find the profit-maximizing level of x, plot all the relevant functions on a diagram like Figure 3.2, then find the demand for x and sketch the demand curve for two different levels of p for each of the following market specifications:

(a) $p = 4 - \frac{3}{8}y$, $r^0 = 6$.

(b) $p^0 = 5$, $r = x$.

(c) $p^0 = 5$, $r^0 = 6$.

3-2. Given the single-factor, quadratic production function, $y = 6x - x^2$, repeat Problem 3-1 for each of the following market specifications:

(a) $p^0 = 3$, $r = 2x$.

(b) $p^0 = 2$, $r^0 = 5$.

3-3. Given the Cobb–Douglas production function, $y = 2x_1^{1/2}x_2^{1/2}$, find the profit-maximizing levels of x_1 and x_2, the expansion path equation, the "short-run" demand for factor x_1, and the "long-run" demand for factor x_1 for each of the following market specifications:

(a) $p = y^{-1/2}$, $r_1^0 = \frac{1}{4}$, $r_2^0 = \frac{1}{9}$.

(b) $p^0 = \frac{1}{2}$, $r_1^0 = \frac{1}{2}$, $r_2 = x_2$.

(c) $p^0 = \frac{1}{2}$, $r_1^0 = 4$, $r_2^0 = 4$.

Table 3.1 Production Functions and Associated Expansion Paths and Conditional and Unconditional Factor Demand Equations for the Two-Factor Model

Production Function		*Expansion Path*[a,b]
Generalized Cobb–Douglas	$y = Ax_1^{b_1}x_2^{b_2}$	$x_2 = \left(\dfrac{r_1 b_2}{r_2 b_1}\right)x_1$
Quadratic	$y = a_0 + a_1 x_1 + a_2 x_2 + \frac{1}{2}b_1 x_1^2 + \frac{1}{2}b_2 x_2^2 + b_3 x_1 x_2$	$x_2 = \dfrac{r_1 a_2 - r_2 a_1 + (r_1 b_3 - r_2 b_1)x_1}{r_2 b_3 - r_1 b_2}$
CES	$y = A[bx_1^{-g} + (1-b)x_2^{-g}]^{-v/g}$	$x_2 = \left(\dfrac{r_1(1-b)}{r_2 b}\right)^{1/(g+1)} x_1$
Transcendental	$y = Ax_1^{a_1}e^{b_1 x_1}x_2^{a_2}e^{b_2 x_2}$	$x_2 = \left(\dfrac{a_2 r_1}{r_2}\right)\left(a_1 x_1^{-1} + b_1 - \dfrac{b_2 r_1}{r_2}\right)^{-1}$

Production Function	*Conditional Factor Demand Equations*[a,b]
Generalized Cobb–Douglas	$\left.\begin{aligned} x_1^c &= y^{1/a}A^{-1/a}\left(\dfrac{r_2 b_1}{r_1 b_2}\right)^{b_2/a} \\[2mm] x_2^c &= y^{1/a}A^{-1/a}\left(\dfrac{r_1 b_2}{r_2 b_1}\right)^{b_1/a} \end{aligned}\right\}$ where $a = b_1 + b_2$ p 24 ✍
Quadratic	Complicated expressions obtained by substituting the expansion path into the production function, then solving for x_1 (or x_2) by applying the quadratic formula; only one root is relevant
CES	$x_1^c = (yA^{-1})^{1/v}\left[b + (1-b)\left(\dfrac{r_1(1-b)}{r_2 b}\right)^{-g/(g+1)}\right]^{1/g}$ Indirect cost function $x_2^c = (yA^{-1})^{1/v}\left[(1-b) + b\left(\dfrac{r_2 b}{r_1(1-b)}\right)^{-g/(g+1)}\right]^{1/g}$
Transcendental	Mathematically intractable[c]

Production Function	*Unconditional Factor Demand Equations*[a,b]
Generalized Cobb–Douglas	$\left.\begin{aligned} x_1^* &= [r_1^{1-b_2}(b_1 pA)^{-1}b_2^{-b_2}(b_1 r_2)^{b_2}]^{1/(a-1)} \\[2mm] x_2^* &= [r_2^{1-b_1}(b_2 pA)^{-1}b_1^{-b_1}(b_2 r_1)^{b_1}]^{1/(a-1)} \end{aligned}\right\}$ where $a = b_1 + b_2$
Quadratic[d]	$x_1^* = \eta_1 + \beta_1\left(\dfrac{r_1}{p}\right) + \beta_3\left(\dfrac{r_2}{p}\right)$ p 24 ✍ $x_2^* = \eta_2 + \beta_3\left(\dfrac{r_1}{p}\right) + \beta_2\left(\dfrac{r_2}{p}\right)$ from indirect Π function
CES	$x_1^* = p^{1/(1-v)}v^{(2-v)/(1-v)}A^{1/(1-v)}b^{1/(1+g)}r_1^{-1/(1+g)}[b^{1/(1+g)}r_1^{g/(1+g)} + (1-b)^{1/(1+g)}r_2^{g/(1+g)}]^{-(v+g)/g(1-v)}$ $x_2^* = p^{1/(1-v)}v^{(2-v)/(1-v)}A^{1/(1-v)}(1-b)^{1/(1+g)}r_2^{-1/(1+g)}[b^{1/(1+g)}r_2^{g/(1+g)}]^{-(v+g)/g(1-v)}$
Transcendental	Mathematically intractable[c]

[a] All prices are assumed fixed.

[b] It is assumed that the production function is strictly concave.

[c] Although the functions are mathematically intractable, points on the functions can be numerically generated given values for the parameters.

[d] Letting $A = (b_1 b_2 - b_3^2)$, then $\beta_1 = b_2/A$; $\beta_2 = b_1/A$; $\beta_3 = -b_3/A$; $\eta_1 = -a_1\beta_1 - a_2\beta_3$; and $\eta_2 = -a_1\beta_3 - a_2\beta_2$. Note that there are some positive as well as negative values of b_3 that locally satisfy the second-order conditions.

3-4. Given $y = Ax_1^{b_1} x_2^{b_2}$, and assuming perfect competition in all markets, show that the expansion path equation and one of the profit-maximization first-order condition equations are sufficient to derive the long-run factor demand equations for factors x_1 and x_2.

3-5. Given the production function, $y = Ax_1^{b_1} x_2^{b_2}$, and perfect competition in product and factor markets, under what conditions does the long-run factor demand function for factor x_2 satisfy the usual properties of a demand function?

3-6. Assume there are only two inputs in the production of wheat—applied nitrogen and irrigation water. If you know that nitrogen and water are being applied in least-cost proportions and that the nitrogen application rate is at the profit-maximizing level, then it follows that water is being applied at its profit-maximizing level also. True or False? (Proof required.)

3-7. Consider max $U(\pi) = \max U(py - r_1 x_1 - r_2 x_2)$ subject to the constraint $y = f(x_1, x_2)$. Assuming that utility, $U(\cdot)$, is a monotonically increasing function of profit (that is, $\partial U / \partial \pi > 0$), derive the factor-side marginal conditions for utility maximization. Do these differ from the classical profit-maximization problem's marginal conditions? Why or why not?

3.7 SELECTED BIBLIOGRAPHY

Allen, R. G. D. *Mathematical Economics.* 2nd ed. London: Macmillan, 1966.

Beightler, C. S., D. T. Phillips, and D. J. Wilde. *Foundations of Optimization*, 2nd ed. Englewood Cliffs, NJ: Prentice-Hall, Inc., 1979.

Chiang, A. C. *Fundamental Methods of Mathematical Economics.* New York: McGraw-Hill Book Co., 1974.

Ferguson, C. E. *The Neoclassical Theory of Production and Distribution.* Cambridge: Cambridge University Press, 1969, Chapters 6, 8 and 9.

Frisch, R. *Theory of Production.* Chicago: Rand McNally, 1965, Chapters 9, 10 and 11.

Gould, J. P. and C. E. Ferguson. *Microeconomic Theory.* Homewood, IL: Irwin, 1980, Chapter 6.

Henderson, J. M. and R. E. Quandt. *Microeconomic Theory: A Mathematical Approach*, 3rd ed. New York: McGraw-Hill, 1980, Chapter 4.

Silberberg, E. *The Structure of Economics: A Mathematical Analysis.* New York: McGraw-Hill, 1978, Chapters 9 and 10.

CHAPTER 4

ECONOMIC ASPECTS OF PRODUCTION: THE OUTPUT PERSPECTIVE

In Chapter 3 we approached the economics of production from the input or factor side, whereas in this chapter we will consider the economics of production from the output side. We will be concerned with such relationships as total revenue, average revenue, marginal revenue, total cost, average cost, and marginal cost as opposed to concepts such as total value product, marginal value productivity, factor cost, and marginal factor cost.

In the preceding chapter we took as given conditions concerning the demand for the firm's output and the supply of its inputs. Combining this information with the production function we were able to deduce profit-maximizing factor levels, culminating with demand functions for factors. In the following sections we will again take as given output demand conditions and factor supply conditions; again we will deduce profit-maximizing conditions—this time culminating with the supply function for the firm's output.

4.1 COST FUNCTIONS

The center of attention in the study of the theory of the firm from an output-side perspective is on the cost functions expressed with output as the independent variable. Most first-year students of economics soon learn that the magic formula—marginal revenue equals marginal cost—will ensure at least a grade C. In fact, in many microeconomic theory courses the discussion of production economics essentially begins with so called costs of production, with only scant attention to the underlying production function (technical force) and optimal factor combinations. Having rather thoroughly explored the technical aspects of production and factor-side issues, our point of departure is to examine the intimate relationship between variable cost in terms of output, the production function, and the expansion path. We begin by considering the single-factor case.

4.1.a Variable Cost—Single-Factor Case

Variable cost, denoted by

$$VC \equiv \tilde{c}(y) \tag{4.1}$$

is defined as the *minimum* cost (thus the tilde over c) necessary to produce y units of output in any particular production period (length of run). Thus, variable cost simply reflects factor costs as we move out an expansion path, rather than factor costs for any point on the production surface. In the case of perfect competition in the factor market, VC will depend on (be a function of) factor price as well as output.

For the single-factor case, the algebra of deriving the variable cost function from the production function is simple and direct, because there is no choice about how much x to use to produce the given level of y (this is not true in the multifactor case). Derivation of the variable cost function for the single-factor case is illustrated by the following example.

Example 4.1 Assume a Cobb–Douglas production function with a single variable factor,

$$y = Ax^b \tag{4.2}$$

Since there is no choice about the input level to use to produce a specified output, the *minimum* cost necessary to produce a particular output, which is variable cost, is simply factor cost expressed in terms of output. To express variable *factor* cost,

$$c \equiv rx \tag{4.3}$$

in terms of output in the single-factor case, we solve the production function for x,

$$x = \left(\frac{y}{A}\right)^{1/b} \tag{4.4}$$

and substitute the resulting function into the factor cost equation,

$$VC \equiv \tilde{c} \equiv \tilde{c}(y) = r\left(\frac{y}{A}\right)^{1/b} \tag{4.5}$$

In (4.5) we use the notation, $\tilde{c}$, rather than c to denote that costs are now expressed in terms of output and that the output is being produced at minimum cost.

It should be noted that derivation of the variable cost function for more than one factor is considerably more complicated because factor costs and variable costs are not necessarily equal; factor costs measure costs for any point on the production surface, while variable costs refer to *minimum* costs for a particular level of output.

The geometry of the basic linkage between the variable cost function and the production function for one variable factor is presented in Figure 4.1.[1] Panel *a* shows the production function; beneath it, in panel *b*, is the cost

---

[1]Figure 4.1 and the discussion related thereto (this paragraph) follows closely a paper by Beattie and Griffin published in the *Southern Journal of Agricultural Economics*, 1980.

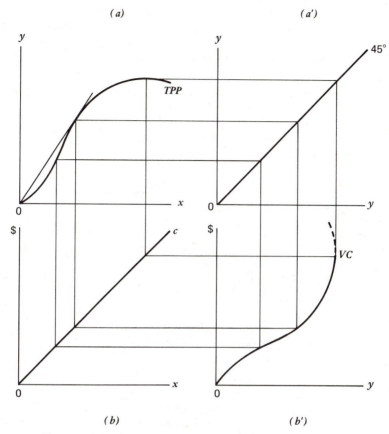

Figure 4.1. Linkage between production function and cost-output relationship. (a) Production function. (a') 45° line. (b) Cost equation. (b') Variable cost function.

equation. The slope of the cost equation depends on the level of the factor price, r. Panel a' is a 45° line that permits the translation of output from the vertical to the horizontal axis; beneath it, in panel b', is the resulting cost-output relationship, (4.5), obtained by "closing the circle" and connecting the points of intersection. From this visual presentation we can see the correspondence of inflection, ray-line tangency, and maximum output points between the production function and the variable cost curve; these points are noted by the connecting lines in Figure 4.1. Also the implication of a three-stage production function for the shape of cost curves is made clear, including the often omitted Stage III (dashed part of VC).

4.1.b Variable Cost—Two-Factor Case

To derive the variable cost function for more than one variable factor, we must translate the expansion path relationship as expressed in terms of factors into output. Since the production function translates inputs into output, it can be used in conjunction with the expansion path equation to express cost in terms of output. To simplify this theoretical derivation, we assume only two variable factors and perfect competition in the factor markets. For the production function, $y = f(x_1, x_2)$, and the associated expansion path, $x_2 = g(x_1, r_1, r_2)$, we can substitute the expansion path into the production function for x_2 to obtain

$$y = f[x_1, g(x_1, r_1, r_2)] \tag{4.6}$$

and by substituting the inverse of the expansion path, $x_1 = g^{-1}(x_2, r_1, r_2)$, into the production function for x_1, gives

$$y = f[g^{-1}(x_2, r_1, r_2), x_2] \tag{4.7}$$

Equations 4.6 and 4.7 relate output to factor prices and to x_1 and x_2, respectively, along an expansion path. As long as we are not in Stage III of production, which is uneconomic, there is a one-to-one mapping between y and x_1 in (4.6) and between y and x_2 in (4.7). Thus, we can uniquely solve (4.6) for x_1, which we denote by

$$x_1 = x_1(r_1, r_2, y) \tag{4.8}$$

where $x_1(\cdot)$ denotes a function, and we can uniquely solve (4.7) for x_2,

$$x_2 = x_2(r_1, r_2, y) \tag{4.9}$$

Substituting (4.8) and (4.9) into the factor cost equation for x_1 and x_2, respectively, we get the variable cost equation. That is,

$$c \equiv r_1 x_1 + r_2 x_2 \tag{4.10}$$

and

$$VC = r_1 x_1(r_1, r_2, y) + r_2 x_2(r_1, r_2, y)$$
$$= \tilde{c}(r_1, r_2, y) \tag{4.11}$$

As in the single-factor case, it is possible to present the geometric equivalence of our mathematical derivation—see Figure 4.2. The large three-dimensional diagram shows the production function with isoquants and an expansion path projected from the x_1, x_2 plane to the production surface. Output levels are projected from the y axis of the three-dimensional diagram to cost-output space; that is, an *inverse* cost function is mapped. From Figure 4.2 the reader can readily observe that the cost function reflects the curvature of the production surface along the expansion path *given* fixed factor prices. Some textbooks refer to this as the mirror image phenomenon.

Notice that the steps we used in deriving (4.8) and (4.9) are exactly the same steps we used in deriving conditional factor demand functions (Section

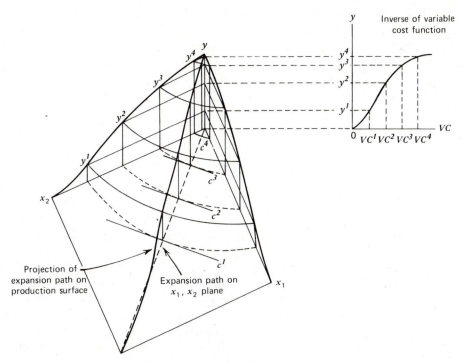

Figure 4.2. An illustration of an expansion path and associated variable cost function.

3.2.h); in fact, (4.8) and (4.9) are the conditional factor demand functions. Therefore, in the case of perfect competition in all factor markets, the cost function (4.11) is equivalent to

$$VC = r_1 x_1^c(r_1, r_2, y) + r_2 x_2^c(r_1, r_2, y) \tag{4.12}$$

where x_1^c and x_2^c are conditional factor demand functions and not quantities.

Example 4.2 In Example 3.12, we derived the conditional factor demand equations for the Cobb–Douglas production function:

$$x_1^c = \left[\frac{y}{A}\right]^{1/(b_1+b_2)} \left[\frac{b_1 r_2}{b_2 r_1}\right]^{b_2/(b_1+b_2)} \tag{4.13}$$

and

$$x_2^c = \left[\frac{y}{A}\right]^{1/(b_1+b_2)} \left[\frac{b_2 r_1}{b_1 r_2}\right]^{b_1/(b_1+b_2)} \tag{4.14}$$

Substituting these into the factor cost equation, we obtain

$$VC = r_1 \left[\frac{y}{A}\right]^{1/(b_1+b_2)} \left[\frac{b_1 r_2}{b_2 r_1}\right]^{b_2/(b_1+b_2)}$$

$$+ r_2 \left[\frac{y}{A}\right]^{1/(b_1+b_2)} \left[\frac{b_2 r_1}{b_1 r_2}\right]^{b_1/(b_1+b_2)}$$

$$= [y A^{-1} r_1^{b_1} r_2^{b_2}]^{1/(b_1+b_2)} \left[\left(\frac{b_1}{b_2}\right)^{b_2/(b_1+b_2)}\right.$$

$$+ \left.\left(\frac{b_2}{b_1}\right)^{b_1/(b_1+b_2)}\right] \qquad (4.15)$$

Notice that in the above example the VC function associated with the Cobb–Douglas production function is homogeneous of degree $1/(b_1 + b_2)$ *in output.* This is a special case of a more general result, namely, that under perfect competition in factor markets, $VC = \bar{c}(y, r_1, r_2)$ is homogeneous of degree $1/\epsilon$ in output, y, if the underlying production function is homogeneous of degree ϵ in factor levels, x_i. Proof of this result is provided in Section 4.1.d.

Because the variable cost function for a Cobb–Douglas production function (Example 4.2) is homogeneous in output, it is characterized by one of the three possibilities shown in Figure 4.3. That is, if a short-run homogeneous

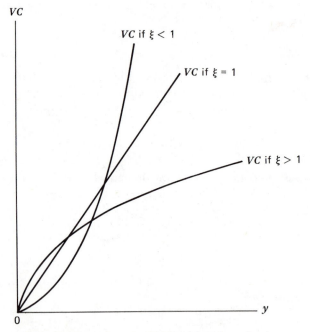

Figure 4.3. Possible variable cost functions for homogeneous production functions (assuming perfect competition in factor markets).

production function exhibits decreasing, constant, or increasing proportional returns to the quasi-scale factor, then the associated short-run variable cost function must increase throughout at an increasing, constant, or decreasing rate, respectively, *assuming perfect competition in the factor markets*. As we will see later, finite profit maximum solutions will not exist for the perfectly competitive firm if the variable cost curve increases at a constant or decreasing rate. Not surprisingly, we will find that second-order conditions are violated in such cases. We will also find that this problem can be resolved if the firm is an imperfect competitor in one or more markets (see Problem 4-3). That is, the key issue regarding second-order conditions is the nature (curvature) of the profit function which embodies *all* technical and economic considerations—the production function, product demand, and factor supplies. The production function (technology) dominates (prevails or dictates the solution) only for the special case of zero product and factor price flexibility.

In the case of imperfect competition in both factor markets, the expansion path does not depend on factor prices and therefore factor prices do not appear in the counterparts of (4.8) and (4.9). Recall that the variable factor cost equation is exclusively a function of input usage, for the imperfect factor market case; that is,

$$c \equiv r_1 x_1 + r_2 x_2 = h^1(x_1)x_1 + h^2(x_2)x_2 \qquad (4.16)$$

where h^1 and h^2 are factor price relationships (supply functions) for x_1 and x_2, respectively. Repeating the derivation of (4.6) through (4.11), using appropriate conditional factor demand notation, the cost function is given by

$$VC = h^1[x_1^c(y)]x_1^c(y) + h^2[x_2^c(y)]x_2^c(y)$$
$$= \tilde{c}(y) \qquad (4.17)$$

which is solely a function of y for this imperfect factor market case.

Two important conclusions pertaining to the variable cost function are: (1) implicit in the output-side cost function is the expansion path; that is, a theoretical cost function for y reflects movements along the expansion path; and (2) cost functions are intimately related to (derived from) the production function.

4.1.c Additional Cost Functions

Total cost (*TC*) is simply variable cost plus a fixed cost component, b; that is,

$$TC \equiv \tilde{c}(y) + b \qquad (4.18)$$

The *average total cost* (*ATC*) function is defined as

$$ATC \equiv \frac{TC}{y} \equiv \frac{\tilde{c}(y) + b}{y} \qquad (4.19)$$

and the *average variable cost* (*AVC*) function is

$$AVC \equiv \frac{VC}{y} \equiv \frac{\bar{c}(y)}{y} \tag{4.20}$$

Finally, the *marginal cost* (*MC*) function is given by the change in total cost or variable cost for an infinitesimal change in output; that is,

$$MC \equiv \frac{dTC}{dy} \equiv \frac{dVC}{dy} \equiv \frac{d[\bar{c}(y) + b]}{dy} \equiv \frac{d\bar{c}(y)}{dy} \tag{4.21}$$

Earlier, we demonstrated how to derive a variable cost function from which the marginal cost function could be obtained by differentiation. However, there is a more direct way of obtaining marginal cost, albeit less intuitively satisfying. To conceptually demonstrate this direct way, recall the Lagrangean factor cost-minimization problem (Section 3.2.a) that was used to obtain the expansion path equation, which in turn was used in deriving the variable cost function. For *s*-variable factors, we can write this function as

$$Lc = \sum_{i=1}^{s} h^i(x_i)x_i + \lambda[y^0 - f(x_1, x_2, \ldots, x_s)] \tag{4.22}$$

where λ is the Lagrangean multiplier.

Note that *if* the first-order conditions for minimization of (4.22) are satisfied, the term in brackets is zero *and* costs are minimum for every output level of interest. Since the term in brackets is zero and the x_i are evaluated at x_i^c (i.e., the *x* levels satisfying the first-order conditions of the cost-minimization problem), the Lagrangean cost function, *Lc* in (4.22), is *minimum* factor cost or factor cost measured along the expansion path. If we substitute $x_i^c = x_i^c(y)$ for x_i in (4.22), then we translate minimum factor cost into variable cost; that is, we go from measuring minimum cost from the factor side to measuring cost from the output side. Thus, if the first-order conditions are satisfied, *Lc* = *VC*. Hence, since $\partial Lc/\partial y = \lambda$, the Langrangean multiplier is marginal cost, *MC*. So by simultaneously solving the first-order conditions associated with (4.22), we obtain

$$\lambda^* = MC = \lambda^*(y) \tag{4.23}$$

To get the variable cost function using this approach, one needs to take the integral of (4.23) between 0 and *y*; that is,

$$VC = \int_0^y MC \, dy = \int_0^y \lambda^*(y) \, dy \tag{4.24}$$

We suggest that the reader obtain *MC* and *VC* in this way for the Cobb–Douglas production function with two variable factors and constant factor prices; then compare *VC* to that obtained in Example 4.2, equation 4.15—the results should be the same.

4.1.d Variable Cost Flexibility

Another cost concept alluded to in the discussion following Example 4.2 was that of the cost-flexibility coefficient. Specifically, we define the *flexibility of variable cost* as

$$\lambda_{vc} \equiv \frac{dVC/VC}{dy/y} \equiv \frac{dVC}{dy}\frac{y}{VC} = \frac{MC}{AVC} \qquad (4.25)$$

That is, λ_{vc} measures the infinitesimal percentage change in variable cost relative to an infinitesimal percentage change in output and, like all elasticities, turns out to be the ratio of the marginal function to the average function. We will see in the next section that, like E_i, ϵ, and ξ for the production function, λ_{vc} is useful in delineating key regions where the cost curves behave in a certain way. (Note that λ_{vc} is different from λ^* in the previous section.)

For a single-factor production function it is easy to show that λ_{vc} is the inverse of the function coefficient *or* quasi-function coefficient *or* factor elasticity (in this case). That is,

$$\lambda_{vc} = \frac{1}{\epsilon} = \frac{1}{\xi} = \frac{1}{E} \qquad (4.26)$$

for the single-factor case.

Generalizing the steps used in deriving *VC* from $c \equiv rx$ and the production function, $y = f(x)$, in Example 4.1, we discover that

$$VC = rf^{-1}(y) \qquad (4.27)$$

which is the general counterpart to (4.5) and to *VC* in panel *b'* of Figure 4.1.

Substituting (4.27) into (4.25) yields

$$\lambda_{vc} \equiv \frac{dVC}{dy}\frac{y}{VC} = \frac{d[rf^{-1}(y)]}{dy}\frac{y}{rf^{-1}(y)} \qquad (4.28)$$

But $f^{-1}(y) = x$, so

$$\lambda_{vc} = \frac{d(rx)}{dy}\frac{y}{rx} = r\frac{dx}{dy}\frac{y}{rx}$$

$$= \frac{dx}{dy}\frac{y}{x} = \frac{1}{\epsilon} \quad \text{or} \quad \frac{1}{\xi} \quad \text{or} \quad \frac{1}{E} \qquad (4.29)$$

Note that the derivation in (4.29) requires that $r \neq h(x)$. That is, the correspondence between cost flexibility and production elasticities requires perfect competition in the factor market(s).

From (4.29) we find that the region where MC is increasing *and* greater than AVC is associated with $\epsilon = \xi = E < 1$ which was Stage II of production. To see this, recall that $\lambda_{vc} = MC/AVC$. In the next section we show that $MC > AVC$ for y values greater than that where AVC is minimum. Therefore, in this range $\lambda_{vc} > 1$, which corresponds to $\epsilon = \xi = E < 1$ from (4.29). In Figure 4.4 the region of y^0 to y^1 on the vertical axis of the production function (top diagram) corresponds to the region of y^0 to y^1 on the horizontal axis of the cost function (lower diagram).

Establishing the correspondence between cost flexibility and the production function related elasticities is, surprisingly, no more difficult for the two-variable factor case. Again, assuming constant factor prices,

$$\tilde{c} \equiv r_1 x_1 + r_2 x_2 = \lambda f_1 x_1 + \lambda f_2 x_2 = \lambda (f_1 x_1 + f_2 x_2) \qquad (4.30)$$

because $\lambda f_1 = r_1$ and $\lambda f_2 = r_2$ if the expansion path conditions are satisfied (i.e., the equivalent equations of (3.82) for perfect competition). Recall that

$$\xi = E_1 + E_2 = f_1 \frac{x_1}{y} + f_2 \frac{x_2}{y} = \frac{f_1 x_1 + f_2 x_2}{y} \qquad (4.31)$$

or

$$f_1 x_1 + f_2 x_2 = y\xi \qquad (4.32)$$

Substituting (4.32) into (4.30), we get

$$\tilde{c} = \lambda y \xi \qquad (4.33)$$

But what are c and λ? Since the expansion path conditions have been imposed $c = VC$ and we know $\lambda = \lambda^*$ is MC from (4.23). Thus, (4.33) may be restated as

$$VC = MC \, y \, \xi \qquad (4.34)$$

Rearranging (4.34),

$$\xi = \frac{VC}{y} \frac{1}{MC} = \frac{AVC}{MC} \qquad (4.35)$$

Since $\lambda_{vc} = MC/AVC$ from (4.25) we see that

$$\xi = \frac{1}{\lambda_{vc}} \quad \text{or} \quad \lambda_{vc} = \frac{1}{\xi} \qquad (4.36)$$

Note that in the above, ξ may be replaced with ϵ if the production function has *only* two factors, that is, if there are no fixed factors.

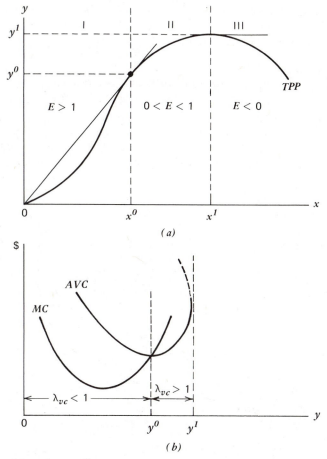

Figure 4.4. Relationship between Stages I and II of the single variable factor production function and the corresponding cost functions. (*a*) Total physical product function. (*b*) Cost functions.

Again for the two-factor case, as for the single-factor case, we find that there is a direct correspondence between the production function and the cost curves in terms of technical elasticities when factor prices are constant. The geometry of this correspondence should be apparent from Figure 4.5 in the following section.

A final point of interest about the correspondence between λ_{vc} and ξ involves the special case of constant proportional return (or homogeneous) functions. Given the general result in (4.36) and given constant factor prices, it follows that if $\xi = k$ (where k is a constant) for all factor levels on the production surface, then $\lambda_{vc} = 1/k$ (λ_{vc} is constant) for all output levels. In other words, homogeneity of degree k of the production function in the variable factors implies homogeneity of degree $1/k$ of the variable cost function in terms of output given perfect competition in the factor markets, as was alluded to in the discussion following Example 4.2. An alternative proof of this result is provided by Silberberg (1978, pp. 303–307).

4.1.e Geometry of Cost Functions

Geometry of the cost functions is shown in Figure 4.5 for the classical three-stage textbook production function. Two important relationships can be seen in this figure. First, notice that total cost and variable cost pass through their respective inflection points when marginal cost is minimum. This can be deduced as follows. From the sufficient conditions for a minimum, expressed

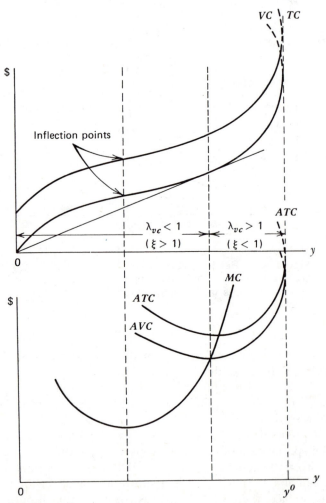

Figure 4.5. The geometry of cost curves and variable cost flexibility.

in terms of marginal cost, we know that $(dMC/dy) = 0$ and $(d^2MC/dy^2) > 0$. Since

$$\frac{dMC}{dy} \equiv \frac{d^2TC}{dy^2} \equiv \frac{d^2VC}{dy^2} \qquad (4.37)$$

TC and *VC* must have inflection points at the level of *y* for which $(dMC/dy) = 0$.

The second important relationship to note in Figure 4.5 is that marginal cost is less than, equal to, or greater than average variable cost when average cost is declining, minimum, or rising, respectively. As proof of this, consider

$$MC \equiv \frac{dVC}{dy} = \frac{d(AVC\ y)}{dy} = AVC + y\frac{dAVC}{dy} \qquad (4.38)$$

Therefore,

$$\frac{dAVC}{dy} < 0 \Rightarrow MC < AVC$$

$$\frac{dAVC}{dy} = 0 \Rightarrow MC = AVC \qquad (4.39)$$

$$\frac{dAVC}{dy} > 0 \Rightarrow MC > AVC$$

The same proof holds for the relationship of *MC* and *ATC* since $MC \equiv dVC/dy \equiv dTC/dy$.

Also, since we know that $\lambda_{vc} = MC/AVC$, it follows that $\lambda_{vc} < 1, = 1,$ and > 1, respectively, for the three cases in (4.39). Further, λ_{vc} is undefined at the point where *VC* and *TC* turn back (at y^0) in Figure 4.5 because $\xi = 0$ at this point. Why? We know at the global maximum of any short-run production function $\xi = 0$. The cost functions represent costs of achieving alternative levels of output *when* inputs are combined in expansion path proportions. Since the expansion path is an isocline it must "pass through" the global maximum as do all isoclines. As in Figures 4.1 and 4.4, we have drawn the "Stage III" portions of *VC*, *TC*, *AVC*, and *ATC* as dashed lines in Figure 4.5. However, note that production in this range violates the expansion path condition because the same level of output could be achieved at lower cost. Thus, although isoclines continue down the back side of the mountain, second-order conditions prevent the expansion path from doing the same. In effect, cost minimization requires that the expansion path be truncated at the global maximum of the production function; that is, one of the two solutions to the first-order conditions is disallowed. However, if an irrational entrepreneur were to continue to add inputs beyond the point where their respective marginal productivities were zero, costs would continue to rise as output fell.

4.2 REVENUE FUNCTIONS

Total revenue (TR) is defined as

$$TR \equiv p\,y \tag{4.40}$$

In the imperfectly competitive case where we assume that $p = g(y)$,

$$TR = g(y)y \tag{4.41}$$

and in the perfectly competitive case where price is constant,

$$TR \equiv p\,y \tag{4.42}$$

Average revenue (AR) is

$$AR \equiv \frac{TR}{y} = \frac{g(y)y}{y} = g(y) \tag{4.43}$$

The firm's average revenue function is given by the demand function for its product. Thus, when perfect competition is assumed, the average revenue function is given by the constant product price:

$$AR = \frac{p\,y}{y} = p \tag{4.44}$$

Marginal revenue (MR) is defined as

$$MR \equiv \frac{dTR}{dy} = \frac{d[g(y)y]}{dy}$$

$$= g(y) + y\frac{d[g(y)]}{dy} = p + y\frac{dp}{dy} \tag{4.45}$$

or when perfect competition is assumed,

$$MR = \frac{d(p\,y)}{dy} = p \tag{4.46}$$

Note that under conditions of perfect competition in the product market the firm's $AR = MR$.

Now let us examine the relationship between marginal revenue and price flexibility, the reciprocal of price elasticity of demand. Recall that price flexibility, λ_p, was defined in Chapter 3 as

$$\lambda_p = \frac{dp}{dy}\frac{y}{p} \tag{4.47}$$

where it is assumed that $p = g(y)$. Accordingly,

$$MR = p + y\frac{dp}{dy} = p + \frac{p}{p}y\frac{dp}{dy}$$
$$= p(1 + \lambda_p) = p(1 + 1/E_p) \tag{4.48}$$

where E_p is the usual price elasticity of demand. That is, the increase in total revenue caused by a unit increment in output is equal to the price multiplied by one plus the product price flexibility. Note that in perfect competition, the price flexibility of demand is zero, thus $MR = p$.

Geometric relationships of the various revenue concepts are illustrated in Figure 4.6. In this figure, panel a shows the case of perfect competition in the product market ($\lambda_p = 0$) and panel b shows the general case for a downward sloping demand curve ($\lambda_p < 0$). One important relationship that can be seen in Figure 4.6 is that total revenue is a maximum when marginal revenue is zero, as expected from the definitions of TR and MR. It is also important to notice that TR is increasing over the elastic region of the demand curve ($E_p < -1$) and decreasing over the inelastic region ($-1 < E_p < 0$). This relationship can be deduced as follows. Rearranging terms in (4.48) gives

$$E_p = \frac{p}{MR - p} \tag{4.49}$$

From (4.49) we see that

$$MR > 0 \Rightarrow E_p < -1$$
$$MR = 0 \Rightarrow E_p = -1 \tag{4.50}$$
$$MR < 0 \Rightarrow -1 < E_p < 0$$

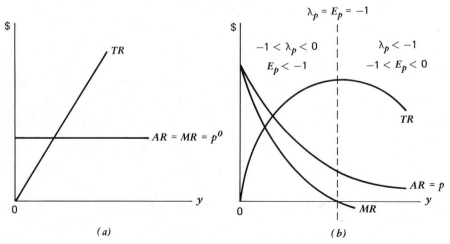

Figure 4.6. Relationship of *TR*, *AR*, and *MR* for $\lambda_p = 0$ and $\lambda_p < 0$. (a) The case of $\lambda_p = 0$. (b) The case of $\lambda_p < 0$.

It is not our intention to confuse the issue by couching our discussion here and Figure 4.6 in terms of both product price flexibility and its reciprocal, price elasticity of demand. Most readers, no doubt, are more at ease with the concept of price elasticity of demand since it is the commonly used concept in economics literature and textbooks. On the other hand, students of production economics will find that many of the classics in production economics use price flexibility (for example, Carlson, 1965, and Frisch, 1965). Price flexibility does have the advantage of being a right-side-up concept from the viewpoint of the imperfectly competitive firm. That is, if we postulate that $p = g(y)$ or $r = h(x)$, then it seems logical to define "elasticity" of those functions as percentage change in the dependent variable relative to percentage change in an independent variable, like most things mathematical.

4.3 PROFIT MAXIMIZATION

In the previous chapter we viewed profit maximization in terms of selecting factor levels. Implicit in this formulation was a profit-maximizing output level obtained by substituting optimal factor levels into the production function. Let us now view the profit-maximization problem from the output side, with cost-minimizing factor levels implicit in the total cost function. Thus, we define

$$\pi \equiv TR - TC \equiv p\,y - [\tilde{c}(y) + b]$$
$$= g(y)y - \tilde{c}(y) - b \tag{4.51}$$

where b is fixed cost. In connection with (4.51), note that when perfect competition in factor and product markets is assumed, we have

$$\pi \equiv p\,y - \tilde{c}(r_1, r_2, y) - b \tag{4.52}$$

The first-order condition for maximization of (4.51) is

$$\frac{d\pi}{dy} = \frac{d[g(y)y - \tilde{c}(y) - b]}{dy}$$
$$= g(y) + y\frac{dg(y)}{dy} - \frac{d\tilde{c}(y)}{dy} = 0 \tag{4.53}$$

Recalling definitions of marginal revenue and marginal cost, it follows from (4.53) that

$$MR = MC \tag{4.54}$$

When perfect competition in the product market is assumed, (4.54) reduces to

$$p = MC \tag{4.55}$$

The second-order condition for maximum profit is that the profit function be concave at the value of y that satisfies the first-order condition, (4.54). That is,

$$
\begin{aligned}
\frac{d^2\pi}{dy^2} &= \frac{d^2[g(y)y - \bar{c}(y) - b]}{dy^2} \\
&= \frac{d\left[g(y) + y\,\frac{dg(y)}{dy} - \frac{d\bar{c}(y)}{dy} \right]}{dy} \\
&= 2\,\frac{dg(y)}{dy} + y\,\frac{d^2g(y)}{dy^2} - \frac{d^2\bar{c}(y)}{dy^2} < 0
\end{aligned}
\qquad (4.56)
$$

which implies that the rate of change of marginal revenue (first two terms) must be less than the rate of change of marginal cost (third term). Or, assuming a downward sloping product demand function, MR must intersect MC from above. The first-order condition, (4.54), taken together with the second-order condition, (4.56), and the total condition that $TR - VC > 0$ are sufficient for maximum positive profit (exclusive of fixed costs).

Example 4.3   Assuming constant product and factor prices, and the cost function derived in Example 4.2, we have the profit function,

$$
\pi = p\,y - y^\alpha r_1^{\alpha b_1} r_2^{\alpha b_2}\left[A^{-\alpha}\left(\frac{b_1}{b_2}\right)^{\alpha b_2} + A^{-\alpha}\left(\frac{b_2}{b_1}\right)^{\alpha b_1} \right] - b
\qquad (4.57)
$$

where $\alpha = 1/(b_1 + b_2)$ and b is fixed cost. To simplify notation, let the term in brackets in (4.57), which is a constant, be denoted by k. Thus,

$$
\pi = p\,y - y^\alpha r_1^{\alpha b_1} r_2^{\alpha b_2} k - b
\qquad (4.58)
$$

The first-order condition is

$$
\frac{d\pi}{dy} = p - \alpha y^{\alpha-1} r_1^{\alpha b_1} r_2^{\alpha b_2} k = 0
\qquad (4.59)
$$

which can be manipulated to give

$$
y^* = [p\, r_1^{-\alpha b_1} r_2^{-\alpha b_2} k^{-1} \alpha^{-1}]^{1/(\alpha-1)}
\qquad (4.60)
$$

Therefore, the critical level of y can be obtained by specifying values for p, r_1, r_2, α, and k in (4.60).

To assure that y^* is associated with maximum rather than minimum profit, we must check the second-order condition,

$$\frac{d^2\pi}{dy^2} = -\alpha(\alpha - 1)y^{\alpha-2}r_1^{\alpha b_1}r_2^{\alpha b_2}k \tag{4.61}$$

Notice that if the associated Cobb–Douglas production function has decreasing proportional returns to the variable inputs (i.e., $\xi = b_1 + b_2 < 1 \Rightarrow \alpha > 1$) then (4.61) is less than zero for all values of y and the second-order condition is satisfied.[2] (If $b_1 + b_2 \geq 1$, the second-order condition will not be satisfied given perfect competition in all markets. Problem 4-3 provides an example where the second-order condition is satisfied despite the fact that $b_1 + b_2 = 1$; the technical force is overridden, so to speak, by the factor supply force.) Whether or not the total condition, $TR - VC > 0$, is satisfied depends on the value of the parameter k (and thus b_1 and b_2) in (4.58).

To introduce an alternative to the Cobb–Douglas production function and associated functions, we present an example using another functional form. This example illustrates that there may be multiple solutions to the first-order condition, only one of which satisfies the second-order condition.

Example 4.4 Find the profit maximizing level of output given

$$VC = .5y^3 - 4y^2 + 12y \tag{4.62}$$

and fixed cost, $b = 4$, and $p = 9.50$. Then

$$\pi = 9.5y - (.5y^3 - 4y^2 + 12y) - 4 \tag{4.63}$$

The first-order condition is

$$\frac{d\pi}{dy} = 9.5 - \underbrace{(1.5y^2 - 8y + 12)}_{MC} = 0 \tag{4.64}$$

where the first term is labeled MR.

Since (4.64) is quadratic in y, we can find its roots by the quadratic formula:

$$y = \frac{-8 \pm \sqrt{8^2 - 4(-1.5)(-2.5)}}{2(-1.5)} = \frac{-8 \pm 7}{-3} \tag{4.65}$$

---

[2] In empirical work with nonexperimental data, we sometimes find that when we estimate parameters for a fully specified (multiple input) Cobb–Douglas function, without constraining the sum of the factor elasticities (coefficients) in the estimation process, that the sum of estimated coefficients is greater than unity. Obviously when this happens longer-run economic implications (long-run factor demand, product supply, etc.) cannot be derived from the estimated model. However, the model still may be fruitful for analyses of shorter-run cases. Satisfaction of second-order conditions for the Cobb–Douglas function requires that $\xi < 1$, not that $\epsilon < 1$. ξ is ϵ only for the long-run case.

Hence, $y = 1/3$ and $y = 5$ at the extreme points of (4.63). To determine which of these two values is associated with a maximum, we must check the second-order condition,

$$\frac{d^2\pi}{dy^2} = -3y + 8 \qquad (4.66)$$

Examining the sign of (4.66) at $y = 1/3$ and $y = 5$, we find

$$\frac{d^2\pi}{dy^2} = \begin{cases} 7 \text{ when } y = 1/3 \\ -7 \text{ when } y = 5 \end{cases} \qquad (4.67)$$

Therefore, profit is maximum when $y = 5$.

The total condition that $TR - VC > 0$ can be examined by substituting $y = 5$ into the profit function, (4.63), *less the fixed cost component*:

$$\pi = 9.5(5) - 0.5(5)^3 + 4(5)^2 - 12(5) = 25 \qquad (4.68)$$

Hence, $y = 5$ is *sufficient* for maximum positive profit (exclusive of fixed cost). The functions used in this example are plotted in Figure 4.7. Note in particular the shape of the profit functions at $y = 1/3$ and $y = 5$.

Suppose in the preceding example that the fixed costs had been $30 instead of $4. How would this alter the optimal level of output? Would it change the firm's decision to produce during this time period? Now suppose that $p = \$2.50$ instead of $9.50. Answer the same questions.[3]

In the case of a single factor and perfect competition in all markets, the technical and economic linkages can be graphically illustrated as shown in Figure 4.8.[4] In this figure one can see the consistency of optimal levels of y, y^*, and x, x^* as viewed from either the factor or product side (see fourth vertical and horizontal rule in panels a, a', b, b'). The reader can verify that the horizontal distance to y^* in panel b' equals the vertical distance in panel a. The addition of panels c, c', d, d', e, and e' permits the completion of the visual linkage in terms of the factor marginal conditions with the product marginal conditions. Panels a, a', e, and e' are the geometric equivalents of the mathematical inverses which permitted the "completion of the circle" in our mathematical derivation of the VC function (Example 4.1).

---

[3] Note that for $p = 2.5$ the first- and second-order conditions are satisfied, yet we assume the firm would choose not to produce in this case—a reversal of our answer to the question when fixed costs rose to $30. Why? Because if we plot the profit function (exclusive of fixed cost) we find that while it has a local maximum at $y = 3$, careful examination reveals that the zero profit level at the origin is greater than the $-\$6$ at the local maximum.

[4] The balance of this section including Figure 4.8 follows closely a paper by Beattie and Griffin published in the *Southern Journal of Agricultural Economics*, 1980.

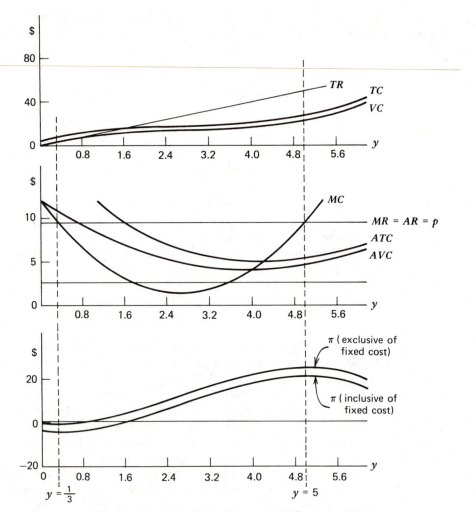

Figure 4.7. Plot of functions used in Example 4.4.

Following the lines in Figure 4.8, one can see the correspondence of breakeven points (first and fifth vertical lines), inflection and maximum and minimum marginal points (second vertical line), ray-line tangency and maximum and minimum average points (third vertical line), profit-maximization point (fourth vertical line), and maximum physical product (sixth vertical line). As in the case of optimal y, the reader can verify that π^* (maximum profit exclusive of fixed cost) in panels b and b' equals π^* in panels d and d'.

Figure 4.8 can be used to demonstrate the impact of improved technology (shifting TPP), changing factor price (change in slope of c), and changes in fixed cost (shifting intercept of c) on a firm's marginal cost curve and optimum factor and product levels. We recommend that students trace through several postulated changes in these parameters.

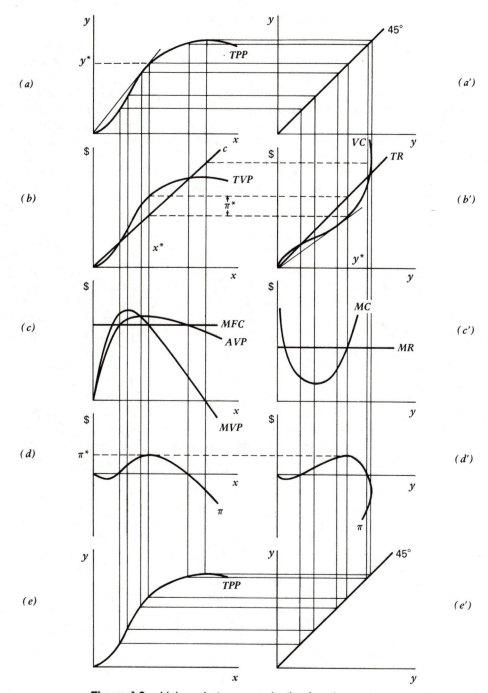

Figure 4.8. Linkage between production function and cost-output relationship with extensions to marginal conditions.

4.4 PRODUCT SUPPLY FUNCTION

The *supply function* of a firm that sells in a perfectly competitive product market gives the quantity that it will produce as a function of product price; moreover, with perfectly competitive factor markets, the quantity supplied is also a function of factor prices. A profit-maximizing firm's supply function can be derived from the first-order conditions for profit maximization. In fact, the supply function is the inverse of the marginal cost function when MC is equated with produce price. Under the assumption of perfect competition in the product market (an essential assumption–see Section 4.4.c) and perfect competition in the factor markets (a convenience assumption), we can derive the supply function as follows. From profit function (4.52) we have the first-order condition,

$$\frac{d\pi}{dy} = p - \frac{\partial \tilde{c}(r_1, r_2, y)}{\partial y} = p - MC = 0 \qquad (4.69)$$

which implies $p = MC$. In (4.69) and throughout the remainder of this chapter, we use $d\pi/dy$ to emphasize that there is only one first-order condition of concern, and we use the partial of $\tilde{c}$ with respect to y on the right-hand side when factor price arguments are included in $\tilde{c}(r_1, r_2, y)$ to emphasize that the r's are treated as parameters or exogenous variables.

Since, in general, marginal cost is a function of y, we can solve (4.69) for the inverse function,

$$y^* = y^*(p, r_1, r_2) \qquad (4.70)$$

However, the entire range of the marginal cost function is not a firm's supply function because satisfaction of the first-order condition at a point where MC

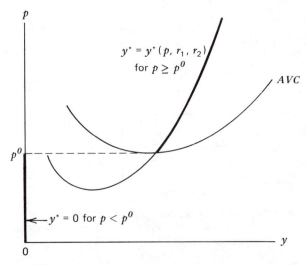

Figure 4.9. A firm's product supply function.

is below *AVC* does not satisfy the total condition. Thus, a firm's supply function is given by the disjointed function,

$$y^* = \begin{cases} y^*(p,r_1,r_2) \text{ for } p \geq \text{minimum } AVC \\ 0 \text{ for } p < \text{minimum } AVC \end{cases} \tag{4.71}$$

A firm's supply function is illustrated by the broad line in Figure 4.9. As can be seen from (4.71), a change in a factor price will shift the firm's supply function. The reader should work through the above logic for a firm that faces imperfectly competitive factor markets to see that factor prices do not appear in the product supply function in that case.

To summarize, a perfectly competitive, profit-maximizing firm's supply function can be obtained in three steps. The first step is to derive the first-order condition for profit maximization in order to get price equal to marginal cost, $p = \partial \bar{c}(y,r_1,r_2)/\partial y$.[5] Given that the marginal cost function equals price, the second step is to take the inverse to get y as a function of price. The final step is to find the price for which *AVC* is a minimum. This determines the discontinuity in the supply function.

Example 4.5   Assume the *VC* function and fixed cost given by (4.62) in Example 4.4. The profit function is

$$\pi = p\,y - (0.5y^3 - 4y^2 + 12y) - 4 \tag{4.72}$$

and the first-order condition is

$$\frac{d\pi}{dy} = p - (1.5y^2 - 8y + 12) = 0 \tag{4.73}$$

which implies

$$p = 1.5y^2 - 8y + 12 \tag{4.74}$$

or $p = MC$. The inverse function can be obtained by solving (4.74) for y using the quadratic formula. That is,

$$y = \frac{8 \pm \sqrt{64 - 4(1.5)(12 - p)}}{2(1.5)} = \frac{8 \pm \sqrt{-8 + 6p}}{3} \tag{4.75}$$

We must now determine the price at which the supply discontinuity occurs. *AVC* is given by

$$AVC = 0.5y^2 - 4y + 12 \tag{4.76}$$

---

[5]An alternative to this is to obtain the marginal cost function by simultaneously solving the first-order conditions for minimization of the Lagrangean cost function; that is, obtain $\lambda^*(r_1,r_2,y) = \partial \bar{c}(y,r_1,r_2)/\partial y$.

which is a minimum when

$$\frac{dAVC}{dy} = y - 4 = 0 \tag{4.77}$$

and when

$$\frac{d^2AVC}{dy^2} = 1 > 0 \tag{4.78}$$

Thus, minimum AVC occurs at $y = 4$. When $y = 4$, AVC is

$$AVC(4) = 0.5(4)^2 - 4(4) + 12 = 4 \tag{4.79}$$

Therefore, the firm's supply function is given by

$$y^* = \begin{cases} \dfrac{8 + \sqrt{6p - 8}}{3} & \text{for } p \geq 4 \\ 0 & \text{for } p < 4 \end{cases} \tag{4.80}$$

Note that the negative square root in (4.75) was dropped because it did not satisfy the second-order condition for maximum profit; equivalently, it was dropped because the associated y values were in the range of decreasing MC.

In Example 4.3 we determined a level of y that maximized profit. But note that the equation used to determine this level, (4.60), is the supply curve if we let p vary. In the Cobb–Douglas example in 4.2, all the cost functions monotonically increase when $b_1 + b_2 < 1$; therefore the entire MC function is the supply function—we do not need to look for a discontinuity point.

Example 4.6   As another example of deriving a supply function, consider the quadratic production function used in Example 3.10. In the preceding example, (4.5), we obtained the supply function by maximizing profit defined as total revenue less total cost. Since it is difficult to directly solve for the cost functions for a quadratic production function, we obtain the supply function by another approach.

Using the matrix notation of Example 3.10, the production function is

$$y = a_0 + A'X + \tfrac{1}{2}X'BX \tag{4.81}$$

Recall that we obtained the following factor demand equation for (4.81):

$$X^* = B^{-1}(R - A) \tag{4.82}$$

where the ith element of the vector, R, is the normalized factor price, r_i/p.

Since factor demand equations 4.82 assume profit-maximizing behavior, we can obtain the product supply equation by substituting (4.82) for X in (4.81). That is, the product supply equation is given by

$$y^* = a_0 + A'X^* + \tfrac{1}{2}(X^*)'BX^* \tag{4.83}$$

Noting that $(X^*)' = (R' - A')(B^{-1})' = (R' - A')B^{-1}$, substitution of (4.82) into (4.83) for X^* gives[6]

$$\begin{aligned}
y^* &= a_0 + A'B^{-1}(R - A) + \tfrac{1}{2}(R' - A')B^{-1}BB^{-1}(R - A) \\
&= a_0 + A'B^{-1}R - A'B^{-1}A + \tfrac{1}{2}(R' - A')B^{-1}(R - A) \\
&= a_0 + A'B^{-1}R - A'B^{-1}A + \tfrac{1}{2}R'B^{-1}R \\
&\quad -\tfrac{1}{2}A'B^{-1}R - \tfrac{1}{2}R'B^{-1}A + \tfrac{1}{2}A'B^{-1}A \\
&= a_0 - \tfrac{1}{2}A'B^{-1}A + \tfrac{1}{2}R'B^{-1}R \tag{4.84}
\end{aligned}$$

To simplify (4.84), let $\gamma_0 = a_0 - \tfrac{1}{2}A'B^{-1}A$, which equals a constant (scalar). Then

$$y^* = \gamma_0 + \tfrac{1}{2}R'B^{-1}R \tag{4.85}$$

In long-hand, (4.85) is

$$\begin{aligned}
y^* &= \gamma_0 + \tfrac{1}{2}[r_1/p \quad r_2/p] \begin{bmatrix} \beta_1 & \beta_3 \\ \beta_3 & \beta_2 \end{bmatrix} \begin{bmatrix} r_1/p \\ r_2/p \end{bmatrix} \\
&= \gamma_0 + \tfrac{1}{2}\beta_1(r_1/p)^2 + \tfrac{1}{2}\beta_2(r_2/p)^2 + \beta_3(r_1/p)(r_2/p) \tag{4.86}
\end{aligned}$$

for the single-product, two-factor case. Therefore, the product supply and factor demand equations associated with maximizing profit subject to a quadratic production function are

$$\begin{aligned}
y^* &= \gamma_0 + \tfrac{1}{2}\beta_1(r_1/p)^2 + \tfrac{1}{2}\beta_2(r_2/p)^2 + \beta_3(r_1/p)(r_2/p) \\
x_1^* &= \eta_1 + \beta_1(r_1/p) + \beta_3(r_2/p) \\
x_2^* &= \eta_2 + \beta_3(r_1/p) + \beta_2(r_2/p)
\end{aligned} \tag{4.87}$$

where $\eta_1 = -a_1\beta_1 - a_2\beta_3$ and $\eta_2 = -a_2\beta_2 - a_1\beta_3$.

It was shown in Example 3.10 that the production function is strictly concave and the second-order conditions are satisfied if $b_1 < 0$, $b_2 < 0$ and

---

[6]Three tricks are involved in simplifying (4.84): The transpose of the right-hand side of (4.82) is given by reversing the order of multiplication of B^{-1} and $(R - A)$; $(B^{-1})' = B^{-1}$ since B (and thus B^{-1}) is symmetric; and $A'B^{-1}R = R'B^{-1}A$.

$|B| = b_1 b_2 - b_3^2 > 0$. To translate the second-order conditions in terms of parameters of the supply and demand equations, consider

$$
B^{-1} = \begin{bmatrix} b_1 & b_3 \\ b_3 & b_2 \end{bmatrix}^{-1} = \frac{1}{|B|} \begin{bmatrix} b_2 & -b_3 \\ -b_3 & b_1 \end{bmatrix}
$$

$$
= \frac{1}{(b_1 b_2 - b_3^2)} \begin{bmatrix} b_2 & -b_3 \\ -b_3 & b_1 \end{bmatrix} \tag{4.88}
$$

Thus,

$$
\beta_1 = b_2/(b_1 b_2 - b_3^2)
$$
$$
\beta_2 = b_1/(b_1 b_2 - b_3^2) \tag{4.89}
$$
$$
\beta_3 = -b_3/(b_1 b_2 - b_3^2)
$$

Therefore, the second-order conditions are satisfied if $\beta_1 < 0$, $\beta_2 < 0$, and $(\beta_1 \beta_2 - \beta_3^2) = 1/(b_1 b_2 - b_3^2) > 0$.

For the three equations in (4.87) of the previous example, note that the parameter β_1 enters equations for y^* and x_1^*, β_2 enters equations for y^* and x_2^*, and β_3 enters all three equations. The relationship between the parameters in this set of equations is not mere happenstance; rather the relationship is a manifestation of the *symmetry* or reciprocity relations that hold for all profit-maximizing firms. Factor-side symmetry was demonstrated in Section 3.2.f, while additional symmetry conditions are proven for the general case in Section 4.4.b.

4.4.a Homogeneity of the Product Supply Function

The reader should note that the product supply and factor demand equations in Example 4.6, namely, (4.87), are all homogeneous of degree zero in prices; that is, a proportional increase in all product and factor prices does not affect the optimal levels of the factors and output. This characteristic, like symmetry, holds for all product supply and factor demand equations based on profit-maximizing behavior of the perfectly competitive firm—irrespective of the form of the production function. Homogeneity of degree zero in prices is not obvious in supply function, (4.80), of Example 4.5 because the factor prices are implicit rather than explicit in the specification of the variable cost function, (4.62). If (4.62) were respecified with explicit factor price arguments in addition to output, it then would be possible to show that the product supply curve derived therefrom was homogeneous of degree zero in prices. Homogeneity of factor demand functions was proven in general in Section 3.2.e. The proof for homogeneity of degree zero in all prices of product supply function follows from that of factor demand. We leave that proof to the reader. However, we note that zero-degree homogeneity for multiproduct-multifactor product supply and factor demand is proven in general in Chapter 6.

4.4.b Comparative Static Relationships and Symmetry

Comparative static analysis viewed from the supply side refers to determination of qualitative information about the partial derivatives, $\partial y^*/\partial r_i$ and $\partial y^*/\partial p$, as related to partial derivatives of the production function. The conventional way of determining comparative static relationships is to simultaneously develop factor-side and product-side relationships. However, given the factor-side relationships developed in Section 3.2.f, there is an indirect method for supply-side comparative static analysis. In this section, we first show this short-cut analysis and then present the conventional method of analysis for the profit-maximization model. Finally, we use these results to demonstrate an important set of symmetry conditions.

To illustrate the short-cut method of developing supply-side comparative static relationships given the factor-side results in Chapter 3, consider the production function, $y = f(x_1, x_2)$. Substituting the factor demand functions, x_i^*, into the production function for the factor quantities, x_i, yields the supply function $y^* = f(x_1^*, x_2^*)$. (Recall that the x_i^*'s are functions of product and factor prices.) Now consider the total differential of the supply function:

$$dy^* = (\partial f/\partial x_1)dx_1^* + (\partial f/\partial x_2)dx_2^* = f_1 dx_1^* + f_2 dx_2^* \quad (4.90)$$

Recall from Section 3.2.f (equations 3.169 and 3.174) that for the profit-maximization model

$$dx_1^* = \frac{f_{22}(dr_1 - f_1 dp) - f_{12}(dr_2 - f_2 dp)}{p(f_{11}f_{22} - f_{12}^2)} \quad (4.91)$$

and

$$dx_2^* = \frac{f_{11}(dr_2 - f_2 dp) - f_{12}(dr_1 - f_1 dp)}{p(f_{11}f_{22} - f_{12}^2)} \quad (4.92)$$

Hence, dy^* as a function of dr_1, dr_2, dp and partial derivatives of the production function can be obtained by substituting (4.91) and (4.92) for dx_1^* and dx_2^*, respectively, in total differential (4.90). This substitution gives

$$
\begin{aligned}
dy^* &= f_1\left(\frac{f_{22}(dr_1 - f_1 dp) - f_{12}(dr_2 - f_2 dp)}{p(f_{11}f_{22} - f_{12}^2)}\right) \\
&\quad + f_2\left(\frac{f_{11}(dr_2 - f_2 dp) - f_{12}(dr_1 - f_1 dp)}{p(f_{11}f_{22} - f_{12}^2)}\right) \\
&= \frac{(f_1 f_{22} - f_2 f_{12})dr_1 + (f_2 f_{11} - f_1 f_{12})dr_2 + (2f_1 f_2 f_{12} - f_1^2 f_{22} - f_2^2 f_{11})dp}{p(f_{11}f_{22} - f_{12}^2)}
\end{aligned}
\quad (4.93)
$$

From (4.93) the following partial derivatives and sign possibilities (discussed later) can be obtained by holding appropriate alternative prices constant: setting $dr_1 = dr_2 = 0$,

$$\frac{\partial y^*}{\partial p} = \frac{2f_1 f_2 f_{12} - f_1^2 f_{22} - f_2^2 f_{11}}{p(f_{11} f_{22} - f_{12}^2)} > 0$$

Setting $dp = dr_2 = 0$,

$$\frac{\partial y^*}{\partial r_1} = \frac{f_1 f_{22} - f_2 f_{12}}{p(f_{11} f_{22} - f_{12}^2)} \begin{cases} < 0 \\ = 0 \\ > 0 \end{cases} \tag{4.94}$$

and setting $dp = dr_1 = 0$,

$$\frac{\partial y^*}{\partial r_2} = \frac{f_2 f_{11} - f_1 f_{12}}{p(f_{11} f_{22} - f_{12}^2)} \begin{cases} < 0 \\ = 0 \\ > 0 \end{cases}$$

which are the output-side comparative static relationships. Similarly, from (4.91) and (4.92), we obtain the factor-side relationships,

$$\frac{\partial x_1^*}{\partial r_1} = \frac{f_{22}}{p(f_{11} f_{22} - f_{12}^2)} < 0$$

$$\frac{\partial x_2^*}{\partial r_2} = \frac{f_{11}}{p(f_{11} f_{22} - f_{12}^2)} < 0$$

$$\frac{\partial x_1^*}{\partial r_2} = \frac{\partial x_2^*}{\partial r_1} = \frac{-f_{12}}{p(f_{11} f_{22} - f_{12}^2)} \begin{cases} < 0 \\ = 0 \\ > 0 \end{cases} \tag{4.95}$$

$$\frac{\partial x_1^*}{\partial p} = \frac{-f_1 f_{22} + f_2 f_{12}}{p(f_{11} f_{22} - f_{12}^2)} \begin{cases} < 0 \\ = 0 \\ > 0 \end{cases}$$

$$\frac{\partial x_2^*}{\partial p} = \frac{-f_2 f_{11} + f_1 f_{12}}{p(f_{11} f_{22} - f_{12}^2)} \begin{cases} < 0 \\ = 0 \\ > 0 \end{cases}$$

Partial derivatives (4.95) together with (4.94) are the full set of comparative static relationships for the profit-maximization model.

Signs of the factor-side relationships were deduced in Chapter 3. Recall that $(\partial x_1^*/\partial r_2) = (\partial x_2^*/\partial r_1)$, $\partial x_1^*/\partial p$, and $\partial x_2^*/\partial p$ could be either positive or negative depending on the sign of f_{12} (i.e., depending on the nature of the technical interdependence of the factors). Consider now the signs of the output-side relationships, (4.94). Note that the denominator in the three partial derivatives in (4.94) is positive if the second-order condition for profit maximization (a strictly concave production function) is satisfied. Note that the sign of the numerator in $\partial y^*/\partial p$ is positive if the production function is strictly quasi-concave. Since a strictly concave function is always strictly quasi-concave (but not necessarily vice versa), then $(\partial y^*/\partial p) > 0$ if the second-order condition for profit maximization is satisfied. The partial derivatives $\partial y^*/\partial r_i$ can be of either sign because $f_{12} > 0$, $= 0$, or < 0, again depending on the technical interdependence of the factors.

In Section 3.2.f, we proved the symmetry condition that $(\partial x_1^*/\partial r_2) = (\partial x_2^*/\partial r_1)$. In addition to this factor-side symmetry, there is a symmetry between some factor-product relationships. Comparison of the partial derivatives in (4.94) and (4.95) proves the following full set of symmetry conditions for the single-product, two-factor profit-maximization model:[7]

$$\partial x_1^*/\partial r_2 = \partial x_2^*/\partial r_1$$
$$\partial x_1^*/\partial p = -\partial y^*/\partial r_1 \qquad (4.96)$$
$$\partial x_2^*/\partial p = -\partial y^*/\partial r_2$$

Again the first equation in (4.96) is the cross-factor price symmetry condition for factor demand functions. The second equation requires that the shift in the demand function for the first factor given a change in product price is equal and opposite of the shift in the supply function for y given a change in the price of the first factor. The third equation is interpreted similarly to the second.

Certainly the opposite directions of the product supply and factor demand shifts seem intuitive. That is, we *normally* expect (*a*) that an increase in the product price will shift the demand function for a factor outward (to the right) and (*b*) that an increase in a factor price will shift the supply function for the product upward (to the left). However, the fact that the magnitudes of those corresponding shifts would be identical is not intuitively obvious (at least to the authors).[8] Nevertheless, it must be emphasized that these symmetry conditions are a general result of the profit-maximization postulate given perfect competition and thus to not impose them in empirical estimation of product supply and factor demand systems results in specification bias in the parameter estimates.

Table 4.1 presents the supply equations for several alternative production functions. Just for the fun of it, establish that the symmetry and homogeneity properties hold for the supply equations in Table 4.1. See Table 3.1 for the

[7]In Chapters 5 and 6 we will also prove that the cross-product price effects for product supply functions are symmetric for the multiproduct model.
[8]Unfortunately, as much as we would like to, we cannot offer the reader further intuitive motivation, explanation or a graphical exposition of symmetry.

Table 4.1 Product Supply Equations Associated With
Various Production Functions

Production Function		Product Supply Equation[a]
Generalized Cobb–Douglas	$y = Ax_1^{b_1}x_2^{b_2}$	$y^* = p^{a/(1-a)}\left[A\left(\dfrac{b_1}{r_1}\right)^{b_1}\left(\dfrac{b_2}{r_2}\right)^{b_2}\right]^{1/(1-a)}$ where $a = b_1 + b_2$
Quadratic[b]	$y = a_0 + a_1x_1 + a_2x_2$ $\quad + \tfrac{1}{2}b_1x_1^2 + \tfrac{1}{2}b_2x_2^2$ $\quad + b_3x_1x_2$	$y^* = \gamma_0 + \beta_1\left[\dfrac{r_1}{p}\right]^2 + \beta_2\left[\dfrac{r_2}{p}\right]^2$ $\quad + \beta_3\left[\dfrac{r_1}{p}\right]\left[\dfrac{r_2}{p}\right]$
CES	$Y = A[bx_1^{-g} + (1 - b)x_2^{-g}]^{-v/g}$	$y^* = p^{v/(1-v)}(va)^{1/(1-v)}[b^{1/(1+g)}r_1^{g/(1+g)}$ $\quad + (1 - b)^{1/(1+g)}r_2^{g/(1+g)}]^{-v(1+g)/g(1-v)}$
Transcendental	$y = Ax_1^{a_1}e^{b_1x_1}x_2^{a_2}e^{b_2x_2}$	Mathematically intractable, but points on the supply function can be numerically generated given values for the parameters

[a]All prices are assumed to be exogenous to the firm. The production function is assumed strictly concave in the region that satisfies the first-order conditions.
[b]Let $A = b_1b_2 - b_3^2$. Then $\beta_1 = b_2/A$; $\beta_2 = b_1/A$; $\beta_3 = -b_3/A$; and $\gamma_0 = a_0 - (b_1a_1^2 + b_2a_2^2 - 2a_1a_2b_3)/A$.

needed factor demand equations. (*Hint*: See Example 4.6 for the quadratic production function.)

In the preceding comparative static derivations, we based output-side relationships on factor-side relationships. It should be noted, however, that the conventional method for deducing the comparative static results involves simultaneous derivation of the factor- and output-side relationships. The conventional method is based on the Lagrangean profit-maximization problem:

$$L\pi = p\,y - r_1x_1 - r_2x_2 + \lambda[y^0 - f(x_1,x_2)] \tag{4.97}$$

with first-order conditions:

$$\begin{aligned}
\partial L\pi/\partial y &= p + \lambda = 0 \\
\partial L\pi/\partial x_1 &= -r_1 - \lambda f_1 = 0 \\
\partial L\pi/\partial x_2 &= -r_2 - \lambda f_2 = 0 \\
\partial L\pi/\partial \lambda &= y - f(x_1,x_2) = 0
\end{aligned} \tag{4.98}$$

Taking the total differentials of (4.98) we get the system of equations:

$$\begin{bmatrix} 0 & 0 & 0 & 1 \\ 0 & -\lambda f_{11} & -\lambda f_{12} & -f_1 \\ 0 & -\lambda f_{21} & -\lambda f_{22} & -f_2 \\ 1 & -f_1 & -f_2 & 0 \end{bmatrix}\begin{bmatrix} dy^* \\ dx_1^* \\ dx_2^* \\ d\lambda^* \end{bmatrix} = \begin{bmatrix} -dp \\ dr_1 \\ dr_2 \\ 0 \end{bmatrix} \tag{4.99}$$

The reader should verify that solution of (4.99) for comparative static relationships results in (4.94) and (4.95).

4.4.c Supply in Noncompetitive Product Markets

While the theory of product supply can accommodate cases of one or more imperfectly competitive factor markets (i.e., $\lambda_{r_i} \neq 0$), it should be noted that the assumption of perfect competition in the product market ($\lambda_p = 0$) is essential for deriving a supply equation. Paralleling the case of $\lambda_r \neq 0$ in factor demand, the reason for this is seen by examining the first-order condition for maximum profit assuming $\lambda_p \neq 0$. That is, given the profit function,

$$\pi = g(y)y - \bar{c}(y) - b \tag{4.100}$$

we know that

$$\frac{d\pi}{dy} = p(1 + \lambda_p) - \frac{d\bar{c}(y)}{dy} = 0 \tag{4.101}$$

which implies

$$MC = MR \neq p \tag{4.102}$$

Product price, p, rather than being given by MR is given by AR and is endogenous to the firm. The problem is that the firm equates MR with MC and in this case MR is *not* product price. Since p is endogenous we are not free to vary p and see what happens to the quantity of y produced. Given $p = g(y)$ and $VC = \bar{c}(y)$, y is uniquely determined as a single point (see Figure 4.10). However, it is crucial to note that a *shift* in the product demand function [i.e., $g(y)$ changes] may result in a different quantity supplied, but of course the locus of such supply points would not yield a supply function in the traditional sense.

4.4.d LeChatelier Principle and Supply Functions

The LeChatelier phenomenon for factor demand functions is also manifested in product supply functions in that the slope of supply functions does not increase (usually decreases) as constraints are added to the optimization problem. (Note that we are viewing slope in terms of a change in y with respect to a change in p, which is graphically inverted from the way in which economists conventionally view the slope of a supply function.) Since mathematical proof of the supply side of this principle is unjustifiably onerous, we offer an intuitive proof for the special case of a two-factor model with perfect competition in all markets. For this case, we will intuitively argue that

$$\frac{\partial y^*(r_1, r_2, p)}{\partial p} \geq \frac{\partial y^*(r_1, p \mid x_2^0)}{\partial p} \tag{4.103}$$

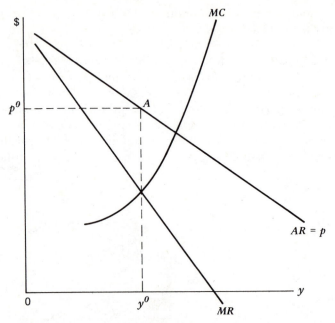

Figure 4.10. Nonexistence of firm's product supply curve when $\lambda_p \neq 0$; supply is given by the single point, A.

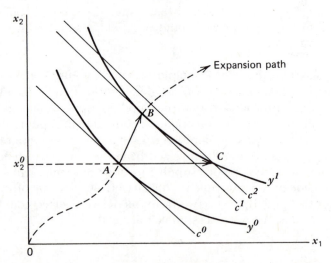

Figure 4.11. The LeChatelier principle related to product supply.

First recall that the product supply function, y^*, is the inverse of the marginal cost function when equated to price for a perfectly competitive firm. Now, with the aid of Figure 4.11, consider the additional cost of increasing output from y^0 to y^1. Suppose that we begin at point A in Figure 4.11. With both factors variable we will move along the expansion path from A to B. However, if x_2 is fixed at x_2^0, we will move from point A to C. Since the expansion path reflects *minimum* cost combinations of x_1 and x_2, the movement from A to C will, by definition, entail costs at least as great as (normally greater than) the cost of going from A to B. That is, given a set of factor prices, the budget line c^1 tangent to B represents less cost than does c^2, which passes through C.

Letting the increment in y approach zero demonstrates that the slope of the marginal cost curve with one factor fixed will be greater than the slope of the marginal cost curve with both factors variable; that is

$$\frac{\partial MC(r_1, r_2, y)}{\partial y} \leq \frac{\partial MC(r_1, y | x_2^0)}{\partial y} \tag{4.104}$$

Since the product supply function, y^*, is the inverse of marginal cost when equated to product price, p, the inequality in (4.103) holds.

4.5 LONG-RUN AND SHORT-RUN COST CURVES

In this section, we geometrically examine the relationship between long-run and short-run cost curves. In addition, we show how to mathematically obtain the long-run cost functions as envelopes of short-run functions. To simplify the presentation we consider only two factors, x_1 and x_2. In the short run, x_1 is variable but x_2 is fixed, while in the long-run both factors are variable. It may be instructive to think of x_2 as measuring plant size, although x_2 can represent any factor in production.

Figure 4.12 illustrates the relationship between long- and short-run cost curves; the upper panel shows total costs (including fixed costs) while the lower panel shows associated average costs. The dark curves represent long-run cost curves while the light curves represent short-run curves. There is a single long-run curve in each case, while there is an infinite number (one for each level of the fixed factor, x_2) of short-run curves, only two of which are shown.

The long-run total cost curve is an *envelope* of the short-run total cost curves. This envelope relationship can be intuitively explained as follows. Consider the cost of producing a level of output, y^1. If x_2 is fixed at x_2^1, then the cost of producing y^1 would be given by point B in the upper panel of Figure 4.12. However, in the long-run x_2 can be adjusted to that level at which cost is minimized given an output level of y^1. From Figure 4.12, it can be seen that the level of x_2 that minimizes cost is that associated with tangency between a short-run curve and the long-run curve. This tangency occurs at point A for output level y^1; costs associated with levels of x_2 other than x_2^0 would be at least as high. Note, however, that this point of tangency does not necessarily

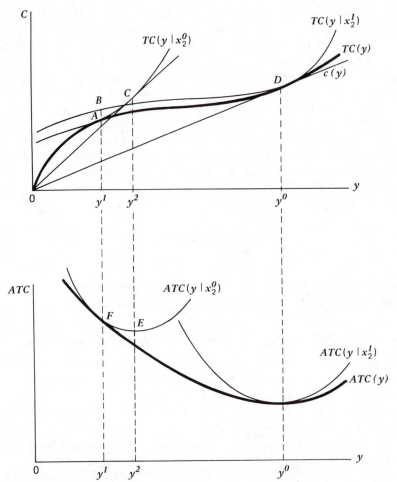

Figure 4.12. The relationship between long- and short-run average and total cost curves.

occur at the minimum point on the short-run ATC curve. In the upper panel, minimum ATC associated with x_2^0 is given by a ray-line that is tangent to $TC(y|x_2^0)$. This tangency occurs at point C (rather than point A) which is given by point E in the lower panel.

The long-run total cost function can be mathematically obtained as the envelope of the family of short-run curves as follows.[9] Let the family of short-run variable cost functions be given by

$$VC(r_1, y|x_2^0) = r_1 x_1^c(r_1, y|x_2^0) \qquad (4.105)$$

---

[9]The long-run total cost curve can be directly obtained by minimizing cost over all factors subject to a specified output level. This approach was illustrated in Section 4.1.c, equations 4.22, 4.23, and 4.24.

where the function, x_1^c, is the cost-minimizing level of x_1 given r_1, y, and x_2.[10] Now let the family of short-run total cost functions, TC, be denoted by

$$TC(r_1,r_2,y|x_2^0) = VC(r_1,y|x_2^0) + r_2 x_2^0 \qquad (4.106)$$

where $r_2 x_2^0$ is short-run fixed costs. In the long-run, the cost-minimizing firm will seek to minimize (4.106) for given output levels.

Since the cost-minimizing level of x_1 and the production relationship between y and x_2 (given x_1^c) are implicit in (4.106), the level of x_2 that minimizes cost given y can be mathematically obtained as the solution to

$$\frac{\partial TC}{\partial x_2} = \frac{\partial VC(r_1,y|x_2)}{\partial x_2} + r_2 = 0 \qquad (4.107)$$

Letting the solution to (4.107) be denoted by $x_2^c(r_1,r_2,y)$, the long-run total cost function is given by substituting x_2^c for x_2^0 in (4.106). Using (4.107) as a basis for eliminating x_2 from (4.106) is precisely the mathematical process used to obtain an envelope to the family of curves given by (4.106).[11]

4.6 PROBLEMS

4-1. Given $y = A x_1^{b_1} x_2^{b_2}$, find VC, TC, ATC, AVC, MC, and product supply. Sketch.

4-2. Given $VC = 2y^3 - 2y^2 + (31/24)y$, $b = 0.1$, and $p^0 = 1$, plot TR, TC, VC, MC, ATC, AVC, and the profit function. Be sure to identify maximums, minimums, and inflection points.

4-3. Given $y = 2 x_1^{1/2} x_2^{1/2}$, $p^0 = 5$, $r_1^0 = 1$, and $r_2 = x_2$, find product supply.

4-4. Derive comparative static relationships for a firm that maximizes profit subject to a cost constraint for a two-factor, single-product production function. Assume that the cost constraint is binding. Is this problem characterized by a counterpart to the Slutsky equation? Why? Does $\partial x_1^c / \partial r_2 = \partial x_2^c / \partial r_1$ (that is, does symmetry hold)? Why or why not?

4-5. Consider a farm that produces both corn and soybeans. Suppose that the production function for corn is $y_c = f(x_1, x_c)$, where x_1 is fertilizer used in corn production and x_c is land devoted to corn production. Let the production function for soybeans be $y_s = f(x_s)$, where x_s is land devoted to soybean production. Find the first-order conditions for profit maximization for this firm assuming a fixed land base, x^0; that is, $x_c + x_s = x^0$.

[10]Note that x_1^c is also the conditional factor demand equation *given* that x_2 is a fixed factor.
[11]In the case of imperfectly competitive factor markets, (4.105), (4.106), and (4.107) would have to be modified to account for factor supply functions.

4.7 SELECTED BIBLIOGRAPHY

Beattie, B. R., and W. L. Griffin. "Production Function, Cost of Production, and Associated Optimality Linkages: A Textbook Supplement." *So. J. Agric. Econ.* 12 (1980):153–155.

Carlson, S. *A Study on the Pure Theory of Production.* New York: Sentry Press, 1965, Chapters 3 and 4.

Ferguson, C. E. *The Neoclassical Theory of Production and Distribution.* Cambridge: Cambridge University Press, 1969, Chapters 7 and 8.

Frisch, R. *Theory of Production.* Chicago: Rand McNally, 1965, Chapters 9, 10, and 11.

Gould, J. P., and C. E. Ferguson. *Microeconomic Theory.* Homewood: Irwin, 1980, Chapter 7.

Henderson, J. M., and R. E. Quandt. *Microeconomic Theory: A Mathematical Approach*, 3rd ed. New York: McGraw-Hill, 1980, Chapters 4 and 5.

Silberberg, Eugene. *The Structure of Economics: A Mathematical Analysis.* New York: McGraw-Hill, 1978, Chapters 7, 9, and 10.

CHAPTER 5

MULTIPRODUCT PRODUCTION

In this chapter we relax the assumption of a single commodity or product. Certainly this seems appropriate as most firms in our economy produce multiple products. In developing the theory of the multiproduct firm, we will find that single product concepts, belabored in previous chapters, are essential to understanding the multiproduct model. That is, multiproduct production can generally be appropriately viewed as production of several single products, but with the products linked through *resource constraints, nonallocable* factors of production and/or through *jointness* in production.

To fully understand the economic principles derived from the multiproduct model, it is imperative that the student master the mathematical representation of multiproduct, multifactor production and master the above terminology. Thus, we turn first to definition of terminology and to a close examination of alternative mathematical representations of a production process. We then develop the classical multiproduct, multifactor model for allocable factors. Finally, a model that includes both allocable and nonallocable factors is presented.

5.1 CONCEPTS, DEFINITIONS, AND ASSUMPTIONS

Economic principles for multiproduct production depend in a critical way on whether factors of production are allocable or nonallocable. By *allocable* we mean that the amount of factor x_i used in producing product y_j can be distinguished from the amount of x_i used in producing $y_k (j \neq k)$. Thus, we define x_{ij} as the amount of factor x_i used in producing y_j. If only two products are produced with a single factor, x_1, then the total amount of x_1 used would be $x_1 = x_{11} + x_{12}$.

On the other hand, a *nonallocable* factor is one for which we cannot distinguish between units used in producing y_j versus that used in producing $y_k (j \neq k)$. In this chapter, we denote nonallocable factors by z and allocable factors by x. Using this notation, y_j and y_k would *both* be produced by the *same units* of factor z. Yet another way of looking at a nonallocable factor is that as z is employed in producing y_j, then one also gets some y_k output whether one wants it or not—a classic example is mutton and wool produced from feeding sheep.

Consider now the mathematical representation of a production function for the multiproduct case, assuming *all* factors are allocable. Mathematically, this case can be represented by either a single function (usually written in implicit form) *or* by a production function for each product. The classical treatment of this case in the economic literature, as well as the standard textbook treatment, is based on the single-equation representation of the process. Let such a production function for a two product, single allocable factor case be denoted in implicit form as

$$F(y_1, y_2, x_1) = 0 \tag{5.1}$$

where y_1 and y_2 are outputs of the products and x_1 is the *total* amount of the single allocable factor used in producing the two products. For reasons to be discussed shortly, we have not explicitly designated the distribution of x_1 to y_1 and y_2 in (5.1); that is, (5.1) is not specified to depend explicitly on x_{11} and x_{12}.

An alternative mathematical representation of the two-product, single allocable factor production process is to specify a separate function for each product. That is,

$$
\begin{aligned}
F^1(y_1, y_2, x_{11}) &= 0 \\
F^2(y_1, y_2, x_{12}) &= 0
\end{aligned}
\tag{5.2}
$$

For convenience, we assume that the functions in (5.2) can be written in explicit form as

$$
\begin{aligned}
y_1 &= f^1(y_2, x_{11}) \\
y_2 &= f^2(y_1, x_{12})
\end{aligned}
\tag{5.3}
$$

Note that we have explicitly allocated $x_1 = x_{11} + x_{12}$ to the products y_1 and y_2; also note that y_2 is an argument in the single equation production function for y_1, and y_1 is an argument in the function for y_2. This specification explicitly recognizes the *jointness* of production of y_1 and y_2. If production of y_1 and y_2 is *nonjoint*, then (5.3) reduces to

$$
\begin{aligned}
y_1 &= f^1(x_{11}) \\
y_2 &= f^2(x_{12})
\end{aligned}
\tag{5.4}
$$

The classical treatments of the multiproduct model (Naylor, 1965; Pfouts, 1961) specified the single implicit functional representation, (5.1), with x_{ij} (as opposed to x_i) as arguments of the function. This, however, gives the illusion that a single-equation representation explicitly distributes (allocates) x_1 to the production of y_1 and y_2. But, as Mittelhammer, Matulich, and Bushaw (1981) show, a *single equation* cannot be used to explicitly allocate x_1 to y_1 and y_2; hence, our specification of (5.1).

As an illustration of the Mittelhammer *et al.* theorem, consider converting

(5.3) to a single equation. On the surface, it might appear that we could simply specify (5.1) as

$$0 = F(y_1, y_2, x_{11}, x_{12}) = F^1(y_1, y_2, x_{11}) + F^2(y_1, y_2, x_{12})$$
$$= [y_1 - f^1(y_2, x_{11})] + [y_2 - f^2(y_1, x_{12})] \tag{5.5}$$

However, this specification does not insure that either production function in (5.3) is satisfied. That is, $F(\cdot)$ could be zero with neither $F^1(\cdot)$ or $F^2(\cdot)$ equaling zero as long as $F^1(\cdot) = -F^2(\cdot)$. The notation $F(\cdot)$ is shorthand for $F(y_1, y_2, x_{11}, x_{12})$. Hence, (5.5) is not an acceptable conversion of (5.2) to a single equation.

Another possibility is to specify (5.1) as

$$0 = F(y_1, y_2, x_{11}, x_{12}) = [F^1(y_1, y_2, x_{11})]^2 + [F^2(y_1, y_2, x_{12})]^2 \tag{5.6}$$

In this case, the only way that $F(\cdot) = 0$ is if both $F^1(\cdot)$ and $F^2(\cdot)$ equal zero. This, however, is not useful because the implicit function rule is rendered inoperable since the gradient (slope) of $F(\cdot)$ vanishes whenever $F^1(\cdot) = F^2(\cdot) = 0$ (Mittelhammer *et al.*, Theorem 2).

The only appropriate way to convert (5.3) into a single equation, (5.1), is to use $x_1 = x_{11} + x_{12}$; this equation implies $x_{12} = x_1 - x_{11}$. Using this identity, we can restate the second function in (5.3) as

$$y_2 = f^2(y_1, x_{12}) = f^2(y_1, x_1 - x_{11}) \tag{5.7}$$

Now let an inverse of $f^1(\cdot)$ in (5.3) be denoted by $x_{11} = g(y_1, y_2)$. Substituting this inverse into (5.7) for x_{11} gives

$$y_2 = f^2[y_1, x_1 - g(y_1, y_2)] \tag{5.8}$$

which can be denoted in implicit form as

$$0 = y_2 - f^2[y_1, x_1 - g(y_1, y_2)] = F(y_1, y_2, x_1) \tag{5.9}$$

Notice that the explicit distribution of x_1 to y_1 and y_2 is lost in converting from (5.3) to the single-equation representation, (5.1) or (5.9). Thus, information is lost in using the single-equation representation as opposed to the multiple-equation representation of the production process.

The single function representation of multiproduct production, (5.1), is used in classical models largely for mathematical convenience, but also because one is not always interested in the explicit allocation of factors to products in theoretical derivations. We follow this convention in presenting the multiproduct model with allocable factors, but the multiequation specification, (5.3), is much more operational for empirical applications.

Figure 5.1 illustrates the two-product cases discussed thus far. Panel *a*

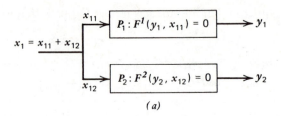

$$x_1 = x_{11} + x_{12}$$

x_{11} → $P_1 : F^1(y_1, x_{11}) = 0$ → y_1

x_{12} → $P_2 : F^2(y_2, x_{12}) = 0$ → y_2

(a)

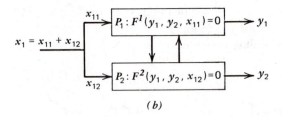

$$x_1 = x_{11} + x_{12}$$

x_{11} → $P_1 : F^1(y_1, y_2, x_{11}) = 0$ → y_1

x_{12} → $P_2 : F^2(y_1, y_2, x_{12}) = 0$ → y_2

(b)

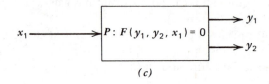

x_1 → $P : F(y_1, y_2, x_1) = 0$ → y_1, y_2

(c)

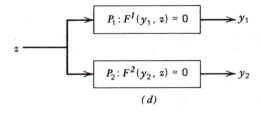

z → $P_1 : F^1(y_1, z) = 0$ → y_1

z → $P_2 : F^2(y_2, z) = 0$ → y_2

(d)

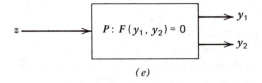

z → $P : F(y_1, y_2) = 0$ → y_1, y_2

(e)

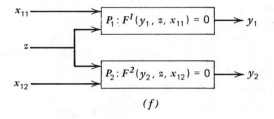

x_{11} → $P_1 : F^1(y_1, z, x_{11}) = 0$ → y_1

z

x_{12} → $P_2 : F^2(y_2, z, x_{12}) = 0$ → y_2

(f)

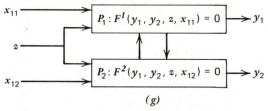

(g)

Figure 5.1. Illustration of allocability of factors of production and alternative mathematical representation of various production processes. (*a*) Nonjoint production from an allocable factor represented by a production function for each product. (*b*) Joint production from an allocable factor represented by a production function for each product. (*c*) Two-product joint or nonjoint production represented by a single production function. (*d*) Production with a nonallocable factor, *z*, represented by a production function for each product. (*e*) Production with a nonallocable factor represented by a single production function. (*f*) Production with a nonallocable factor and an allocable factor represented by a production function for each product. (*g*) Joint production with a nonallocable factor and an allocable factor represented by a production function for each product.

represents the two-equation representation of nonjoint production from a single allocable factor. Panel *b* shows joint production from a single allocable factor; the process P_1 designates production of y_1 while P_2 designates production of y_2, with interrelated processes due to jointness in production. Panel *c* shows the single-equation representation of the processes in panel *a* or panel *b*. Conceptually, we can convert from panel *a* or panel *b* to panel *c*, but it is usually impossible to *decompose* the single equation in panel *c* to either of the cases in panels *a* or *b*. This is because we cannot ascertain how to allocate (decompose) x_1 to x_{11} and x_{12} solely on the basis of $F(y_1,y_2,x_1) = 0$.

Panel *d* in Figure 5.1 represents the case of a nonallocable factor of production, *z*—a case to which we now turn. An example of this case is sheep production resulting in two products—mutton and wool—from a nonallocable factor of production—feed. Panels *e* and *f* are discussed later. Panel *g* of Figure 5.1, while not discussed, is presented for completeness. It is a logical extension (complication) of the process depicted in panel *f*; that is, jointness is added.

Our point of departure for mathematical representation of production of two products from a nonallocable factor is the two production functions,

$$y_1 = f^1(z)$$
$$y_2 = f^2(z)$$

(5.10)

Can the two-equation representation of production be reduced to a single equation? In this case, the answer is yes, but something important is lost in the conversion; namely, *z* is lost as an argument of the function. To see this, suppose the inverse of the first equation in (5.10) exists; let this inverse be denoted by $z = g(y_1)$. Substitution of $g(\cdot)$ into the second equation of (5.10) for z gives

$$y_2 = f^2[g(y_1)] \tag{5.11}$$

which can be written in implicit form as

$$0 = y_2 - f^2[g(y_1)] = F(y_1, y_2) \tag{5.12}$$

In the case of an allocable factor, x, we saw that conversion from the multiple-equation representation to the single-equation representation, (5.1), resulted in a loss of explicit distribution of the factor. With a nonallocable factor the loss of information is more serious. Since z is not an argument in (5.11) or (5.12), the single-equation representation of production with a nonallocable factor is useless for economic analysis of the optimal level of z. In fact, rather than being a restatement (conversion) of the production functions in (5.10), equation (5.11) is effectively an output expansion path—a locus of attainable combinations of y_1 and y_2 as the nonallocable factor, z, is (implicitly) increased. Thus, (5.11) is not an alternative specification of (5.10) in the usual sense. We will amplify on this point in the discussion relating to the output expansion path for a conventional allocable factor (see Section 5.2.c). For the above reasons, we must use (5.10) to represent multiproduct production with a nonallocable factor.

In Section 5.2 we develop the case of two products produced from a single allocable factor.[1] This model is generalized to m products and n-allocable factors in Section 5.3. The important distinction between supply and marginal cost for the multiproduct case is discussed in Section 5.4. Section 5.5 presents the case of two products produced from a single nonallocable factor and a single allocable factor (see panel f of Figure 5.1). This case simultaneously demonstrates the marginal economic principles for a nonallocable factor and for an allocable factor. Generalization of this case, while straightforward, is not presented as the necessary notation is unwieldy. The chapter concludes with additional discussion of the applicability and efficacy of multiproduct production theory for the applied economist.

5.2 TWO-PRODUCT PRODUCTION WITH A SINGLE ALLOCABLE FACTOR

When two products are produced by a firm using a single allocable factor, it is possible, although not necessary, to represent the production process by a single implicit function,

$$F(y_1, y_2, x) = 0 \tag{5.13}$$

---

[1]The case of *nonjoint* production of two-products from an allocable factor that is fixed in total supply (i.e., $x_1 = x_{11} + x_{12} =$ fixed) is not presented. This case can be analyzed with single product concepts, but with the products linked through the resource constraint (see Problem 4-5).

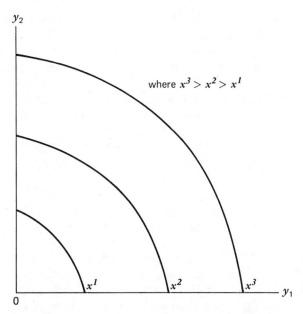

Figure 5.2.   A family of product transformation curves.

as discussed in Section 5.1. The subscript is dropped from x for notational convenience in this section.

With only one factor of production, the production function can usually be explicitly expressed as[2]

$$x = w(y_1, y_2) \tag{5.14}$$

That is, the amount of the factor used is expressed in terms of the quantities of each product produced, y_1 and y_2.

5.2.a Product Transformation Curve

Using the concept of a *product transformation curve*, which is also called a production possibilities curve, we can represent the production function, (5.13) or (5.14), in two-dimensional space. We define a product transformation curve as the locus of output combinations that can be obtained from a given amount of the variable factor. A family of product transformation curves is illustrated in Figure 5.2.

The notion of a product transformation curve is analogous to that of an isoquant—the only difference being that the former reflects output combinations holding the factor constant, while the latter shows input combinations holding output constant. If one thinks of the factor, x, in terms of cost of production or outlay, then the product transformation curve reflects a constant cost or outlay curve.

---

[2]We have said "usually" because expressions such as $0 = a_1 y_1^2 + a_2 y_2^2 + a_3 e^x + a_4 x$ cannot be *explicitly* solved for x.

In Chapter 2 we discussed isoquant patterns at some length. An analagous section could be developed here. In Figure 5.2 the product transformation curves are shown with negative slopes and are concave toward the origin, which is the typical pattern. However, there is one special case of product transformation curves that is common in the literature—the case of *fixed proportions*. This case, Figure 5.3, is represented for an allocable factor by right-angle product transformation curves that are concave toward the origin. This case is not of interest in this chapter, as such a problem is easily converted to a single product case by defining a new composite product with a composite price, both represented by output combinations along the ray-line, OA, in Figure 5.3.

The reader should be aware that if the factor were *nonallocable* rather than allocable, then a product transformation curve cannot be defined [recall (5.11)]. That is, for every level of z there is one and only one attainable combination of y_1 and y_2. In effect the idea of a product transformation curve degenerates to a single point for the nonallocable factor case. It will be seen shortly that (5.11), rather than being an alternative representation of the production function from which one can obtain a family of production possibility curves, is akin to an output expansion path in the nonallocable factor case.

5.2.b Rate of Product Transformation

An important technical concept pertaining to multiproduct production is that of the *rate of product transformation (RPT)*, defined as the negative of the slope of a product transformation curve,

$$RPT_{12} \equiv -\frac{dy_2}{dy_1} \tag{5.15}$$

The rate of product transformation can be derived from the explicit form of the production function, (5.14). Taking the total differential of this function, we obtain

$$dx = \frac{\partial x}{\partial y_1} dy_1 + \frac{\partial x}{\partial y_2} dy_2 = w_1 dy_1 + w_2 dy_2 \tag{5.16}$$

where w_1 and w_2 are *akin to* inverse marginal productivities for x in the production of y_1 and y_2, respectively. The term "akin to" is important, for w_1 and w_2 are not, strictly speaking, inverse marginal productivities as we normally think of the concept.[3] Consider the marginal productivity of x in the production of y_1, MPP_{11}. Most of us are conditioned to think of MPP_{11} as having as its arguments, x and y_2. That is, we normally think of MPP_{11} as $\partial y_1/\partial x \equiv f_1^1(x,y_2)$ where this partial derivative is of the function, $y_1 = f^1(y_2,x)$.

---

[3] Some authors, for example, Carlson, refer to w_1 and w_2 as marginal coefficients of production, presumably to avoid this complication.

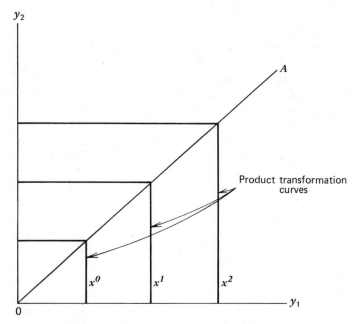

Figure 5.3.   Product transformation curves for the fixed proportions case.

Now what about $w_1 \equiv \partial x/\partial y_1$? By the inverse function rule, $\partial x_1/\partial y_1 = 1/(\partial y_1/\partial x)$; that is, the reciprocal (inverse) of the marginal productivity of x in y_1, or so it would seem. But is $1/(\partial y_1/\partial x)$ the same as $1/MPP_{11}$? Not exactly. Why? Recall that $\partial x/\partial y_1$ was obtained from the function, $x = w(y_1,y_2)$, so the arguments in w_1 are *not* x and y_2 but rather y_1 and y_2. If we can explicitly solve the function, $x = w(y_1,y_2)$, for y_1, say $y_1 = w^{-1}(x,y_2)$, then we could substitute $w^{-1}(x,y_2)$ into $w_1(y_1,y_2)$ for y_1 and get $w_1[w^{-1}(x,y_2),y_2] = 1/f_1(x,y_2)$ which can be properly interpreted as the reciprocal of the marginal productivity of x in the production of y_1. (Notice that y_1 no longer appears as an independent variable in w_1.)[4]

The message is that we must be careful when giving economic interpretation to results that were derived using the inverse function rule and its cousin, the implicit function rule. Notice, we do not say, "*avoid* economic interpretation." Rather we stress the need to be careful because the inverse and implicit function rules are deceptively simple, albeit they are powerful analytic tools.

---

[4]As an example, consider the function, (1) $y = 4x^{1/2}$, and its inverse, (2) $x = y^2/16$. From (1), $dy/dx = 2x^{-1/2}$ and from (2) $dx/dy = y/8$. Now, the question is: Does $1/(dx/dy) = dy/dx$ as it must according to the inverse function rule? Indeed it does, *when* the appropriate *ex post* variable substitution is made. That is, $1(dx/dy) = 1/(y/8) = 8/y = 8/4x^{1/2} = 2x^{-1/2}$. Thus, $1(dx/dy)$ can be interpreted as dy/dx when $4x^{1/2}$ is substituted in for y *after* the derivative, dx/dy, is taken.

Getting back to the main theme: the w_1 and w_2 in (5.16) may be interpreted as inverse marginal productivities (in the conventional sense) only when the appropriate right-hand-side variable substitutions are made (*ex post*), so that the resulting marginal functions contain the correct explanatory (independent) variables. Throughout the remainder of this chapter we will be interpreting functions like w_1 and w_2 as inverse marginal productivities, or whatever, under the presumption that the appropriate variable substitutions can and have been made.

Continuing with our derivation of the *RPT*, the change in x along a given product transformation curve is zero by definition. Thus, (5.16) becomes simply

$$0 = w_1 dy_1 + w_2 dy_2 \tag{5.17}$$

Therefore,

$$\frac{dy_2}{dy_1} = -\frac{w_1}{w_2} \tag{5.18}$$

and

$$RPT_{12} \equiv -\frac{dy_2}{dy_1} = \frac{w_1}{w_2} = \frac{\partial x/\partial y_1}{\partial x/\partial y_2} = \frac{1/(\partial y_1/\partial x)}{1/(\partial y_2/\partial x)} = \frac{\partial y_2/\partial x}{\partial y_1/\partial x} \tag{5.19}$$

(Again, the next-to-last step in (5.19) utilizes the inverse function rule, so be careful.) Thus the rate of product transformation equals the ratio of the marginal physical productivity of x in production of y_2 to the marginal physical productivity of x in the production of y_1.

As in the single-product case, rational production requires that MPPs be positive; hence, the slopes of the product transformation curves are negative and RPT is positive in the region of economic interest.

5.2.c Constrained Revenue Maximization

Now let us examine economic concepts pertinent to multiproduct production. The first concept that we wish to examine is the *output expansion path*, which is defined to be a locus of points, (y_1, y_2), that maximizes revenue subject to a fixed amount of the variable factor. An output expansion path is similar in concept to the factor expansion path, except that the former pertains to products and the latter relates to factors. An output expansion path is derived by maximizing revenue subject to a given amount of the factor.

In the general case of imperfect competition, total revenue is given by

$$TR \equiv p_1 y_1 + p_2 y_2 = g^1(y_1) y_1 + g^2(y_2) y_2 \tag{5.20}$$

where $g^1(y_1)$ and $g^2(y_2)$ are the demand functions for y_1 and y_2, respectively.[5] Total revenue, (5.20), is to be maximized subject to the constraint that $x = x^0$. This constrained maximization problem can be converted into an unconstrained maximization problem using the Lagrangean approach. Thus, we form the Lagrangean function,

$$LTR = g^1(y_1)y_1 + g^2(y_2)y_2 + \eta[x^0 - w(y_1,y_2)] \qquad (5.21)$$

The first-order conditions for maximization of (5.21) are

$$\frac{\partial LTR}{\partial y_1} = g^1(y_1) + y_1\,g_1^1 - \eta w_1 = 0$$

$$\frac{\partial LTR}{\partial y_2} = g^2(y_2) + y_2\,g_2^2 - \eta w_2 = 0 \qquad (5.22)$$

$$\frac{\partial LTR}{\partial \eta} = x^0 - w(y_1,y_2) = 0$$

Solving the first two equations in (5.22) for the Lagrangean multiplier, η, and equating the results, we obtain a necessary condition for constrained revenue maximization,

$$\frac{g^1(y_1) + y_1\,g_1^1}{w_1} = \frac{g^2(y_2) + y_2\,g_2^2}{w_2} \qquad (5.23)$$

or

$$\frac{g^1(y_1) + y_1\,g_1^1}{g^2(y_2) + y_2\,g_2^2} = \frac{w_1}{w_2} \qquad (5.24)$$

Thus, a necessary condition is that

$$\frac{MR_1}{MR_2} = \frac{w_1}{w_2} = \frac{\partial x/\partial y_1}{\partial x/\partial y_2} = \frac{\dfrac{1}{MPP_{11}}}{\dfrac{1}{MPP_{12}}} = \frac{MPP_{12}}{MPP_{11}} \qquad (5.25)$$

In geometric terms, the first-order condition, (5.25), requires that the *isorevenue* curve be tangent to the product transformation curve as in Figure

---

[5]A more general case is given by interrelated demand functions; that is, $p_1 = g^1(y_1,y_2)$ and $p_2 = g^2(y_1,y_2)$. To simplify derivations, we have assumed independent demand functions, but we encourage the reader to consider constrained revenue maximization in the case of interdependent demand functions.

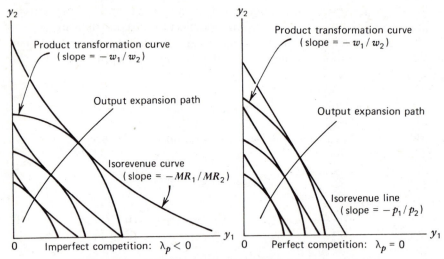

Figure 5.4. Output expansion path for imperfectly and perfectly competitive product market cases.

5.4. Of course, the shape of the isorevenue curve depends on the nature of the demand functions for y_1 and y_2. The locus of points traced out by tangency of isorevenue curves and product transformation curves, (5.25), is defined as the *output expansion path* (see Figure 5.4).

The second-order condition for constrained revenue maximization requires that the bordered Hessian determinant be positive, namely that

$$
\begin{vmatrix}
\dfrac{\partial^2 TR}{\partial y_1^2} & \dfrac{\partial^2 TR}{\partial y_1 \partial y_2} & \dfrac{\partial^2 TR}{\partial y_1 \partial \eta} \\[2ex]
\dfrac{\partial^2 TR}{\partial y_2 \partial y_1} & \dfrac{\partial^2 TR}{\partial y_2^2} & \dfrac{\partial^2 TR}{\partial y_2 \partial \eta} \\[2ex]
\dfrac{\partial^2 TR}{\partial \eta \partial y_1} & \dfrac{\partial^2 TR}{\partial \eta \partial y_2} & \dfrac{\partial^2 TR}{\partial \eta^2}
\end{vmatrix} > 0 \tag{5.26}
$$

With downward sloping demand functions, the isorevenue curves will always be convex to the origin. In this case, the second-order condition, (5.26), allows for concave or convex product transformation curves; however, convex product transformation curves must be less convex than the isorevenue curves. For linear isorevenue curves (i.e., perfect competition) the second-order condition requires concave product transformation curves.

In the case of perfectly competitive product markets, the Lagrangean revenue function is

$$
LTR = p_1 y_1 + p_2 y_2 + \eta[x^0 - w(y_1, y_2)] \tag{5.27}
$$

and the first-order conditions are

$$\frac{\partial LTR}{\partial y_1} = p_1 - \eta w_1 = 0$$

$$\frac{\partial LTR}{\partial y_2} = p_2 - \eta w_2 = 0 \tag{5.28}$$

$$\frac{\partial LTR}{\partial \eta} = x^0 - w(y_1, y_2) = 0$$

Using the first two equations to eliminate η yields the marginal condition, or output expansion path,

$$\frac{p_1}{p_2} = \frac{w_1}{w_2} = \frac{MPP_{12}}{MPP_{11}} \tag{5.29}$$

Simultaneous solution of (5.28) gives the conditional product supply equations and the Lagrangean multiplier function,

$$y_j^c = y_j^c(p_1, p_2, x) \qquad \text{for } j = 1,2 \tag{5.30}$$
$$\eta^c = \eta^c(p_1, p_2, x)$$

The y_j^c functions in (5.30) are called *conditional* product supply functions because of their dependence on the factor level, x, which is presumed to be fixed. In (5.30) the fixed factor is represented merely as x, rather than x^0, as it is permissible to consider variation in x in the context of conditional product supply analysis. In contrast, ordinary or unconditional product supply equations depend on factor prices and not factor levels. The economic interpretation of the Lagrangean multiplier in (5.30) is that it shows the effect on gross revenue of an infinitesimal change in x (i.e., $\eta^c = \partial LTR^c / \partial x$) allowing the y_j to adjust in an optimal manner.

With perfect competition, the second-order condition reduces to

$$\begin{vmatrix} -\eta w_{11} & -\eta w_{12} & -w_1 \\ -\eta w_{21} & -\eta w_{22} & -w_2 \\ -w_1 & -w_2 & 0 \end{vmatrix} > 0 \tag{5.31}$$

Expanding this determinant, we obtain

$$\eta(w_{11}w_2^2 - 2w_{12}w_1w_2 + w_{22}w_1^2) > 0 \tag{5.32}$$

Note that since $\eta = (\partial LTR/\partial x) > 0$, the second-order condition in the competitive case requires that

$$(w_{11}w_2^2 - 2w_{12}w_1w_2 + w_{22}w_1^2) > 0 \tag{5.33}$$

which is equivalent to requiring that the production function in explicit form, (5.14), be strictly quasi-convex, thus implying product transformation curves concave to the origin (see Figure 5.4—perfectly competitive case).

Example 5.1   Assume the implicit production function,

$$x - y_1^2 - y_2^2 = 0 \tag{5.34}$$

which in explicit form is

$$x = y_1^2 + y_2^2 \tag{5.35}$$

Assuming perfect competition in product markets, the Lagrangean revenue function is

$$LTR = p_1 y_1 + p_2 y_2 + \eta(x^0 - y_1^2 - y_2^2) \tag{5.36}$$

with first-order conditions,

$$\frac{\partial LTR}{\partial y_1} = p_1 - 2\eta y_1 = 0$$

$$\frac{\partial LTR}{\partial y_2} = p_2 - 2\eta y_2 = 0 \tag{5.37}$$

$$\frac{\partial LTR}{\partial \eta} = x^0 - y_1^2 - y_2^2 = 0$$

Solving each of the first two equations for η and equating the results gives

$$\frac{p_1}{y_1} = \frac{p_2}{y_2} \tag{5.38}$$

Expressing (5.38) in terms of y_2 gives the output expansion path,

$$y_2 = \frac{p_2}{p_1} y_1 \tag{5.39}$$

Substituting the output expansion path into the last equation in (5.37), in other words, the production function, and rearranging terms gives the conditional supply equation for the first product,

$$y_1^c = \frac{p_1 x^{1/2}}{(p_1^2 + p_2^2)^{1/2}} \tag{5.40}$$

Substitution of (5.40) back into the production function gives the conditional supply equation for the second product,

$$y_2^c = \frac{p_2 x^{1/2}}{(p_1^2 + p_2^2)^{1/2}} \qquad (5.41)$$

Checking the second-order condition, (5.33), we find that

$$2(2y_2)^2 - 2(0)(2y_1)(2y_2) + 2(2y_1)^2 = 8y_2^2 + 8y_1^2 > 0 \text{ for } y_1, y_2 > 0 \quad (5.42)$$

Thus, the second-order condition is satisfied in this example.

An item worthy of note from (5.40) and (5.41) in the example is that the conditional product supply functions are, not surprisingly, homogeneous of degree zero in prices. This particular result can be proven in general by applying the homogeneity test to the derivation in (5.27) through (5.30). The proof is analogous to that for conditional factor demand in Chapter 3. Also taking $\partial y_1^c / \partial p_2$ from (5.40) and $\partial y_2^c / \partial p_1$ from (5.41) will verify that the symmetry condition holds. The symmetry and homogeneity results for conditional supply are formally proven (in general) in Chapter 6.

Before moving on, it may be instructive to compare the case presented in this section with the case of a *nonallocable* factor. Recall that for a nonallocable factor, (5.11) was the output expansion path. No matter what the ratio of marginal revenues, there is only one possible combination of y_1 and y_2 that can be produced for alternative levels of a nonallocable factor, z; that is, there are no product transformation curves in the nonallocable factor case (see Figure 5.5). Unlike the allocable factor case, product price arguments do not appear in the output expansion path for a nonallocable factor.

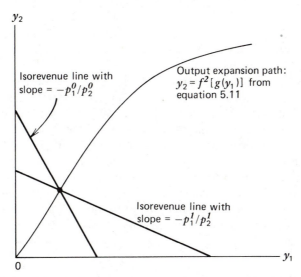

Figure 5.5. Output expansion path for the case of a single-nonallocable factor.

5.2.d Profit Maximization

We now examine the conditions for maximum profit in the two-product, single allocable factor case. As in the single-product case, the mathematics of profit maximization can be approached as either a constrained optimization problem or an unconstrained optimization problem formulated by substituting the explicit form of the production function into the profit function for x. In this section, we focus on the unconstrained approach but suggest that the reader also consider the constrained (Lagrangean) method using the production function in implicit form.[6] The constrained approach is used in Section 5.3.b, equation 5.87.

With imperfect competition in factor and product markets, the profit function (exclusive of fixed cost) is given by

$$\pi \equiv TR - c \equiv p_1 y_1 + p_2 y_2 - rx$$
$$= g^1(y_1)y_1 + g^2(y_2)y_2 - h(x)x \qquad (5.43)$$

where $r = h(x)$ is the factor supply function and other terms are as defined previously. Since only a single factor is used, there are no factor–factor tradeoffs to be considered in producing given levels of both y_1 and y_2; thus, $c \equiv rx = h(x)x = h[w(y_1,y_2)]w(y_1,y_2) = VC$. That is, the VC function can be obtained by substituting the explicit form of the production function, (5.14), for x in the variable factor cost equation, c.

To treat the problem of maximizing (5.43) subject to the production function, (5.14), as an unconstrained problem, we can substitute the production function, (5.14), for x in (5.43); as shown above, this is equivalent to substituting the VC function for c in (5.43). Thus,

$$\pi \equiv TR - VC = g^1(y_1)y_1 + g^2(y_2)y_2 - h[w(y_1,y_2)]w(y_1,y_2) \qquad (5.44)$$

Notice that in specifying a profit function for which we can apply unconstrained optimization methods, we have expressed profit exclusively in terms of output levels. By comparison, we most often expressed profit exclusively in terms of factor levels in the multifactor single product case in Chapter 3. In this multiproduct single-factor case, we eliminate the factor level from the profit function simply because we have an explicit production function that allows us to easily eliminate x but not to easily eliminate y_1 or y_2 or both. In general, this substitution can only be done in the single-factor case. In the multiproduct–multifactor case with the production process represented by a single equation, we must use a Lagrangean optimization approach with the implicit production function as a constraint, or first determine the multiproduct cost function as in the first part of Section 5.3.b. With a single factor, we use profit function (5.44) to simplify optimization and to focus on selection of output levels.

---

[6]The setup is $L\pi = p_1y_1 + p_2y_2 - rx + \theta[x^0 - w(y_1,y_2)]$, where θ is a Lagrangean multiplier.

Taking the first-partial derivatives of profit function (5.44) with respect to y_1 and y_2, then setting each of the resulting equations equal to zero, we obtain the first-order conditions,

$$\frac{\partial \pi}{\partial y_1} = g^1(y_1) + y_1 g_1^1 - h[w(\cdot)]w_1 - w(\cdot)h_1[w(\cdot)] = 0$$

$$\frac{\partial \pi}{\partial y_2} = g^2(y_2) + y_2 g_2^2 - h[w(\cdot)]w_2 - w(\cdot)h_2[w(\cdot)] = 0$$

(5.45)

again where $w(\cdot)$ is shorthand for $w(y_1,y_2)$. Rearranging terms in (5.45) we find that

$$g^1(y_1) + y_1 g_1^1 = h[w(\cdot)]w_1 + w(\cdot)h_1[w(\cdot)]$$
$$g^2(y_2) + y_2 g_2^2 = h[w(\cdot)]w_2 + w(\cdot)h_2[w(\cdot)]$$

(5.46)

or, substituting notation, we have

$$MR_1 = MC_1$$
$$MR_2 = MC_2$$

(5.47)

which is the familiar output-side economic principle that marginal revenue equals marginal cost. Note that MC_j depends, in general, on both y_1 and y_2; thus, (5.47) must be simultaneously solved to obtain profit-maximizing values, y_1^* and y_2^*. The profit-maximizing level of factor usage is obtained by substituting y_j^* for y_j in the production function, (5.14); that is, $x^* = w(y_1^*,y_2^*)$.

The right-hand side of (5.47), MC_j, can be restated as a factor-side relationship as follows. Since $VC = h[w(y_1,y_2)]w(y_1,y_2)$, we have

$$MC_j \equiv \frac{\partial VC}{\partial y_j} = h[w(y_1,y_2)]w_j(y_1,y_2) + w(y_1,y_2)\frac{\partial h}{\partial y_j} \qquad \text{for } j = 1,2 \quad (5.48)$$

Recalling that $x = w(y_1,y_2)$, (5.48) can be expressed as

$$MC_j = h(x)w_j + x\frac{\partial h}{\partial x} \cdot \frac{\partial x}{\partial y_j}$$

$$= h(x)w_j + xh_1 \cdot w_j$$

$$= w_j[h(x) + xh_1]$$

(5.49)

What is the term in brackets in (5.49)? Since $c \equiv rx = h(x)\,x$, $MFC_1 \equiv \frac{\partial c}{\partial x} = h(x) + xh_1$. Substitution of this relationship into (5.49) gives

$$MC_j = w_j MFC_1 = \frac{MFC_1}{MPP_{1j}} \qquad \text{for } j = 1,2 \quad (5.50)$$

Thus, (5.47) can be restated as a factor-side economic principle:

$$MR_1 = MC_1 = \frac{MFC_1}{MPP_{11}}$$

$$MR_2 = MC_2 = \frac{MFC_1}{MPP_{12}}$$

(5.51)

That is, the first-order conditions for profit maximization require that

$$MR_1 \cdot MPP_{11} = MFC_1 \Rightarrow MVP_{11} = MFC_1$$

$$MR_2 \cdot MPP_{12} = MFC_1 \Rightarrow MVP_{12} = MFC_1$$

(5.52)

Notice that with a perfectly competitive factor market, (5.52) reduces to

$$MVP_{11} = r$$

$$MVP_{12} = r$$

(5.53)

and with perfect competition in all markets, the first-order conditions are simply that

$$p_1 MPP_{11} = r$$

$$p_2 MPP_{12} = r$$

(5.54)

The first-order conditions when expressed as in (5.52) and (5.53) give the familiar economic principle of *equal marginal value in use*. That is, since the marginal factor cost is the same no matter what the use, we find that profit maximization requires that *MVP*s be equal among uses. We should also note that the results obtained in (5.52) and (5.53) are due to the fact that the factor is *allocable* to the individual products, which in effect allowed us to subscript the factor to distinguish between that used in y_1 production, x_{11}, and that used in y_2 production, x_{12}, as was discussed in Section 5.1. We will see later that this marginal principle is invalid for nonallocable factors.

For the single allocable factor, two product case, we see that the familiar first-order conditions that marginal revenues must equal marginal costs on the output side can be manipulated to produce the parallel input side conditions that marginal value productivities must equal marginal factor cost. The reader is cautioned that the appealing result which allowed this transformation, chiefly that $MC_j = MFC_1/MPP_{1j}$, holds *only* for the single-factor case. That is, $MC_j \neq MFC_i/MPP_{ij}$ when there is more than one variable factor (see footnote 9).

As a final note, the reader is encouraged to develop a proof (parallel to the one developed in Chapter 3 concerning the relationship between the profit-maximizing conditions and the input expansion path) showing that the profit-maximizing solution for the multiproduct firm lies on the output expansion path.

The second-order condition for maximum profit requires that the determinants of the principal minors of the unbordered Hessian alternate in sign, beginning with a negative sign. Thus, the second-order condition requires that

$$\frac{\partial^2 \pi}{\partial y_1^2} < 0$$

$$\frac{\partial^2 \pi}{\partial y_2^2} < 0 \tag{5.55}$$

$$\begin{vmatrix} \dfrac{\partial^2 \pi}{\partial y_1^2} & \dfrac{\partial^2 \pi}{\partial y_1 \partial y_2} \\[2ex] \dfrac{\partial^2 \pi}{\partial y_2 \partial y_1} & \dfrac{\partial^2 \pi}{\partial y_2^2} \end{vmatrix} > 0$$

with all of the above evaluated at the values of y_1 and y_2 that satisfy the first-order conditions, in other words, y_1^* and y_2^*.

In the case of perfect competition in all markets, the second-order condition requires that

$$\frac{\partial^2 \pi}{\partial y_1^2} = -rw_{11} < 0 \Rightarrow w_{11} > 0$$

$$\frac{\partial^2 \pi}{\partial y_2^2} = -rw_{22} < 0 \Rightarrow w_{22} > 0 \tag{5.56}$$

$$\begin{vmatrix} \dfrac{\partial^2 \pi}{\partial y_1^2} & \dfrac{\partial^2 \pi}{\partial y_1 \partial y_2} \\[2ex] \dfrac{\partial^2 \pi}{\partial y_2 \partial y_1} & \dfrac{\partial^2 \pi}{\partial y_2^2} \end{vmatrix} = \begin{vmatrix} -rw_{11} & -rw_{12} \\[1ex] -rw_{21} & -rw_{22} \end{vmatrix}$$

$$= r^2(w_{11}w_{22} - w_{12}w_{21}) > 0$$
$$\Rightarrow (w_{11}w_{22} - w_{12}^2) > 0$$

which implies that the factor-dependent explicit form of the production function must be strictly convex. Restrictions on the shape of the production function in the case of imperfectly competitive markets depends upon product demand and factor supply relationships as close examination of (5.55) will reveal.

Example 5.2   Assuming perfect competition in all markets and the production function used in Example 5.1, we can express profit as

$$\pi = p_1 y_1 + p_2 y_2 - r(y_1^2 + y_2^2) \tag{5.57}$$

To maximize profit, we must satisfy the first-order conditions,

$$\frac{\partial \pi}{\partial y_1} = p_1 - 2ry_1 = 0$$

$$\frac{\partial \pi}{\partial y_2} = p_2 - 2ry_2 = 0$$

(5.58)

Solving for y_1 and y_2 we find that

$$y_1^* = \frac{p_1}{2r}$$

(5.59)

$$y_2^* = \frac{p_2}{2r}$$

(5.60)

To obtain the profit-maximizing factor level, we substitute (5.59) and (5.60) into the production function, (5.35), which gives

$$x^* = \left[\frac{p_1}{2r}\right]^2 + \left[\frac{p_2}{2r}\right]^2 = \frac{p_1^2 + p_2^2}{4r^2}$$

(5.61)

If we allow prices to vary, (5.59) and (5.60) are product supply equations for y_1 and y_2, respectively, and (5.61) is the factor demand equation. It is interesting to note that cross-product prices do not appear in the product supply equations for this particular multiproduct specification. This is because the products are technically independent when viewed from the factor side; that is, $(\partial^2 x / \partial y_1 \partial y_2) = 0$.[7] However, for this production function, (5.35), product transformation curves are negatively sloped and strictly concave to the origin implying that the products do compete for the fixed amount of x. Again, the reader is cautioned not to confuse the idea of technical interdependence with the shape of a particular product transformation curve. The situation is analogous to that in Chapter 2 where we considered isoquant patterns as one issue and factor interdependence as another.

The homogeneity and symmetry conditions are easy to verify for the unconditional product supply and factor demand functions in the above example. We leave that as an exercise for the reader.

5.2.e Technical Interdependence of Products

The technical interrelationship between two products produced from an allocable factor may be viewed in terms of the change in marginal productivity of the factor in the production of one product due to a change in the amount

---

[7]In general we expect that products will be technically interdependent, in which case the cross-price arguments will appear in the product supply functions.

of another product produced *when only a single variable factor* is involved in the production process. That is, when the multiproduct production function is given by $x = w(y_1, y_2)$, then we define the following:

1. If $\partial^2 x / \partial y_1 \partial y_2 \equiv \partial \left(\dfrac{\partial x}{\partial y_1} \right) \Big/ \partial y_2 \equiv w_{12} < 0 \Rightarrow y_1$ and y_2 are *technically complementary.*

2. If $\partial^2 x / \partial y_1 \partial y_2 \equiv w_{12} > 0 \Rightarrow y_1$ and y_2 are *technically competing.*
3. If $\partial^2 x / \partial y_1 \partial y_2 \equiv w_{12} = 0 \Rightarrow y_1$ and y_2 are *technically independent.*

The above definition states that if one product is increased and as a result the inverse marginal productivity [remember the *ex post* variable substitution required here per the discussion following (5.16)] of the factor employed in the other product decreases, increases, or remains unchanged, then the two products are respectively technically complementary, competing, or independent.

Although not immediately obvious, this classification does have intuitive appeal. Consider the case of technical complementarity. That is, if $w_{12} < 0$, then $\partial x / \partial y_1$ decreases as y_2 is increased, which is to say that MPP_{11} increases. Increasing marginal productivity in response to an increase in the level of an alternative product seems consistent with the notion of complementarity. Similarly, if marginal productivity is diminished, the jargon, *competing*, seems appropriate as does *independence* for the case of no change.

5.2.f Economic Interdependence of Products, Comparative Statics, Symmetry, and Homogeneity

Two products are said to be economically interdependent if a change in the price of one product influences the quantity supplied of the other product (here we are referring to *unconditional* product supply). We define the following:

1. If $\partial y_j^* / \partial p_k < 0$, then y_j and y_k are *economically competing.*
2. If $\partial y_j^* / \partial p_k = 0$, then y_j and y_k are *economically independent.*
3. If $\partial y_j^* / \partial p_k > 0$, then y_j and y_k are *economically complementary* for $j \neq k$ and $j,k = 1,2$.

To fully develop economic interdependence of products, it is useful to examine the total differential of the first-order conditions for profit maximization. Of course, economic interdependence as defined above makes sense only with perfectly competitive product markets. For simplicity and so that we might consider comparative static results from a factor-price as well as product-price perspective, we also assume a perfectly competitive factor market. Under these assumptions, the first-order conditions are

$$p_j - rw_j = 0 \qquad \text{for } j = 1,2 \tag{5.62}$$

and the total differentials of (5.62) are

$$-rw_{11}dy_1^* - rw_{12}dy_2^* = -dp_1 + w_1dr$$
$$-rw_{21}dy_1^* - rw_{22}dy_2^* = -dp_2 + w_2dr \qquad (5.63)$$

Recall that the w_i's are first-partial derivatives of $x = w(y_1,y_2)$, so the differentials, dy_1 and dy_2, appear in (5.63), in addition to the price differentials. The differentials, dy_1^* and dy_2^*, are used in place of dy_1 and dy_2 to emphasize that the comparative static results must be evaluated and interpreted in terms of optimal (as opposed to any) output levels.

In matrix notation, the system of simultaneous equations in (5.63) is represented as

$$\begin{bmatrix} -rw_{11} & -rw_{12} \\ -rw_{21} & -rw_{22} \end{bmatrix} \begin{bmatrix} dy_1^* \\ dy_2^* \end{bmatrix} = \begin{bmatrix} -dp_1 + w_1dr \\ -dp_2 + w_2dr \end{bmatrix} \qquad (5.64)$$

Using Cramer's rule to obtain the solution to (5.64) for the variables dy_1^* and dy_2^*, yields

$$dy_1^* = \frac{\begin{vmatrix} (-dp_1 + w_1dr) & -rw_{12} \\ (-dp_2 + w_2dr) & -rw_{22} \end{vmatrix}}{\begin{vmatrix} -rw_{11} & -rw_{12} \\ -rw_{21} & -rw_{22} \end{vmatrix}}$$

$$= \frac{rw_{22}(dp_1 - w_1dr) - rw_{12}(dp_2 - w_2dr)}{r^2(w_{11}w_{22} - w_{12}w_{21})} \qquad (5.65)$$

Similarly,

$$dy_2^* = \frac{rw_{11}(dp_2 - w_2dr) - rw_{21}(dp_1 - w_1dr)}{r^2(w_{11}w_{22} - w_{12}w_{21})} \qquad (5.66)$$

Holding factor price and own-product price constant in (5.65) and/or (5.66), we find

$$\frac{dy_j^*}{dp_k} \equiv \frac{\partial y_j^*}{\partial p_k} = \frac{-w_{jk}}{r(w_{11}w_{22} - w_{12}^2)} \gtreqless 0 \qquad \text{for } j \neq k \text{ and } j,k = 1,2 \quad (5.67)$$

Assuming the second-order condition is satisfied, the denominator in (5.67) will be positive [see (5.56)], so economic interdependence of the products will be determined by the negative of the cross-partial derivative of the explicit form of the production function, which was what we used to establish our technical classification. That is, in the previous section we argued that if

$w_{12} < 0, = 0, > 0$, then y_1 and y_2 were technically complementary, independent, or competitive, respectively.

From (5.67) we note that $\partial y_j^*/\partial p_k > 0$ if $w_{jk} < 0$, equals zero if $w_{jk} = 0$, and is negative if $w_{jk} > 0$. If $\partial y_j^*/\partial p_k > 0$, we say that y_j and y_k are *economic complements*; if $\partial y_j^*/\partial p_k = 0$, y_j and y_k are *economically independent*; and if $\partial y_j^*/\partial p_k < 0$, y_j and y_k are *economically competitive*—consistent with our technical classification. Fortunately, the classification system also makes intuitive sense. If when the price of y_2 is increased, we find that the entrepreneur increases y_1 as well as y_2, it would seem to make sense to call this relationship complementary. On the other hand, if an increase in p_2 induces the expected increase in y_2 but engenders a decrease in y_1, then it seems appropriate to call this relationship competitive.

Total differentials, (5.65) and (5.66), which were used to establish the comparative static relationships given by (5.67), can also be used to deduce the remaining comparative static relationships for the two-product, single-factor profit-maximization model. Letting $dp_1 = dp_2 = 0$ in (5.65) and (5.66), respectively, gives

$$
\begin{aligned}
\frac{dy_1^*}{dr} &\equiv \frac{\partial y_1^*}{\partial r} = \frac{-w_1 w_{22} + w_2 w_{12}}{r(w_{11} w_{22} - w_{12}^2)} \gtreqless 0 \\
\frac{dy_2^*}{dr} &\equiv \frac{\partial y_2^*}{\partial r} = \frac{-w_2 w_{11} + w_1 w_{12}}{r(w_{11} w_{22} - w_{12}^2)} \gtreqless 0
\end{aligned}
\tag{5.68}
$$

Moreover, letting dr and the appropriate alternative product price differential equal zero in (5.65) and (5.66) gives

$$
\begin{aligned}
\frac{dy_1^*}{dp_1} &\equiv \frac{\partial y_1^*}{\partial p_1} = \frac{w_{22}}{r(w_{11} w_{22} - w_{12}^2)} \geq 0 \\
\frac{dy_2^*}{dp_2} &\equiv \frac{\partial y_2^*}{\partial p_2} = \frac{w_{11}}{r(w_{11} w_{22} - w_{12}^2)} \geq 0
\end{aligned}
\tag{5.69}
$$

The suggested signs are discussed later.

Factor-side comparative static relationships can be derived taking the total differential of the production function evaluated at optimal values of y_1 and y_2 (and thus x):

$$
dx^* = w_1 dy_1^* + w_2 dy_2^*
\tag{5.70}
$$

We know dy_1^* and dy_2^* from (5.65) and (5.66), respectively. Making these substitutions into (5.70) and collecting like terms gives

$$
dx^* = \frac{(w_1 w_{22} - w_2 w_{12})dp_1 + (w_2 w_{11} - w_1 w_{12})dp_2 + (2 w_1 w_2 w_{12} - w_1^2 w_{22} - w_2^2 w_{11})dr}{r(w_{11} w_{22} - w_{12}^2)}
\tag{5.71}
$$

Therefore, setting appropriate differentials equal to zero, yields

$$\frac{dx^*}{dp_1} \equiv \frac{\partial x^*}{\partial p_1} = \frac{w_1 w_{22} - w_2 w_{12}}{r(w_{11} w_{12} - w_{12}^2)} \gtreqless 0$$

$$\frac{dx^*}{dp_2} \equiv \frac{\partial x^*}{\partial p_2} = \frac{w_2 w_{11} - w_1 w_{12}}{r(w_{11} w_{22} - w_{12}^2)} \gtreqless 0 \qquad (5.72)$$

$$\frac{dx^*}{dr} \equiv \frac{\partial x^*}{\partial r} = \frac{2 w_1 w_2 w_{12} - w_1^2 w_{22} - w_2^2 w_{11}}{r(w_{11} w_{22} - w_{12}^2)} \leq 0$$

Sign possibilities for the partial derivatives in (5.67), (5.68), (5.69), and (5.72) follow from strict convexity of the production function.

A comparative examination of (5.67), (5.68), and (5.72) reveals the following symmetry conditions:

$$\frac{\partial y_1^*}{\partial p_2} = \frac{\partial y_2^*}{\partial p_1}$$

$$\frac{\partial y_1^*}{\partial r} = -\frac{\partial x^*}{\partial p_1} \qquad (5.73)$$

$$\frac{\partial y_2^*}{\partial r} = -\frac{\partial x^*}{\partial p_2}$$

As noted in earlier chapters, these symmetry conditions are often overlooked in theoretical and empirical analyses. Again, it is important to emphasize that these conditions follow from the deterministic, static, profit-maximization model regardless of the underlying production function. While it is important that symmetry conditions be recognized, we caution the reader not to over generalize. For example, symmetry does not hold for some types of dynamic and/ or stochastic utility, profit, or cost optimization models.

Finally, it is easy to show for the two-product, single-factor model that the unconditional factor demand and product supply functions are homogeneous of degree zero in product and factor prices. We know that $x^*(r, p_1, p_2)$, $y_1^*(r, p_1, p_2)$, and $y_2^*(r, p_1, p_2)$ are derived from the first-order conditions in (5.62) in a manner analogous to Example 5.2. By replacing p_j and r in (5.62) with tp_j and tr, we get

$$(tp_j) - (tr)w_j = 0 \Rightarrow t(p_j - rw_j) = 0 \Rightarrow p_j - rw_j = 0/t = 0 \qquad (5.74)$$

Since the first-order conditions are homogeneous of degree zero in prices, it follows that x^*, y_1^*, and y_2^* will also not depend on t and, thus, are also homogeneous of degree zero in prices.

5.3 MULTIPRODUCT PRODUCTION WITH *n*-ALLOCABLE FACTORS

In the case of multiproduct, multifactor production with allocable factors, specification of *RPT*, the output expansion path, the input expansion path, profit-maximizing conditions and cost-minimizing conditions is much more difficult than in the single-factor case. One can no longer define a technical product transformation curve merely by fixing a single factor to reduce the dimension of the problem enough to show technical and economic concepts geometrically. Consequently, treatment of the multiproduct, multifactor case must be done through abstract mathematical means. Thus, in this section we move directly to the bottom line issues, namely, conditional and unconditional factor demand and unconditional product supply.

We assume perfect competition in all markets, not because this is an essential assumption, but to simplify derivations and notation. Readers interested in imperfectly competitive cases can follow the logic shown for the competitive case, taking note to introduce the relevant product demand and factor supply functions into the optimization process. Again, it is also assumed that *all* factors are *allocable*.

5.3.a Cost Minimization and Conditional Factor Demand

We begin the general case by considering the cost-minimization problem and derivation of conditional factor demand functions. Conditional factor demand functions are important because they allow us to obtain the variable cost function on the output side, similar to what was done in the single-product case in Chapter 4.

Let the implicit production function be denoted by

$$F(y_1, \ldots, y_m, x_1, \ldots, x_n) = 0 \tag{5.75}$$

For this implicit production function, the Lagrangean cost function is

$$LC = \sum_{i=1}^{n} r_i x_i + \phi F(y_1, \ldots, y_m, x_1, \ldots, x_n) \tag{5.76}$$

with first-order conditions,

$$\frac{\partial LC}{\partial x_i} = r_i + \phi F_i = 0 \qquad \text{for } i = 1, \dots, n$$

$$\frac{\partial LC}{\partial \phi} = F(\cdot) = 0$$

(5.77)

where the subscript, i, relates *only* to factors and factor prices.[8]

Simultaneously solving the $(n + 1)$ equations for the $(n + 1)$ unknowns, $x_1, \dots, x_n$ and ϕ in (5.77) gives the conditional factor demand equations,

$$x_i^c = x_i^c(r_1, \dots, r_n, y_1, \dots, y_m) \qquad \text{for } i = 1, \dots, n \qquad (5.78)$$

As in the single-product case, the variable cost function on the output side is given by minimum factor cost for producing specified outputs, expressed in terms of output. That is,

$$VC = \sum_{i=1}^{n} r_i x_i^c(r_1, \dots, r_n, y_1, \dots, y_m)$$

$$= \bar{c}(r_1, \dots, r_n, y_1, \dots, y_m)$$

(5.79)

The second-order condition for cost minimization requires that the determinants of the principal minors of the bordered Hessian be negative. (The reader is reminded that the subscripts in the following determinants denote factors, *not* products.) Thus,

$$\begin{vmatrix} 0 & F_1 & F_2 \\ F_1 & \phi F_{11} & \phi F_{12} \\ F_2 & \phi F_{21} & \phi F_{22} \end{vmatrix} < 0$$

$$\begin{vmatrix} 0 & F_1 & F_2 & F_3 \\ F_1 & \phi F_{11} & \phi F_{12} & \phi F_{13} \\ F_2 & \phi F_{21} & \phi F_{22} & \phi F_{23} \\ F_3 & \phi F_{31} & \phi F_{32} & \phi F_{33} \end{vmatrix} < 0 \qquad (5.80)$$

$$\vdots$$

$$\begin{vmatrix} 0 & F_1 & F_2 & \cdots & F_n \\ F_1 & \phi F_{11} & \phi F_{12} & \cdots & \phi F_{1n} \\ F_2 & \phi F_{21} & \phi F_{22} & \cdots & \phi F_{2n} \\ \vdots & \vdots & \vdots & & \vdots \\ F_n & \phi F_{n1} & \phi F_{n2} & \cdots & \phi F_{nn} \end{vmatrix} < 0$$

[8]Although not presented here, expansion path conditions for the cost-minimization model can be obtained by solving alternative pairs of the first n equations in (5.77) for ϕ and equating the results.

which is equivalent to requiring that the production function be strictly quasi-convex over the relevant domain.

Completeness would suggest a section at this point developing constrained revenue maximization for the multiproduct, multifactor case parallel to Section 5.2.c for the single-factor case. The development would culminate with the specification of conditional product supply functions. However, this development is left to the student as an exercise and we move directly to profit maximization and the usual unconditional product supply and factor demand ideas.

5.3.b Profit Maximization, Product Supply, and Factor Demand

In this section we establish necessary and sufficient conditions for profit maximization for a competitive multiproduct, multifactor firm with all factors allocable to the individual products. As noted earlier, optimization can be approached either as an unconstrained problem using the variable cost equation, 5.79, or as a constrained problem using the implicit production function.

We begin with the unconstrained formulation. Profit (exclusive of fixed cost) is given by

$$\pi \equiv TR - VC \equiv \sum_{j=1}^{m} p_j y_j - \bar{c}(r_1, \ldots, r_n, y_1, \ldots, y_m) \tag{5.81}$$

Taking first-partial derivatives of (5.81) and setting each equal to zero, we obtain the first-order conditions,

$$\frac{\partial \pi}{\partial y_j} = p_j - \frac{\partial \bar{c}}{\partial y_j} = 0 \qquad \text{for } j = 1, \ldots, m \tag{5.82}$$

which imply

$$p_j = \frac{\partial \bar{c}}{\partial y_j} \qquad \text{for } j = 1, \ldots, m \tag{5.83}$$

or the familiar profit-maximizing requirement that

$$MR_j = MC_j \qquad \text{for } j = 1, \ldots, m \tag{5.84}$$

Although many pairs can be formulated, it turns out that $(n - 1)$ equations of the form $r_i/r_l = F_i/F_l$ for $i, l = 1, \ldots, n$ and $i \neq l$ are sufficient to fully specify the input expansion path conditions.

The second-order condition for maximum profit requires that the principal minors of the unbordered Hessian alternate in sign, beginning with a negative sign. Thus,

$$\frac{\partial^2 \pi}{\partial y_j^2} < 0$$

$$\begin{vmatrix} \dfrac{\partial^2 \pi}{\partial y_1^2} & \dfrac{\partial^2 \pi}{\partial y_1 \partial y_2} \\[2ex] \dfrac{\partial^2 \pi}{\partial y_2 \partial y_1} & \dfrac{\partial^2 \pi}{\partial y_2^2} \end{vmatrix} > 0$$

$$\vdots$$

$$(-1)^k \begin{vmatrix} \dfrac{\partial^2 \pi}{\partial y_1^2} & \dfrac{\partial^2 \pi}{\partial y_1 \partial y_2} & \cdots & \dfrac{\partial^2 \pi}{\partial y_1 \partial y_k} \\[2ex] \vdots & \vdots & & \vdots \\[2ex] \dfrac{\partial^2 \pi}{\partial y_k \partial y_1} & \dfrac{\partial^2 \pi}{\partial y_k \partial y_2} & \cdots & \dfrac{\partial^2 \pi}{\partial y_k^2} \end{vmatrix} > 0 \qquad \text{for } k = 3, \ldots, m$$

$$(5.85)$$

which is equivalent to requiring that marginal cost of any output increase at an increasing rate and that the variable and/or total cost equation is strictly convex in all y in the neighborhood of the y values that satisfy the first-order conditions.

Solving the m equations in (5.83) for the m unknowns, y_j, we obtain the product supply equations,

$$y_j^* = y_j^*(r_1, r_2, \ldots, r_n, p_1, p_2, \ldots, p_m) \qquad \text{for } j = 1, \ldots, m \qquad (5.86)$$

Unconditional factor demand equations cannot be obtained directly from this formulation of the profit-maximization problem; however, they can be obtained by substituting (5.86) into the implicit production function and using the input expansion path conditions, alluded to in footnote 8, to eliminate all x_i except one, say x_l, to give the factor demand equation for x_l.

An alternative profit-maximization formulation which highlights determination of factor levels and factor demand as well as product levels and product supply is a Lagrangean approach. The Lagrangean profit function is expressed as

$$L\pi = \sum_{j=1}^{m} p_j y_j - \sum_{i=1}^{n} r_i x_i + \lambda F(x_1, \ldots, x_n, y_1, \ldots, y_m) \qquad (5.87)$$

Taking first-partial derivatives and setting each equal to zero, we obtain the following:

$$\frac{\partial L\pi}{\partial y_j} = p_j + \lambda \frac{\partial F}{\partial y_j} = 0 \qquad \text{for } j = 1, \dots, m \tag{5.88}$$

$$\frac{\partial L\pi}{\partial x_i} = -r_i + \lambda \frac{\partial F}{\partial x_i} = 0 \qquad \text{for } i = 1, \dots, n \tag{5.89}$$

$$\frac{\partial L\pi}{\partial \lambda} = F(\cdot) = 0 \tag{5.90}$$

From the *m* equations in (5.88) we obtain the output–output first-order conditions,

$$\frac{p_j}{p_k} = \frac{\partial F/\partial y_j}{\partial F/\partial y_k} \qquad \text{for } j,k = 1, \dots, m \tag{5.91}$$

which, by the implicit function rule, gives

$$\frac{p_j}{p_k} = -\frac{\partial y_k}{\partial y_j} \Rightarrow \frac{MR_j}{MR_k} = RPT_{jk} \qquad \text{for } j,k = 1, \dots, m \tag{5.92}$$

The *n* equations in (5.89) yield the factor–factor first-order conditions,

$$\frac{r_i}{r_l} = \frac{\partial F/\partial x_i}{\partial F/\partial x_l} \qquad \text{for } i,l = 1, \dots, n \tag{5.93}$$

Applying the implicit function rule to the right-hand side of (5.93) gives

$$\frac{r_i}{r_l} = -\frac{\partial x_l}{\partial x_i} \Rightarrow \frac{MFC_i}{MFC_l} = RTS_{il} \qquad \text{for } i,l = 1, \dots, n \tag{5.94}$$

Finally, combining the *j*th equation in (5.88) with the *i*th equation in (5.89) gives the factor–output first-order conditions,

$$-p_j \left[\frac{\partial F/\partial x_i}{\partial F/\partial y_j} \right] = r_i \qquad \text{for } \begin{cases} i = 1, \dots, n \\ j = 1, \dots, m \end{cases} \tag{5.95}$$

which, by the implicit function rule, gives

$$-p_j \left(-\frac{\partial y_j}{\partial x_i} \right) = r_i \Rightarrow MVP_{ij} = MFC_i \qquad \text{for } \begin{cases} i = 1, \dots, n \\ j = 1, \dots, m \end{cases} \tag{5.96}$$

Thus, in (5.92), (5.94), and (5.96) we have the output expansion path conditions, the factor expansion path conditions, and the profit-maximizing factor usage conditions, respectively, all from a single optimization problem. The only thing missing is the optimal output conditions, that is to say, $MR_j = MC_j$.[9]

Simultaneous solution of the first-order conditions, (5.88), (5.89), and (5.90), yields unconditional long-run factor demand [first equation in (5.97)] and product supply equations [second equation in (5.97)]. That is,

$$x_i^* = x_i^*(r_1, \ldots, r_n, p_1, \ldots, p_m) \quad \text{for } i = 1, \ldots, n$$

$$y_j^* = y_j^*(r_1, \ldots, r_n, p_1, \ldots, p_m) \quad \text{for } j = 1, \ldots, m \quad (5.97)$$

$$\lambda^* = \lambda^*(r_1, \ldots, r_n, p_1, \ldots, p_n)$$

In previous constrained optimization problems, the Lagrangean multiplier was given an economic interpretation such as marginal cost or marginal revenue; however, for (5.97) the Lagrangean multiplier, λ^*, does not have any useful economic interpretation. In earlier problems, our constraint was formed by taking the explicit form of an equation of interest and *creating* an implicit form by moving the independent variables to the left-hand side of the equation. In general, we were dealing with a constraint of the form $u - f(q_1, q_2) = 0$. In such cases, taking the partial of the Lagrangean function, say L, with respect to u yielded simply the Lagrangean multiplier, say λ. Thus, it was possible to interpret λ as the $\partial L / \partial u$, in other words, as a marginal revenue, marginal cost, or whatever. In the multiproduct, multifactor case, it is not clear what the dependent variable, u, might be or even that an explicit form exists. We have m possible y's and n possible x's, any or all of which could play the role of u or q's. Taking the partial of L with respect to a particular y, for example, does not give λ, but rather $\lambda \partial F / \partial y$, which has no obvious economic interpretation. Nevertheless, it should be noted that solution of the first-order conditions for this problem gives a solution for λ^*.

Any number of shorter-run factor demand functions or product supply functions could be deduced by holding various factors and/or products fixed in our derivations, in which case the fixed factors or product quantities would not be treated as choice variables in (5.87). Hence, the fixed factors or fixed product quantities would replace their corresponding prices in (5.97).

Using the Lagrangean approach we have deduced most of the familiar first-order (marginal) conditions for profit maximization for a multiproduct, multiallocable-factor firm from a single optimization problem. Unlike our

---

[9]Again, we caution the reader *not* to jump to the conclusion that the marginal revenue equal marginal cost condition can be deduced from (5.96) by merely rearranging terms such that $p_j = r_i / (\partial y_j / \partial x_i)$. Clearly p_j is marginal revenue for the perfectly competitive firm. But, as noted earlier, $r_i / (\partial y_j / \partial x_i)$ is *not* marginal cost in terms of output for the multifactor case as in the single-factor case. Marginal productivity of x_i in the production of y_j presumes that all factors and products except one of each are being held constant, whereas marginal cost presumes that all variable factors are expanded or contracted in least cost proportions. That is, $r_i / (\partial y_j / x_i)$ is not the marginal cost *function*, although it is equal to marginal cost at the optimal y and x levels.

previous formulations where all component parts were expressed solely as functions of inputs or of outputs, here revenue is expressed in terms of output, cost is expressed in terms of inputs, and the production function is used as a constraint to derive the various optimality relationships between pairs of outputs and inputs.

The second-order condition for maximum profit in this case requires that the relevant principal minors of the bordered Hessian alternate in sign, beginning with positive. To simplify statement of the second-order condition, consider the new notation, F_{uv}, to represent the second-order cross-partial derivative of F with the indices $u,v = 1,2,\ldots,m,m + 1,\ldots,m + n$. Then

$$\begin{vmatrix} 0 & F_1 & F_2 \\ F_1 & \lambda F_{11} & \lambda F_{12} \\ F_2 & \lambda F_{21} & \lambda F_{22} \end{vmatrix} > 0$$

$$\vdots$$

$$(-1)^s \begin{vmatrix} 0 & F_1 & F_2 & \cdots & F_s \\ F_1 & \lambda F_{11} & \lambda F_{12} & \cdots & \lambda F_{1s} \\ \vdots & \vdots & \vdots & & \vdots \\ F_s & \lambda F_{s1} & \lambda F_{s2} & \cdots & \lambda F_{ss} \end{vmatrix} > 0 \qquad \text{for } s = 3,\ldots,m + n \tag{5.98}$$

Second-order condition (5.98) is equivalent to requiring that the production function in implicit form be strictly convex in input/output space.

5.3.c Technical Interdependence

In the case of a single allocable factor the technical interdependence between two products was described in terms of a shift in marginal productivity. With two or more allocable factors, description of product interrelationships in this manner is not possible. That is, the production function cannot be expressed exclusively in terms of a *single* factor and the several products. For the two-factor case, for example, the mixed partial derivative, $\partial^2 x_1/\partial y_1 \partial y_2$ holding x_2 constant, is not conclusive regarding the interdependence between y_1 and y_2 since $\partial^2 x_2/\partial y_1 \partial y_2$ holding x_1 constant may differ in sign.

Likewise, the mixed partial derivative $\partial^2 y_j/\partial x_i \partial x_l$ is not conclusive regarding the interrelationship between factor pairs. Thus, it is not possible to develop a general technical factor interdependence or technical product interdependence classification scheme based solely on partial derivatives of a multiproduct, multifactor production function.[10] However, we can develop a limited notion of technical product interdependence by resorting to the mul-

---

[10]Additional discussion of the problem associated with defining and evaluating technical product interdependence in the multiproduct, multifactor case can be found in Carlson (1965, pp. 77–83). Also, Carlson discusses why the assumption of constant factor prices is essential to the classification.

tiproduct cost function rather than the production function as a basis for the classification scheme.

For the single-factor case it can be shown that a product–product classification based on $\partial^2 VC/\partial y_1 \, \partial y_2$ is equivalent to $\partial^2 x/\partial y_1 \, \partial y_2$ if the factor price is constant; that is,

$$r(\partial^2 x/\partial y_1 \, \partial y_2) = \partial^2(rx)/\partial y_1 \, \partial y_2 = \partial^2 VC/\partial y_1 \, \partial y_2 = \partial MC_1/\partial y_2$$

Thus, the products, y_1 and y_2, are said to be technically competing, independent, or complementary if the marginal cost of producing one product is increased, unchanged, or decreased, respectively, as the level of the other product is increased. This classification may be generalized to the multiproduct, multifactor case by taking appropriate partial derivatives of the cost function, $VC = \phi(y_1, \ldots, y_m, r_1, \ldots, r_n)$. That is, any pair of products, y_j and y_k, are technically competing, independent, or complementary as the sign of $\partial^2 VC/\partial y_j \, \partial y_k$ is positive, zero, or negative, respectively. The advantages of stating the technical classification in terms of changes in marginal costs are (1) the classification has intuitive appeal and (2) unlike the classification based on inverse marginal productivities, it is conclusive—there is only one mixed derivative for each pair of products.[11]

It was demonstrated in the single-product, multifactor case and in the multiproduct, single allocable factor case, that the concepts of technical interdependence and economic interdependence were consistent if perfect competition exists in all markets. In the multiproduct, multifactor case, consistency between technical and economic interdependence can be established between pairs of products using the technical classification based on multiproduct cost; however, only for the most short-run cases (where all factors but one are fixed) can a relationship between technical and economic factor–factor interdependence be established. In the authors' view, the more powerful and useful concept, to which we now turn, is that of economic interdependence. Concepts of technical interdependence are subsumed within economic interdependence in any event.

5.3.d Economic Interdependence

Consideration of the interrelationship between two factors, two products, or a product and a factor in an economic sense involves determining what happens to quantity demanded or quantity supplied as a particular price changes.

---

[11]The reader should note that while it is possible to develop a conclusive product–product classification system for the multiproduct, multifactor case, it is not possible to develop a conclusive factor–factor classification scheme. There is not an appropriate equivalent to the multiproduct cost function that allows the combining, so to speak, of the products in the same way that cost was the common denominator of dissimilar factors. Actually, one presumably could develop a parallel idea using joint revenue as a common denominator. However, we see no added conceptual or analytical leverage in such an undertaking.

To be more specific, consider the following definitions for factor interdependence, with $i \neq l$:

$$\frac{\partial x_i^*}{\partial r_l} < 0 \Rightarrow x_i \text{ and } x_l \text{ are } economically\ complementary$$

$$\frac{\partial x_i^*}{\partial r_l} > 0 \Rightarrow x_i \text{ and } x_l \text{ are } economically\ competing \text{ (or rival in demand)}$$

$$\frac{\partial x_i^*}{\partial r_l} = 0 \Rightarrow x_i \text{ and } x_l \text{ are } economically\ independent$$

Rationale for this classification was provided in Section 3.2.g.
For product interdependence, $j \neq k$,

$$\frac{\partial y_j^*}{\partial p_k} < 0 \Rightarrow y_j \text{ and } y_k \text{ are } economically\ competing$$

$$\frac{\partial y_j^*}{\partial p_k} > 0 \Rightarrow y_j \text{ and } y_k \text{ are } economically\ complementary$$

$$\frac{\partial y_j^*}{\partial p_k} = 0 \Rightarrow y_j \text{ and } y_k \text{ are } economically\ independent$$

the rationale for which was provided in Section 5.2.f.

Although we do not develop any classification for factor–product or product–factor cross-price effects, the reader should nevertheless note that $\partial y_j^*/\partial r_i$ and $\partial x_i^*/\partial p_j$ are also obtainable from (5.97), the profit-maximizing factor demand and product supply functions. For normal products and normal factors we would expect that $\partial y_j^*/\partial r_i < 0$ and $\partial x_i^*/\partial p_j > 0$. That is, we would expect an increase in a factor price to reduce the quantity supplied of any product utilizing that factor and conversely that an increase in a product price would engender an increase in factor usage. We will see in a moment that, not surprisingly, symmetry conditions require that $\partial y_j^*/\partial r_i = -\partial x_i^*/\partial p_j$.

5.3.e Comparative Statics of the Profit-Maximization Model

Another way of obtaining economic interdependence relationships is the traditional comparative statics approach involving total differentiation of the first-order conditions for profit maximization. In addition to economic interdependence relationships, which we now know can be obtained directly from the multiproduct supply and factor demand equations, the traditional approach conveniently allows deducing the signs of own- and cross-price effects and symmetry as related to properties of the underlying production function.

Comparative statics of the multiproduct, multifactor profit-maximization model can be examined by taking the total differential of first-order conditions, (5.88), (5.89), and (5.90). Using the notation F_{uv} to represent second-order cross-partial derivatives of F with $u,v = 1, \ldots, m, m + 1, \ldots, m + n$, the total differentials of the first-order conditions are

$$\lambda F_{11} dy_1^* + \cdots + \lambda F_{1,m+n} dx_n^* + F_1 d\lambda^* = -dp_1$$

$$\cdots\cdots\cdots\cdots\cdots\cdots\cdots\cdots\cdots\cdots\cdots\cdots\cdots\cdots\cdots\cdots\cdots\cdots\cdots$$

$$\lambda F_{m+n,1} dy_1^* + \cdots + \lambda F_{m+n,m+n} dx_n^* + F_{m+n} d\lambda^* = dr_n \qquad (5.99)$$

$$F_1 dy_1^* + \cdots + F_{m+n} dx_n^* = 0$$

With given price changes, (5.99) can be treated as a system of $(m + n + 1)$ equations in $(m + n + 1)$ unknowns, dy_j, dx_i, and $d\lambda$.

In matrix notation, this system of equations is given by

$$
\begin{bmatrix}
\lambda F_{11} & \cdots & \lambda F_{1,m+n} & F_1 \\
\vdots & & \vdots & \vdots \\
\lambda F_{m+n,1} & \cdots & \lambda F_{m+n,m+n} & F_{m+n} \\
F_1 & \cdots & F_{m+n} & 0
\end{bmatrix}
\begin{bmatrix}
dy_1^* \\
\vdots \\
dy_m^* \\
dx_1^* \\
\vdots \\
dx_n^* \\
d\lambda^*
\end{bmatrix}
=
\begin{bmatrix}
-dp_1 \\
\vdots \\
-dp_m \\
dr_1 \\
\vdots \\
dr_n \\
0
\end{bmatrix}
\qquad (5.100)
$$

Now let us solve the system of equations, 5.100, for dy_j^* and dx_i^*. Applying Cramer's rule, we obtain

$$dy_j^* = \frac{-D_{1j} dp_1 - \cdots - D_{mj} dp_m + D_{m+1,j} dr_1 + \cdots + D_{m+n,i} dr_n}{D} \qquad (5.101)$$

and

$$dx_i^* = \frac{-D_{1i} dp_1 - \cdots - D_{mi} dp_m + D_{m+1,i} dr_1 + \cdots + D_{m+n,i} dr_n}{D} \qquad (5.102)$$

where D is the determinant of the coefficient matrix in (5.100) and D_{uv} is the determinant of the cofactor of the element in the uth row and vth column of the coefficient matrix.

Equation 5.101 can be used to examine the effects on the quantity of a product supplied of changes in one or more prices, whereas equation 5.102 can be used to examine effects of price changes on the quantity of a factor demanded.

Setting all price differentials except one equal to zero, we find

$$\frac{\partial y_j^*}{\partial p_k} = -\frac{D_{kj}}{D}$$

$$\frac{\partial y_j^*}{\partial r_i} = \frac{D_{m+i,j}}{D}$$

$$\frac{\partial x_i^*}{\partial r_l} = \frac{D_{m+l,m+i}}{D} \qquad (5.103)$$

$$\frac{\partial x_i^*}{\partial p_j} = -\frac{D_{j,m+i}}{D}$$

Notice that economic interdependence can be deduced from the signs of D_{uv} and D. Assuming that the implicit production function is strictly convex, cross-partial derivatives of product supply and factor demand functions can be positive, negative, or zero, depending on the production function; not surprisingly, product supply functions must have a positive slope [$j = k$ in the first equation of (5.103)] and factor demand functions must have a negative slope [$i = l$ in the third equation of (5.103)]. We leave formal proof of these assertions to the reader. In the next section, the symmetry conditions are shown to follow from (5.103).

5.3.f Symmetry

Since the coefficient matrix in (5.100) is symmetric, the cofactor matrix is also symmetric. Therefore, $D_{uv} = D_{vu}$ for all u and v. Consequently, we deduce the following *symmetry conditions* from (5.103):

$$\frac{\partial y_j^*}{\partial p_k} = \frac{\partial y_k^*}{\partial p_j}$$

$$\frac{\partial y_j^*}{\partial r_i} = -\frac{\partial x_i^*}{\partial p_j} \qquad (5.104)$$

$$\frac{\partial x_i^*}{\partial r_l} = \frac{\partial x_l^*}{\partial r_i}$$

That is, the effect of a product price change on the production of an alternative product must be the same as a change in the price of the latter on the quantity produced of the former. The effect of a change in an input price on the production of a particular product must be opposite the effect of a change of the corresponding product price on usage of that factor. And, the effect of a change in an input price on the quantity employed of an alternative input must equal the effect of a change in the price of the latter on the former.

It is important to note that the symmetry conditions *always* hold for a profit-maximizing firm operating in a static, deterministic environment.[12] These conditions have important implications for empirical studies of factor demand and product supply. If an empirical study begins with an estimated production function, then the derived demand and supply functions will automatically satisfy the symmetry conditions. However, many empirical studies begin with specification of functional forms for the demand and supply equations rather than the production function. In this case, there is no assurance that the symmetry conditions are satisfied. Consequently, the analyst must make sure that the set of supply and demand equations is specified such that the symmetry requirements are met, *if* the demand and supply functions pertain to a *profit-maximizing firm.* Unfortunately, one finds few applications in the literature where symmetry conditions are imposed or statistically tested, yet profit maximization is presumed.

5.4 A DIGRESSION ON SUPPLY VERSUS MARGINAL COST

Since *Principles of Economics*, you have likely been taught that the product supply curve is the (inverse) marginal cost curve for a firm that operates in a competitive product market. In the case of single product production, this is indeed the case; however, in the multiproduct case the two concepts are not generally synonymous, as shall be demonstrated. Only if all other product quantities are held constant (a nearly trivial case) will inverse marginal cost be the supply function.

First consider the single product case. In Chapter 4, it was established that profit maximization for a competitive firm required that

$$p = MC = MC(r_1, \ldots, r_n, y) \tag{5.105}$$

Carefully note the arguments of the marginal cost function. Since marginal condition (5.105) shows optimal levels of y for given p and given factor prices, it follows that (5.105) is an inverse supply function. Thus, the supply equation can be obtained by solving (5.105) for y:

$$y = MC^{-1}(p, r_1, r_2, \ldots, r_n) = y^*(p, r_1, r_2, \ldots, r_n) \tag{5.106}$$

Now consider the multiproduct case. Arguments of the cost function, and thus the marginal cost functions, are factor prices and *quantities of products produced*:

$$MC_j = MC_j(r_1, \ldots, r_n, y_1, y_2, \ldots, y_m) \tag{5.107}$$

---

[12]It should be noted that cross-price effects are not symmetric in certain types of uncertainty models (see Pope, 1982) or in certain types of stochastic, dynamic models (see Taylor, 1984).

For multiproduct production with all output quantities variable, we know that the profit-maximizing conditions are $p_j = MC_j$ for all j; thus,

$$p_j = MC_j(r_1, \ldots, r_n, y_1, \ldots, y_m) \tag{5.108}$$

Taking the inverse of (5.108) to obtain y_j gives

$$y_j = MC_j^{-1}(r_1, \ldots, r_n, y_1, \ldots, y_{j-1}, p_j, y_{j+1}, \ldots, y_m) \tag{5.109}$$

Note, however, that the arguments of the supply function are

$$y_j^* = y_j^*(r_1, \ldots, r_n, p_1, \ldots, p_m) \tag{5.110}$$

A comparison of (5.109) and (5.110) shows that the (p_j, y_j) points traced out by MC_j are based on the assumption that all other outputs are fixed in quantity, while the points generated by the supply curve, (5.110), are based on the assumption that all other outputs are at their respective optimal levels. Hence, the inverse marginal cost curve when equated to p, and the supply curve are not, in general, synonymous in the multiproduct case.

As something of an aside, note that the jth supply function can be obtained from the jth inverse marginal cost function by substituting product supplies for the other y (not y_j) into (5.109). That is,

$$
\begin{aligned}
y_j^* &= MC_j^{-1}(r_1, \ldots, r_n, y_1^*, \ldots, y_{j-1}^*, p_j, y_{j+1}^*, \ldots, y_m^*) \\
&= MC_j^{-1}(r_1, \ldots, r_n, p_1, \ldots, p_m) \\
&= y_j^*(r_1, \ldots, r_n, p_1, \ldots, p_m)
\end{aligned}
\tag{5.111}
$$

Not surprisingly, the process represented in (5.111) gives the same result as the process in Section 5.3.b—equations 5.81 through 5.86.

5.5 TWO-PRODUCT PRODUCTION WITH AN ALLOCABLE AND A NONALLOCABLE FACTOR

Consider the case of production of two products, y_1 and y_2, produced with a single nonallocable factor, z, and a single allocable factor, $x_1 = x_{11} + x_{12}$, where x_{1j} is the amount of x_1 used in producing $y_j, j = 1,2$. Assuming that the process is decomposable, we can represent production with the two production functions,

$$
\begin{aligned}
y_1 &= f^1(x_{11}, z) \\
y_2 &= f^2(x_{12}, z)
\end{aligned}
\tag{5.112}
$$

That is, the process is like that represented in Figure 5.1f and discussed in Section 5.1.

Throughout this section we assume perfect competition in all markets to avoid quite messy notation for the mathematical derivations. However, after completing mathematical derivations for the competitive case, we state the marginal economic principles for the more general case of imperfect competition.

5.5.a Constrained Cost Minimization

Let us examine the conditions for minimization of cost for the firm that produces given levels of y_1 and y_2 using the technology described by the production functions in (5.112). Variable factor cost for the firm is

$$c \equiv r_1 x_{11} + r_1 x_{12} + r_z z = r_1(x_{11} + x_{12}) + r_z z \qquad (5.113)$$

which we want to minimize subject to (5.112). For this constrained minimization, we form the Lagrangean,

$$Lc = r_1(x_{11} + x_{12}) + r_z z + \lambda_1[y_1 - f^1(x_{11}, z)] + \lambda_2[y_2 - f^2(x_{12}, z)] \qquad (5.114)$$

where λ_j is the Lagrangean multiplier associated with the production function for y_j, $j = 1,2$. (For additional discussion of the Lagrangean technique for multiple constraints, see Chiang, 1974, Chap. 12.)

First-order conditions for minimization of (5.114) are

$$\frac{\partial Lc}{\partial x_{11}} = r_1 - \lambda_1 f^1_{x_{11}} = 0$$

$$\frac{\partial Lc}{\partial x_{12}} = r_1 - \lambda_2 f^2_{x_{12}} = 0$$

$$\frac{\partial Lc}{\partial z} = r_z - \lambda_1 f^1_z - \lambda_2 f^2_z = 0 \qquad (5.115)$$

$$\frac{\partial Lc}{\partial \lambda_1} = y_1 - f^1(x_{11}, z) = 0$$

$$\frac{\partial Lc}{\partial \lambda_2} = y_2 - f^2(x_{12}, z) = 0$$

where $f^1_{x_{11}}$ and $f^2_{x_{12}}$ denote $\partial f^1/\partial x_{11}$ and $\partial f^2/\partial x_{12}$, respectively, and f^1_z and f^2_z denote $\partial f^1/\partial z$ and $\partial f^2/\partial z$, respectively. These necessary conditions can be simultaneously solved for the conditional factor demand equations,

$$x^c_{11} = x^c_{11}(r_1, r_z, y_1, y_2)$$
$$x^c_{12} = x^c_{12}(r_1, r_z, y_1, y_2) \qquad (5.116)$$
$$z^c = z^c(r_1, r_z, y_1, y_2)$$

and for the Lagrangean multiplier functions,

$$\lambda_1^c = \lambda_1^c(r_1, r_z, y_1, y_2)$$

$$\lambda_2^c = \lambda_2^c(r_1, r_z, y_1, y_2)$$

(5.117)

Perhaps the only unusual feature of the factor demand functions in (5.116) is that *both* y_1 and y_2 are, in general, arguments of both allocable factor demand functions. For example, x_{11}^c depends on y_2 even though x_{11} is not used in producing y_2. This occurs because any change in y_2 will induce a cost-minimizing change in x_{12} and z. Since the nonallocable factor, z, changes in response to a change in y_2 we would then expect adjustment in x_{11} to the new level of z, as z is an argument in the y_1 production function as well as in the y_2 production function. Finally, the total demand for the allocable factor, x_1, is given by

$$x_1^c = x_{11}^c + x_{12}^c$$

$$= x_{11}^c(r_1, r_z, y_1, y_2) + x_{12}^c(r_1, r_z, y_1, y_2)$$

$$= x_1^c(r_1, r_z, y_1, y_2)$$

(5.118)

For this model, the Lagrangean multipliers, λ_j, are interpreted as follows: from (5.114) we have $\partial Lc/\partial y_j = \lambda_j$. If production function constraints are satisfied, then Lc in (5.114) is factor cost. Furthermore, if x_{1j} and z are evaluated at the cost-minimizing levels given by (5.116), then Lc represents the minimum cost of producing y_1 and y_2; hence, λ_j is the marginal cost of producing the jth output. That is, $\lambda_j^c = MC_j$ for $j = 1,2$. (The envelope theorem, presented in Chapter 6, is a formal proof of this relationship.)

How can we interpret the first-order conditions in (5.115) in economic terminology? First, note that if we solve the first equation of (5.115) for λ_1 and the second equation for λ_2 we obtain $\lambda_j = r_1/f_{x_{1j}}^j$. Substituting this result into the third equation for λ_1 and λ_2, and rearranging terms gives

$$\frac{r_z}{r_1} = \frac{f_z^1}{f_{x_{11}}^1} + \frac{f_z^2}{f_{x_{12}}^2}$$

(5.119)

which can be stated as

$$\frac{r_z}{r_1} = \frac{MPP_{z1}}{MPP_{11}} + \frac{MPP_{z2}}{MPP_{12}}$$

$$= RTS_{z,x_{11}}^1 + RTS_{z,x_{12}}^2$$

(5.120)

where MPP_{z1} and MPP_{z2} denote the marginal productivity of the nonallocable factor, z, in the production of y_1 and y_2, respectively; where MPP_{11} and MPP_{12} are the marginal productivity of the allocable factor, x_1, in the production of

y_1 and y_2, respectively; and where $RTS^1_{z,x_{11}}$ and $RTS^2_{z,x_{12}}$ denote the rate of technical substitution of the nonallocable factor for the allocable factor in the production of y_1 and y_2, respectively. Therefore, (5.120) tells us that we must *equate the sum of the RTSs of a nonallocable factor for an allocable factor to the factor–price ratio*, which is considerably different from the marginal economic principle for allocable factors used to produce a single product. In a loose sense, the summation in (5.120) results because z is used in producing two products of value and we must sum these two components of value.

5.5.b Profit Maximization

We now consider the economic and mathematical conditions for maximization of profit for the firm that produces y_1 and y_2 using the process described by the production functions in (5.112). Profit associated with y_1 cannot be treated separately from profit associated with y_2 because the nonallocable factor, z, links the products on the cost side. Thus, we define profit for the firm as

$$\begin{aligned} \pi &\equiv p_1 y_1 + p_2 y_2 - r_1 x_{11} - r_1 x_{12} - r_z z \\ &= p_1 y_1 + p_2 y_2 - r_1(x_{11} + x_{12}) - r_z z \end{aligned} \tag{5.121}$$

To convert the problem of maximizing (5.121) subject to (5.112) into an unconstrained optimization problem, we can substitute the production functions in (5.112) for y_j into (5.121). Hence,

$$\pi = p_1 f^1(x_{11},z) + p_2 f^2(x_{12},z) - r_1(x_{11} + x_{12}) - r_z z \tag{5.122}$$

First-order conditions for maximization of (5.122) are

$$\frac{\partial \pi}{\partial x_{11}} = p_1 f^1_{x_{11}} - r_1 = 0$$

$$\frac{\partial \pi}{\partial x_{12}} = p_2 f^2_{x_{12}} - r_1 = 0 \tag{5.123}$$

$$\frac{\partial \pi}{\partial z} = p_1 f^1_z + p_2 f^2_z - r_z = 0$$

Simultaneous solution of (5.123) for x_{11}, x_{12}, and z gives the ordinary (unconditional) factor demand equations,

$$\begin{aligned} x^*_{11} &= x^*_{11}(p_1,p_2,r_1,r_z) \\ x^*_{12} &= x^*_{12}(p_1,p_2,r_1,r_z) \\ z^* &= z^*(p_1,p_2,r_1,r_z) \end{aligned} \tag{5.124}$$

Product supply equations can be obtained by appropriate substitution of (5.124) into the production functions in (5.112). That is,

$$y_1^* = f^1(x_{11}^*, z^*) = y_1^*(p_1, p_2, r_1, r_z)$$
$$y_2^* = f^2(x_{12}^*, z^*) = y_2^*(p_1, p_2, r_1, r_z)$$

(5.125)

Notice that factor demand and product supply equations depend, in general, on all prices and not just the prices directly associated with each respective product. For example, y_1^* depends on p_2 because the products y_1 and y_2 are linked via the nonallocable factor, z.

Using terminology first introduced in Chapter 3 and given the assumption of perfect competition in all markets, first-order conditions (5.123) can be restated as

$$p_1 MPP_{11} = VMP_{11} = r_1$$
$$p_2 MPP_{12} = VMP_{12} = r_1$$
$$p_1 MPP_{z1} + p_2 MPP_{z2} = r_z$$

(5.126)

Thus, from the first two conditions in (5.126) we see that the marginal principle for an *allocable* factor requires that the value of the marginal productivity of the factor in production of each product must equal the price of the factor. Not surprisingly, this is the same marginal principle found for optimal factor usage for the single product case in Chapter 3. Taken together, the first two conditions in (5.126) imply that $VMP_{11} = VMP_{12}$, which makes intuitive sense since x_{11} and x_{12} are the same factor. Again, this is the familiar *principle of equimarginal value in use*.

The third condition in (5.126) is the marginal principle for a *nonallocable* factor; namely, that the value of the marginal productivity of z used in producing y_1 *plus* the value of the marginal productivity of z used in producing y_2 must equal the price of z. This also makes intuitive sense as z produces not only y_1 but also y_2; thus, z produces a dual value and we must sum the marginal values to measure the total contribution of z at the margin.

As in the single-product case, the factor-side marginal conditions may be expressed, for imperfect competition in all product and factor markets, as

$$MVP_{11} = MFC_{x_1}$$
$$MVP_{12} = MFC_{x_1}$$
$$MVP_{z1} + MVP_{z2} = MFC_z$$

(5.127)

The reader familiar with the theory of consumer behavior will note that the last equation of (5.127) is analogous to the case of a "pure public good" (see Henderson and Quandt, 1980, Chap. 11).

Output-side marginal economic principles for the decomposable two-product, single-allocable, and single-nonallocable factor model can be obtained by specifying profit (exclusive of fixed cost) as

$$\pi \equiv p_1 y_1 + p_2 y_2 - VC = p_1 y_1 + p_2 y_2 - \tilde{c}(y_1, y_2, r_1, r_z) \qquad (5.128)$$

where VC is obtained from the cost-minimization problem in the previous section. That is,

$$
\begin{aligned}
VC &= r_1(x_{11} + x_{12}) + r_z z \\
&= r_1(x_{11}^c + x_{12}^c) + r_z z^c \\
&= r_1[x_{11}^c(r_1, r_z, y_1, y_2) + x_{12}^c(r_1, r_z, y_1, y_2)] + r_z z^c(r_1, r_z, y_1, y_2) \\
&= \tilde{c}(y_1, y_2, r_1, r_z) \qquad (5.129)
\end{aligned}
$$

where x_{11}^c, x_{12}^c, and z^c are the conditional factor demand equations given by (5.116).

Maximizing (5.128) with respect to y_1 and y_2 results in the first-order conditions,

$$
\begin{aligned}
\frac{\partial \pi}{\partial y_1} &= p_1 - \frac{\partial \tilde{c}}{\partial y_1} = 0 \\[2mm]
\frac{\partial \pi}{\partial y_2} &= p_2 - \frac{\partial \tilde{c}}{\partial y_2} = 0
\end{aligned}
\qquad (5.130)
$$

which can be stated as

$$
\begin{aligned}
p_1 &= MC_1 = \lambda_1^c(y_1, y_2, r_1, r_z) \\
p_2 &= MC_2 = \lambda_2^c(y_1, y_2, r_1, r_z)
\end{aligned}
\qquad (5.131)
$$

where λ_j^c are solutions to the cost-minimization problem, namely, (5.117).

Notice that in general, the first-order conditions (5.130) or (5.131) must be *simultaneously* solved to obtain y_1^* and y_2^*, the product supply equations. This is because effects of the nonallocable factor on profit maximizing marginal conditions are reflected in the multiproduct cost function, $VC = \tilde{c}(y_1, y_2, r_1, r_z)$. If all factors of production were allocable to the individual products produced by a firm, then the variable cost function would be *additively separable*; that is, $VC = \tilde{c}^1(y_1, r_1, r_z) + \tilde{c}^2(y_2, r_1, r_z)$. However, because z is a nonallocable factor of production, the associated variable cost function is not additively separable, and we cannot solve first-order conditions *individually* for y_1 and y_2 to obtain the product supply functions.

For the case of imperfect competition in the product markets, (5.131) would be expressed as

$$
\begin{aligned}
MR_1 &= MC_1 \\
MR_2 &= MC_2
\end{aligned}
\qquad (5.132)
$$

With imperfect competition in the factor markets, factor prices will not appear as arguments in the variable cost function; that is, $VC = \tilde{c}(y_1, y_2)$. Again, $\tilde{c}(y_1, y_2)$ is not additively separable into $\tilde{c}^1(y_1) + \tilde{c}^2(y_2)$ because z is a nonallocable factor of production.

For allocable factors, we find that the marginal rules for resource allocation for the multiproduct firm are rather straightforward extensions of the single-product case. However, the marginal rule *for a nonallocable factor* requires that marginal value productivity of the factor in the production of each product must be summed and then equated with marginal factor cost.

5.6 ADDITIONAL REMARKS

The reader has undoubtedly noticed that we gave only one example problem in this chapter, and this problem was for a single allocable factor. We did not provide examples in the multiproduct, multifactor case represented by a single production function because we know of no *single equation* production function specifications that (*a*) are flexible, (*b*) satisfy the second-order conditions globally, (*c*) exhibit economic interdependence, and (*d*) are reasonably easy to manipulate mathematically. From an operational standpoint, the only workable alternative is to use the multiequation representation of the multiproduct, multifactor production process, *or* to use a dual approach which allows the analyst to bypass direct mathematical specification of a production function. Mathematical forms of production functions presented in Tables 2.1, 3.1, and 4.1 are suitable for use in the multiequation representations of multiproduct production, whereas the dual approach, and some appropriate mathematical specifications related thereto, are presented in the next chapter.

5.7 PROBLEMS

5-1. Consider $x = y_1^\alpha + y_2^\beta$. For what parameter values will the function be strictly quasi-convex? Strictly convex?

5-2. Develop comparative static relationships for the two-product, two-factor constrained cost-minimization problem.

5-3. Develop comparative static relationships for the two-product, two-factor constrained revenue-maximization problem.

5-4. Determine the profit-maximizing conditions and derive the factor demand and product supply equations for the production function

$$x = a_0 + a_1 y_1 + a_2 y_2 + \tfrac{1}{2} b_1 y_1^2 + \tfrac{1}{2} b_2 y_2^2 + b_3 y_1 y_2$$

$$= a_0 + A'Y + Y'BY \text{ in matrix form}$$

5-5. Derive the marginal economic principles for the two-product, single allocable factor case using the two-production function representation $y_1 = f^1(x_{11}, y_2)$ and $y_2 = f^2(x_{12}, y_1)$. How do the marginal principles differ for nonjoint production; that is, if $y_1 = f^1(x_{11})$ and $y_2 = f^2(x_{12})$? Deduce comparative static relationships for this model.

5-6. Obtain factor demand and product supply equations for the two-product, single allocable factor and single nonallocable factor case represented by the production functions, $y_1 = A_1 x_{11}^{\alpha} z^{\beta}$ and $y_2 = A_2 x_{12}^{\delta} z^{\gamma}$. What are the second-order conditions for profit maximization for this problem? (Note: Closed form solutions cannot be obtained except for special cases.)

5-7. Deduce comparative static relationships for the model given in Section 5.5.

5.8 SELECTED BIBLIOGRAPHY

Beattie, B. R., S. Thompson, and M. Boehlje. "Product Complementarity in Production: The By-Product Case." *So. J. Agric. Econ.* 6 (1974): 161–165.

Carlson, S. *A Study on the Pure Theory of Production.* New York: Sentry Press, 1965, Chapter 5.

Chiang, A. C. *Fundamental Methods of Mathematical Economics.* New York: McGraw-Hill, 1974.

Dano, Sven. *Industrial Production Models.* Vienna: Springer-Verlag, 1966. This book gives one of the most complete treatments of multiproduct production.

French, B. C., L. L. Sammet, and R. G. Bressler. "Economic Efficiency in Plant Operations with Special Reference to the Marketing of California Pears." *Hilgardia* 24 (1956). This report discusses some important elaborations to the conventional marginalist economic theory of production with special reference to the time dimension, plant segmentation, and multiple- rather than single-stage plants. The discussion provides a good example of the need for careful thought in defining variables and specifying production processes for mathematical and economic analysis.

Henderson, J. M., and R. E. Quandt. *Microeconomic Theory: A Mathematical Approach,* 3rd ed. New York: McGraw-Hill, 1980, Section 4-5.

Mittelhammer, R. C., S. C. Matulich, and D. Bushaw, "On Implicit Forms of Multiproduct–Multifactor Production Functions." *Amer. Jour. Agri. Econ.* 63 (1981): 164–168. This paper examines several issues regarding implicit function representation of multiproduct, multifactor production. Both single-equation and vector-equation representations of implicit production functions are discussed. Two important theorems pertaining to the single-equation representation of production are given in the paper.

Naylor, T. H. "A Kuhn–Tucker Model of the Multi-Product, Multi-Factor Firm." *So. Econ. J.* 31 (1965): 324–330.

Pfouts, R. W. "The Theory of Cost and Production in the Multi-Product Firm." *Econometrica* 29 (1961): 650–658.

Pope, R. D. "To Dual or Not to Dual?" *West. J. Agric. Econ.* 7 (1982): 337–351.

Taylor, C. R. "Stochastic Intertemporal Duality Theory." *Amer. J. Agric. Econ.* 66 (1984): 351–357.

CHAPTER 6

DUALITY THEORY

"Curiouser and curiouser!" cried Alice.
Alice's Adventures in Wonderland by Lewis Carroll.

To the uninitiated there seems to be something almost magical or hocus-pocus about duality. To the recently baptized, it seems almost too good to be true. To the veteran dualist some doubts begin to creep in about the generality of static, deterministic duality relationships. Thus, the comment by Alice seems appropos in the context of duality as well as for her particular "adventure in Wonderland."

Our purpose in this chapter is to introduce the serious student of production economics to the thrill and beauty, the theoretical and practical leverage, and the shortcomings of the duality approach. It was intimated in Chapter 1 that duality was useful to (or safe in the hands of) only those who thoroughly understand the primal approach. We strongly believe that. Because duality is so attractive, and yet so deceptive, we must chart our course carefully. Accordingly, in this chapter we proceed as follows. We begin with some background ideas about duality and then move to an illustration of the what and how of duality. We then establish the why of duality by providing proof and geometric interpretation of the fundamental theorems and lemmas underlying duality theory. Next is a discussion of properties that must reside in the parent functions utilized in duality, if the approach is to yield valid results. Finally, we conclude with some comments about alternative functional forms and implications of duality for empirical work.

6.1 BACKGROUND COMMENTS

Product supply and factor demand equations consistent with a firm's optimizing behavior can be obtained by two different but equivalent approaches. One approach, which was illustrated in previous chapters, is to explicitly solve an optimization problem. This approach is often called the primal setup. Another approach, called the *dual approach*, allows one to obtain product supply and factor demand equations by partial differentiation of an indirect objective function. (An indirect function will be defined shortly.)

Duality theory does not offer any particularly profound insights into production economics theory; nevertheless it is often quite useful because it is a more convenient way to obtain supply and demand equations than is the traditional (primal) approach. The dual approach is also useful (but there are pitfalls to be avoided) in generating a functional specification for a consistent set of supply and demand equations for econometric estimation. Because of the theoretical convenience offered by duality, it behooves us to fully understand duality theory. In recent years, this approach has become commonplace in economic literature.

All derivations provided in this chapter pertain only to a price-taking firm, although duality can be extended to some types of imperfect competition. Throughout this chapter, y and x refer to quantities, whereas y^*, y^r, x^*, and x^c can refer to either functions or quantities. Although both quantities and functions are denoted with the same symbol, interpretation of the notation should be apparent from the context in which it is used. In this chapter as in Chapter 5, all derivations implicitly assume a long-run production period or that all factors are variable (i.e., $i = 1, \ldots, n$). Accordingly, profit equations are presented without a fixed-cost component. At appropriate times the implications of a shorter-run situation (where certain factors are fixed) are discussed.

6.2 AN ILLUSTRATION OF DUALITY

To give a feel for what is generally involved in duality theory, we first present an illustration and examples. In Chapters 3 and 4, factor demand and product supply equations were derived for the single-product case from maximization of the profit function,

$$\pi \equiv py - \sum_{i=1}^{n} r_i x_i \tag{6.1}$$

subject to a production function,

$$y = f(x_1, \ldots, x_n) \tag{6.2}$$

Profit function (6.1) is referred to in duality literature as a *direct* profit function.

An important concept in duality is that of an *indirect profit function*, defined as the *maximum* profit associated with given product and factor prices. One way to obtain an indirect profit function, although impractical, would be to solve the primal problem as in Chapters 3 and 4 for (unconditional) factor demand and product supply functions. That is, assuming a single-product, two-factor case we ended up with

$$
\begin{aligned}
x_1^* &= x_1^*(p, r_1, r_2) \\
x_2^* &= x_2^*(p, r_1, r_2) \\
y^* &= y^*(p, r_1, r_2)
\end{aligned}
\tag{6.3}
$$

which were our demand functions for x_1 and x_2 and our supply function for y, respectively. Substituting (6.3), the optimal x's and y, into (6.1) gives

$$\tilde{\pi} \equiv py^*(p,r_1,r_2) - r_1x_1^*(p,r_1,r_2) - r_2x_2^*(p,r_1,r_2) \tag{6.4}$$

or, more compactly,

$$\tilde{\pi} = \tilde{\pi}(p,r_1,r_2) \tag{6.5}$$

That is, maximum profit, $\tilde{\pi}$, is now expressed as a function of the product and input prices.[1]

Of course, as alluded to above, such a procedure would be a self-defeating way to get an indirect profit function. (Nevertheless, it is an appropriate way to theoretically view the concept.) If one had to get an indirect profit function this way, one would not bother, because after all, we promised a short-cut method for obtaining the desired supply and demand functions. A procedure that requires one to use the supply and demand functions in order to derive the same is, of course, of questionable value. However, our purpose here is to make certain that we have a complete conceptual understanding of an indirect profit function.

Let a general indirect profit function for the single-product, n-variable factor case be denoted by

$$\tilde{\pi} = \tilde{\pi}(p,r_1, \ldots ,r_n) \tag{6.6}$$

Recall that in a profit-maximizing context, the optimal levels of the product and the factors are functions of the product and factor prices. Thus, a profit function that represents maximum profit associated with *given* product and factor prices, quite naturally, will have as arguments the appropriate prices with the variable factor quantities eliminated. [An indirect profit function can accommodate fixed factor quantities, although not shown in (6.6).]

Another important concept in duality is the *envelope theorem*. We prove the envelope theorem in the next section, but first show its applicability in economic optimization. A very important result of the envelope theorem, which is sometimes referred to as Hotelling's lemma, is that

$$\frac{\partial \tilde{\pi}}{\partial p} = y^*(p,r_1, \ldots ,r_n) \tag{6.7}$$

---

[1]It is conventional in duality literature to represent an indirect function (profit, cost, or utility) with a tilde (˜) overhead rather than an asterisk (∗) in the superscript position. That is, in duality literature, $\tilde{\pi}$ (rather than π^*) represents maximum or optimal profit whereas x^* and y^* represent optimal (profit-maximizing) input and output levels or functions, consistent with our usage in preceding chapters. Why a tilde rather than an asterisk, we are not sure, but we adopt the convention for the sake of consistency with other literature.

which is the product supply equation, and that

$$\frac{\partial \tilde{\pi}}{\partial r_i} = - x_i^*(p, r_1, \ldots, r_n) \tag{6.8}$$

which is the negative of the ith factor demand equation.

Before we prove these powerful results, consider the following illustration of Hotelling's lemma.

Example 6.1 Suppose we have the indirect profit function,

$$\tilde{\pi} = 2p^2 r_1^{-0.5} r_2^{-0.5} \tag{6.9}$$

By Hotelling's lemma we obtain the product supply equation,

$$\frac{\partial \tilde{\pi}}{\partial p} = y^* = 4pr_1^{-0.5} r_2^{-0.5} \tag{6.10}$$

and the factor demand equations,

$$\frac{\partial \tilde{\pi}}{\partial r_1} = -x_1^* = -p^2 r_1^{-1.5} r_2^{-0.5} \tag{6.11}$$

$$\frac{\partial \tilde{\pi}}{\partial r_2} = -x_2^* = -p^2 r_1^{-0.5} r_2^{-1.5} \tag{6.12}$$

The convenience of duality should be apparent. *If* we know the indirect profit function we can get the unconditional factor demand and product supply functions by simple partial differentiation—quite an analytical advantage, indeed.

Conceptually similar to an indirect profit function is an indirect cost function, defined as the minimum cost required to produce a specified output, y, at given factor prices. That is,

$$\tilde{c} = \tilde{c}(r_1, \ldots, r_n, y) \tag{6.13}$$

Another important envelope theorem result, usually referred to as Shephard's lemma, is that

$$\frac{\partial \tilde{c}}{\partial r_i} = x_i^c(r_1, \ldots, r_n, y) \tag{6.14}$$

which is the factor demand equation for the ith factor *conditional* on the output level, y (i.e., conditional factor demand).

Example 6.2   Suppose that we know the indirect cost function,

$$\tilde{c} = \frac{1}{8}y^2 r_1^{0.5} r_2^{0.5} \tag{6.15}$$

By Shephard's lemma, (6.14), we obtain the conditional factor demand equations associated with (6.15):

$$\frac{\partial \tilde{c}}{\partial r_1} = x_1^c = \frac{1}{16}y^2 r_1^{-0.5} r_2^{0.5} \tag{6.16}$$

$$\frac{\partial \tilde{c}}{\partial r_2} = x_2^c = \frac{1}{16}y^2 r_1^{0.5} r_2^{-0.5} \tag{6.17}$$

The analytical convenience, and thus appeal, of duality for deriving product supply and factor demand functions is vividly demonstrated in the two preceding examples. That is, if one knows the indirect profit and indirect cost functions, the desired conditional factor demands and unconditional product supply and factor demand functions fall out immediately by simple partial differentiation of the appropriate parent indirect function. Contrast this with what we went through in Chapters 3 and 4 using the primal approach. The trick, of course, lies in knowing (appropriately specifying) the parent indirect functions—functions that will yield supply and demand equations that have the necessary (desirable) properties of symmetry, zero-degree homogeneity in prices, and so forth. Another concern is whether the underlying production function is tractable or recoverable from the indirect functions. These matters are addressed in later sections. We turn now to proof of the envelope theorem—a crucial theorem underlying duality theory.

6.3 THE ENVELOPE THEOREM

Hotelling's lemma and Shephard's lemma are specific cases of a general result called the envelope theorem. To prove the envelope theorem, consider the problem of maximizing, with respect to the w's, the function,

$$q = f(w_1, \ldots, w_n; \alpha) \tag{6.18}$$

where α is a parameter (e.g., a price) or a set of parameters. Assuming that $f(\cdot)$ is once continuously differentiable, the first-order conditions for maximization of (6.18) are

$$\partial f / \partial w_i = 0 \quad \text{for } i = 1, \ldots, n \tag{6.19}$$

It was shown in previous chapters that equations like (6.19) can be solved for functions of the form:

$$w_i^* = w_i^*(\alpha) \tag{6.20}$$

That is, a set of optimal w's in terms of the parameter (or parameter vector), α, is implied by (6.19). Substituting (6.20) into the objective function, (6.18), gives the indirect objective function,

$$q^* = f[w_1^*(\alpha), \ldots, w_n^*(\alpha); \alpha] \tag{6.21}$$

According to the envelope theorem, the rate of change of a maximum function, q^*, with respect to a parameter change, α, allowing all w_i to adjust, is equal to the rate of change in the direct function, q, with respect to a change *in α, holding all w_i constant.* To see this, consider the partial derivative of (6.21) with respect to α; that is,

$$\frac{\partial q^*}{\partial \alpha} = \sum_{i=1}^{n} \frac{\partial f}{\partial w_i^*} \frac{\partial w_i^*}{\partial \alpha} + \frac{\partial f}{\partial \alpha} \tag{6.22}$$

Since the $\partial f / \partial w_i^*$ are all zero *when the first-order conditions,* (6.19), *are satisfied,* it follows that (6.22) simplifies to

$$\frac{\partial q^*}{\partial \alpha} = \frac{\partial f}{\partial \alpha} \tag{6.23}$$

which establishes the envelope theorem.

The left-hand side of (6.23) is the change in the maximum value of q, allowing all w_i to adjust, whereas the right-hand side of (6.23) is the change in q holding all w_i fixed. Again, remember that (6.23) holds only for $\partial f / \partial \alpha$ evaluated at w_i^*. After proving the product supply property of Hotelling's lemma in the next section, we will graphically illustrate the envelope theorem as applied to direct and indirect profit functions and then return to a proof of the factor demand property of Hotelling's lemma.

6.3.a Hotelling's Lemma

Consider applying the envelope theorem to an indirect profit function. For generality, we will consider the multiproduct, multifactor case. Recall that previous derivations have shown that the profit-maximizing output levels are a function of prices (i.e., the product supply equations) and that profit-maximizing factor levels are functions of prices (i.e., factor demand equations). Let these output and factor levels be denoted by y_j^* and x_i^*, respectively. Given y_j^* and x_i^*, maximum or indirect profit is given by

$$\tilde{\pi} \equiv \sum_j p_j y_j^* - \sum_i r_i x_i^* \tag{6.24}$$

for the perfectly competitive firm. (The notation, Σ_j and Σ_i is shorthand for $\Sigma_{j=1}^{m}$ and $\Sigma_{i=1}^{n}$, respectively.)

Consider the change in maximum profit when the kth product price changes. Since y_j^* and x_i^* are differentiable functions of prices, we have

$$\frac{\partial \tilde{\pi}}{\partial p_k} = y_k^* + \sum_j p_j \frac{\partial y_j^*}{\partial p_k} - \sum_i r_i \frac{\partial x_i^*}{\partial p_k} \tag{6.25}$$

[Note: the summation over j in the second term of (6.25) includes $j = k$ because *all* y_j^*s are a function of *all* product and factor prices including the kth product price.] For Hotelling's lemma to hold, the last two terms in (6.25) must sum to zero. To show this, recall that the first-order conditions for profit maximization in the multiproduct, multifactor case are

$$\begin{aligned} p_j + \lambda(\partial F/\partial y_j) &= 0 && \text{for } j = 1, \ldots, m \\ -r_i + \lambda(\partial F/\partial x_i) &= 0 && \text{for } i = 1, \ldots, n \end{aligned} \tag{6.26}$$

where λ is the Lagrangean multiplier and F is the implicit production function, $F(y_1, \ldots, y_m, x_1, \ldots, x_n) = 0$.

Substitution of (6.26) into (6.25) for r_i and p_j gives

$$\frac{\partial \tilde{\pi}}{\partial p_k} = y_k^* - \left[\lambda \sum_j \frac{\partial F}{\partial y_j^*} \frac{\partial y_j^*}{\partial p_k} + \lambda \sum_i \frac{\partial F}{\partial x_i^*} \frac{\partial x_i^*}{\partial p_k} \right] \tag{6.27}$$

Consider now the production function associated with profit-maximizing output and factor levels:

$$0 = F(y_1^*, \ldots, y_m^*, x_1^*, \ldots, x_n^*) \tag{6.28}$$

Since the x_i^* and the y_j^* are differentiable functions of prices, the right-hand side of (6.28) is a differentiable function of prices, and we have

$$\frac{\partial(0)}{\partial p_k} = 0 = \sum_j \frac{\partial F}{\partial y_j^*} \frac{\partial y_j^*}{\partial p_k} + \sum_i \frac{\partial F}{\partial x_i^*} \frac{\partial x_i^*}{\partial p_k} \tag{6.29}$$

Substitution of (6.29) into (6.27) gives

$$\frac{\partial \tilde{\pi}}{\partial p_k} = y_k^* - \lambda(0) = y_k^* \tag{6.30}$$

as was to be shown.

The final step in proving Hotelling's lemma is to show that the function, y_k^*, is equal to the quantity, y_k. This step is made by noting that from the direct profit function, π, we have $\partial \pi / \partial p_k = y_k$, and from the envelope theorem,

(6.23), we have $\partial\tilde{\pi}/\partial p_k = \partial\pi/\partial p_k$. Thus, we have established the product supply property of Hotelling's lemma, namely, that

$$\frac{\partial\tilde{\pi}}{\partial p_k} = y_k^*(p_1, \ldots, p_m, r_1, \ldots, r_n) = y_k \quad (6.31)$$

The envelope theorem as applied to direct and indirect profit functions, that is, $\partial\tilde{\pi}/\partial p_k = \partial\pi/\partial p_k$ can be illustrated with the aid of Figure 6.1. In Figure 6.1, $\tilde{\pi}$ represents the indirect profit function (for the single product, single-factor case) as related to product price for a given factor price, r^0.[2] Since direct profit does not involve optimization, there is a family of direct profit equations that can be drawn in Figure 6.1; π^0, π^1, π^2, and π^3, which differ only by the fixed levels of x and y, illustrate four equations in this family. The direct profit equations are linear because product price enters the direct profit equation linearly; for example, $\pi^0 = py^0 - r^0x^0$ where y^0, r^0, and x^0 are constants.

It follows from our maximization postulate that for a given product price, say p^0, indirect profit will equal direct profit only if direct profit is evaluated at $x^*(p^0,r^0)$ and $y^*(p^0,r^0)$; that is, at maximum profit given (p^0,r^0). Thus, if $x^0 = x^*(p^0,r^0)$ and $y^0 = y^*(p^0,r^0)$, then π^0 in Figure 6.1 will equal $\tilde{\pi}(p^0,r^0)$ at point A. Note, however, that if $y^0 = y^*(p^0,r^0)$ but $x^3 \neq x^*(p^0,r^0)$, then $\pi^3 < \tilde{\pi}$. Thus, it intuitively follows from profit maximization that $\tilde{\pi}$ is an (upper) *envelope* to the family of direct profit equations.

The *envelope theorem* follows from this envelope relationship. The partial derivative $\partial\tilde{\pi}/\partial p$ gives the slope of $\tilde{\pi}$ in Figure 6.1 evaluated at a particular point, say A, for the price p^0. Since this is the slope of a tangent to $\tilde{\pi}$ at point A, $\partial\tilde{\pi}/\partial p = \partial\pi^0/\partial p = y^0$. Again, this envelope relationship holds *only for* $\partial\pi/\partial p$ evaluated at x^* and y^*. For example, if $y^1 \neq y^*(p^0,r^0)$, then $\partial\tilde{\pi}/\partial p \neq \partial\pi^1/\partial p = y^1$ evaluated at p^0, since π^1 is not tangent to $\tilde{\pi}$ at point A (rather it is tangent at point B).

In other words, the envelope theorem says that $\partial\tilde{\pi}/\partial p$, which allows y and x to adjust to the price change [see (6.25)], is equal to $\partial\pi/\partial p$, which does not allow y and x to adjust to the price change, as long as $\partial\pi/\partial p$ is evaluated at y^* and x^*.

To prove the factor demand property of Hotelling's lemma, consider

$$\frac{\partial\tilde{\pi}}{\partial r_l} = \sum_j p_j \frac{\partial y_j^*}{\partial r_l} - \sum_i r_i \frac{\partial x_i^*}{\partial r_l} - x_l^* \quad (6.32)$$

Substitution of first-order conditions (6.26) into (6.32) for r_i and p_j gives

$$\frac{\partial\tilde{\pi}}{\partial r_l} = -\left(\lambda \sum_j \frac{\partial F}{\partial y_j^*}\frac{\partial y_j^*}{\partial r_l} + \lambda \sum_i \frac{\partial F}{\partial x_i^*}\frac{\partial x_i^*}{\partial r_l}\right) - x_l^* \quad (6.33)$$

---

[2]In Section 6.5.b, we will prove that $\tilde{\pi}$ is convex in all prices if the underlying production function, $y = f(x)$, is strictly concave.

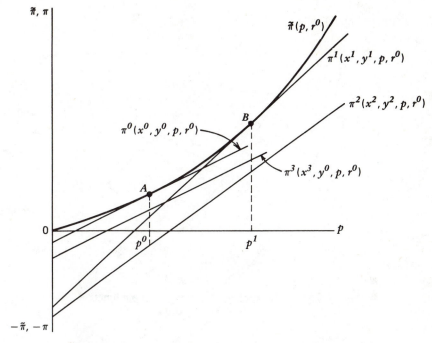

Figure 6.1. An illustration of the envelope theorem applied to profit functions.

Partial differentiation of (6.28) with respect to r_l yields

$$0 = \sum_j \frac{\partial F}{\partial y_j^*} \frac{\partial y_j^*}{\partial r_l} + \sum_i \frac{\partial F}{\partial x_i^*} \frac{\partial x_i^*}{\partial r_l} \tag{6.34}$$

Substituting (6.34) into (6.33) gives

$$\frac{\partial \tilde{\pi}}{\partial r_l} = (0) - x_l^* = - x_l^* \tag{6.35}$$

From the direct profit function, we have $\partial \pi / \partial r_l = -x_l$ and from the envelope theorem we know $\partial \pi / \partial r_l = \partial \tilde{\pi} / \partial r_l$, thus establishing the factor demand property of Hotelling's lemma:

$$\frac{\partial \tilde{\pi}}{\partial r_l} = -x_l^*(p, r_1, \ldots, r_n) = - x_l \tag{6.36}$$

Figure 6.2 shows an indirect profit function in three dimensions for a single-product, single-factor case. Notice that $\tilde{\pi}$ gets smaller as r increases; and $\tilde{\pi}$ increases as p increases, as one would expect. Convexity of $\tilde{\pi}$ for a

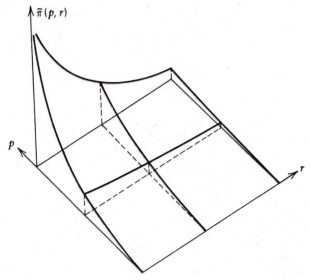

Figure 6.2. An illustration of an indirect profit function.

production function that satisfies second-order conditions is established in Section 6.5.b.

6.3.b Shephard's Lemma

Derivation of Shephard's lemma is parallel to the derivation of Hotelling's lemma. It was shown in Chapter 4 that the factor levels that minimize the cost of producing fixed levels of the products depend on factor prices and all output quantities. Letting x_i^c denote the level of factor i that minimizes cost, the indirect cost function is given by

$$\bar{c} \equiv \sum_i r_i x_i^c \tag{6.37}$$

Since the x_i^c are differentiable functions of all factor prices, we have

$$\frac{\partial \bar{c}}{\partial r_l} = \sum_i r_i \frac{\partial x_i^c}{\partial r_l} + x_l^c \tag{6.38}$$

For Shephard's lemma to hold, the first term on the right-hand side of (6.38) must equal zero. To show this, recall the Lagrangean for the constrained cost-minimization problem:

$$Lc = \sum_i r_i x_i + \lambda F(y_1, \ldots, y_m, x_1, \ldots, x_n) \tag{6.39}$$

with first-order conditions,

$$r_i + \lambda \frac{\partial F}{\partial x_i} = 0 \qquad \text{for } i = 1, \dots, n \qquad (6.40)$$

Substitution of (6.40) into (6.38) for r_i gives

$$\frac{\partial \tilde{c}}{\partial r_l} = -\lambda \sum_i \frac{\partial F}{\partial x_i^c} \frac{\partial x_i^c}{\partial r_l} + x_l^c \qquad (6.41)$$

Now consider the production function constraint evaluated at cost-minimizing factor levels:

$$0 = F(y_1, \dots, y_m, x_1^c, \dots, x_n^c) \qquad (6.42)$$

Partial differentiation of (6.42) with respect to r_l gives

$$\frac{\partial(0)}{\partial r_l} = 0 = \sum_i \frac{\partial F}{\partial x_i^c} \frac{\partial x_i^c}{\partial r_l} \qquad (6.43)$$

Substitution of (6.43) into (6.41) gives

$$\frac{\partial \tilde{c}}{\partial r_l} = -\lambda(0) + x_l^c = x_l^c \qquad (6.44)$$

which was to be shown. And, from the envelope theorem, we have

$$\frac{\partial \tilde{c}}{\partial r_l} = \frac{\partial Lc}{\partial r_l} = x_l^c = x_l \qquad (6.45)$$

thus establishing Shephard's lemma.

The envelope theorem applied to direct and indirect cost functions is illustrated in Figure 6.3. In this case, indirect cost is a *lower* envelope to the family of direct cost equations given by $c \equiv r_1 x_1 + r_2 x_2$. The envelope theorem says that at point A, the slope of the indirect cost equation is equal to the slope of the direct cost equation *if* the slope of the direct cost equation is evaluated at the cost-minimizing values, x_1^0 and x_2^0. Note that for suboptimal values of x, such as x_1^2 and x_2^2, the slope of the direct cost equation does not necessarily equal the slope of the indirect cost equation.

An indirect cost function, in terms of isocost curves, is illustrated in Figure 6.4. Note that the isoindirect cost curves are for a single level of y, y^0. Moving away from the origin represents an increase in both factor prices, thus costs, $\tilde{c}$, increase for given y^0. There is another set of isoindirect cost curves for another value of y.

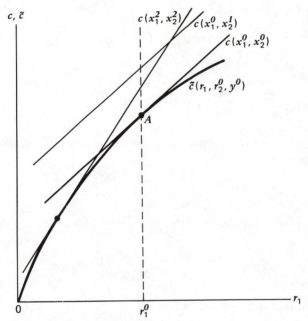

Figure 6.3. An illustration of the envelope theorem applied to cost functions.

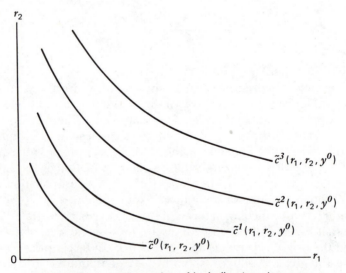

Figure 6.4. An illustration of isoindirect cost curves.

234

6.3.c A Revenue Counterpart to Shephard's Lemma

Although rarely used, a revenue counterpart to Shephard's lemma exists. Letting y_j^c denote the level of y_j that maximizes revenue subject to fixed levels of the factors of production, we can define the indirect revenue function,

$$\tilde{R} \equiv \sum_j p_j y_j^c \tag{6.46}$$

Since the conditional product supply equations, y_j^c, are differentiable functions of product prices, partial differentiation of (6.46) with respect to p_k gives

$$\frac{\partial \tilde{R}}{\partial p_k} = \sum_j p_j \frac{\partial y_j^c}{\partial p_k} + y_k^c \tag{6.47}$$

The Lagrangean formulation of the constrained revenue-maximization problem is

$$LR = \sum_j p_j y_j + \eta F(y_1, \dots, y_m, x_1, \dots, x_n) \tag{6.48}$$

with first-order conditions

$$\frac{\partial LR}{\partial y_j} = p_j + \eta \frac{\partial F}{\partial y_j} = 0 \tag{6.49}$$

which implies that

$$p_j = - \eta \frac{\partial F}{\partial y_j} \qquad \text{for } j = 1, \dots, m \tag{6.50}$$

Substitution of (6.50) into (6.47) for p_j gives

$$\frac{\partial \tilde{R}}{\partial p_k} = - \eta \sum_j \frac{\partial F}{\partial y_j^c} \frac{\partial y_j^c}{\partial p_k} + y_k^c \tag{6.51}$$

From the implicit production function evaluated at y_j^c, we have

$$\frac{\partial (0)}{\partial p_k} = 0 = \sum_j \frac{\partial F}{\partial y_j^c} \frac{\partial y_j^c}{\partial p_k} \tag{6.52}$$

Therefore,

$$\frac{\partial \tilde{R}}{\partial p_k} = - \eta(0) + y_k^c \tag{6.53}$$

and from the envelope theorem $\partial \tilde{R}/\partial p_k = \partial LR/\partial p_k$; thus

$$\frac{\partial \tilde{R}}{\partial p_k} = y_k^c = y_k \qquad (6.54)$$

which is the revenue counterpart to Shephard's lemma.

6.3.d Symmetry Conditions

Envelope results for the profit-maximization, cost-minimization, and revenue-maximization models provide an easy means for establishing the symmetry conditions for these models.

First consider the profit-maximization model. From Hotelling's lemma we have

$$\frac{\partial \tilde{\pi}}{\partial r_i} = - x_i^* \qquad (6.55)$$

Consider now the partial derivative of (6.55) with respect to some other factor price, r_l; that is,

$$\frac{\partial^2 \tilde{\pi}}{\partial r_i \partial r_l} = - \frac{\partial x_i^*}{\partial r_l} \qquad (6.56)$$

From Young's theorem, we know that a cross-partial derivative is invariant with respect to the order of differentiation; that is,

$$\frac{\partial^2 \tilde{\pi}}{\partial r_i \partial r_l} \equiv \frac{\partial^2 \tilde{\pi}}{\partial r_l \partial r_i} \qquad (6.57)$$

Thus, from (6.56) and (6.57)

$$\frac{\partial x_i^*}{\partial r_l} = \frac{\partial x_l^*}{\partial r_i} \qquad \text{for } i \neq l \qquad (6.58)$$

Similarly, it can be shown that

$$\frac{\partial y_j^*}{\partial r_i} = - \frac{\partial x_i^*}{\partial p_j}$$

$$\frac{\partial y_j^*}{\partial p_k} = \frac{\partial y_k^*}{\partial p_j} \qquad \text{for } j \neq k \qquad (6.59)$$

Equations (6.58) and (6.59) represent the full set of symmetry conditions for the competitive profit-maximizing firm.

Using the above logic, one can establish for the constrained cost-minimization problem that

$$\frac{\partial x_i^c}{\partial r_l} = \frac{\partial x_l^c}{\partial r_i} \qquad \text{for } i \neq l \tag{6.60}$$

and that

$$\frac{\partial y_j^c}{\partial p_k} = \frac{\partial y_k^c}{\partial p_j} \qquad \text{for } j \neq k \tag{6.61}$$

for the constrained revenue-maximization model.

6.4 PRIMAL–DUAL–PRIMAL EXAMPLE

It was noted earlier that product supply and factor demand relationships obtained from profit maximization or from constrained cost minimization (the primal problems) are implicit in indirect profit and cost functions, which are the foundation for the dual approach. Thus, by now we should be comfortable (at least intuitively) with the notion that the two approaches are equivalent. However, since the preceding derivations were rather abstract, it may be instructive to consider a concrete example. Be forewarned that the primal–dual–primal circle that we will follow in this example is not illustrative of how duality is used for theoretical derivations or for empirical applications; the usual starting point for duality is specification of an indirect function rather than specification of a production function.

6.4.a Profit Maximization

Let us begin with a primal approach and maximize profit for the production function,

$$y = 2x_1^{0.5}x_2^{0.25} \tag{6.62}$$

Substitution of (6.62) into the profit function gives

$$\pi = 2px_1^{0.5}x_2^{0.25} - r_1x_1 - r_2x_2 \tag{6.63}$$

The first-order conditions for maximum profit are

$$r_1 = px_1^{-0.5}x_2^{0.25} \tag{6.64}$$

$$r_2 = 0.5px_1^{0.5}x_2^{-0.75} \tag{6.65}$$

Simultaneous solution of (6.64) and (6.65) gives the demand equation for factor 1,

$$x_1^* = 0.5p^4r_1^{-3}r_2^{-1} \tag{6.66}$$

and the demand equation for factor 2,

$$x_2^* = 0.25p^4r_2^{-2}r_1^{-2} \tag{6.67}$$

The product supply equation can be obtained by substitution of (6.66) and (6.67) into the production function, (6.62), yielding

$$y^* = p^3r_1^{-2}r_2^{-1} \tag{6.68}$$

Before turning to the dual approach, note that the symmetry conditions are satisfied for the primal problem; namely,

$$\frac{\partial x_1^*}{\partial r_2} = \frac{\partial x_2^*}{\partial r_1} = -0.5p^4r_1^{-3}r_2^{-2} \tag{6.69}$$

$$\frac{\partial y^*}{\partial r_1} = -\frac{\partial x_1^*}{\partial p} = -2p^3r_1^{-3}r_2^{-1} \tag{6.70}$$

and

$$\frac{\partial y^*}{\partial r_2} = -\frac{\partial x_2^*}{\partial p} = -p^3r_1^{-2}r_2^{-2} \tag{6.71}$$

Now consider the same problem in a duality setting. Substitution of the product supply equation, (6.68), and the factor demand equations, (6.66) and (6.67), into the direct profit function, (6.1), gives the indirect profit function,

$$\tilde{\pi} = 0.25p^4r_1^{-2}r_2^{-1} \tag{6.72}$$

Specification of an indirect profit function, such as (6.72), is usually the starting point for a dual approach; that is, one would normally not know the supply and demand equations, for that is what one typically wishes to deduce in an empirical application using the dual approach.

Applying Hotelling's lemma to (6.72) we obtain the product supply equation,

$$\frac{\partial \tilde{\pi}}{\partial p} = p^3r_1^{-2}r_2^{-1} = y^* \tag{6.73}$$

which checks with (6.68), and the factor demand equations,

$$\frac{\partial \tilde{\pi}}{\partial r_1} = -0.5 p^4 r_1^{-3} r_2^{-1} = -x_1^* \tag{6.74}$$

and

$$\frac{\partial \tilde{\pi}}{\partial r_2} = -0.25 p^4 r_1^{-2} r_2^{-2} = -x_2^* \tag{6.75}$$

which check with (6.66) and (6.67), respectively.

6.4.b Cost Minimization

Let us now consider duality from a cost of production standpoint. The direct (variable) cost function is

$$c \equiv r_1 x_1 + r_2 x_2 \tag{6.76}$$

which we want to minimize for a given level of output, y, subject to the production function (6.62). As shown in Chapter 3, the cost-minimizing bundle of inputs can be found by solving the Lagrangean minimization problem,

$$Lc = r_1 x_1 + r_2 x_2 + \lambda(y - 2x_1^{0.5} x_2^{0.25}) \tag{6.77}$$

Cost-minimizing values of x_1 and x_2 are obtained by simultaneous solution of

$$\frac{\partial Lc}{\partial x_1} = r_1 - \lambda x_1^{-0.5} x_2^{0.25} = 0 \tag{6.78}$$

$$\frac{\partial Lc}{\partial x_2} = r_2 - 0.5\lambda x_1^{0.5} x_2^{-0.75} = 0 \tag{6.79}$$

$$\frac{\partial Lc}{\partial \lambda} = y - 2x_1^{0.5} x_2^{0.25} = 0 \tag{6.80}$$

From (6.78) and (6.79) we can obtain the expansion path,

$$x_2 = \frac{r_1 x_1}{2r_2} \tag{6.81}$$

Substitution of (6.81) into (6.80) for x_2 gives the conditional demand equation for factor 1,

$$x_1^c = 0.5 y^{1.33} r_1^{-0.33} r_2^{0.33} \tag{6.82}$$

Solving the expansion path (6.81) for x_1 as a function of x_2, r_1, and r_2, and substituting the result into (6.80) gives the conditional demand equation for factor 2,

$$x_2^c = 0.25y^{1.33}r_1^{0.67}r_2^{-0.67} \tag{6.83}$$

The indirect cost function can be obtained by substituting the conditional factor demand equations, (6.82) and (6.83), into the direct cost function, (6.76), which yields

$$\tilde{c} = 0.75y^{1.33}r_1^{0.67}r_2^{0.33} \tag{6.84}$$

As noted previously, specification of an indirect cost function is usually the starting point for duality derivations involving cost. Note that application of Shephard's lemma to (6.84) will yield the conditional factor demand equations, (6.82) and (6.83). Also note that

$$\frac{\partial \tilde{c}}{\partial y} = y^{0.33}r_1^{0.67}r_2^{0.33} = MC \tag{6.85}$$

which is, as it should be, the inverse of the product supply equation, (6.68), when MC is equated to p.

We have shown how an indirect cost function can be derived on the basis of a production function. Let us now pose the question: Can we derive a production function from an indirect cost function? As long as the cost function is homogeneous of degree one in factor prices and satisfies the curvature properties, which are discussed in a later section, the answer to this question is yes, except in a special case (Silberberg, 1978, p. 311). For our example, it is relatively easy to obtain the production function, but for most indirect cost functions it is a quite difficult task.

In general, the production function can be derived from the set of conditional factor demand equations that are obtained by applying Shephard's lemma to the indirect cost function. Variables in this set of equations are y, x_1, x_2, r_1, and r_2, so the object of the game is to eliminate r_1 and r_2 by simultaneous solution of the conditional factor demand equations for y as a function of x_1 and x_2. Since the factor demand equations are homogeneous of degree zero in factor prices, we can express $r = r_1/r_2$ (an explanation of this property of homogeneous functions is given in Section 2.2.j). So doing simplifies the factor demand equations, (6.82) and (6.83), to

$$x_1^c = 0.5y^{1.33}r^{-0.33} \tag{6.86}$$

and

$$x_2^c = 0.25y^{1.33}r^{0.67} \tag{6.87}$$

respectively.

Squaring each side of (6.86) and rearranging terms in both equations yields

$$r^{0.67} = 0.25y^{2.67}(x_1^c)^{-2} \tag{6.88}$$

and

$$r^{0.67} = 4x_2^c y^{-1.33} \tag{6.89}$$

Equating (6.88) and (6.89) to eliminate r gives

$$4x_2^c y^{-1.33} = 0.25y^{2.67}(x_1^c)^{-2} \tag{6.90}$$

which, upon rearranging terms and dropping the superscript, c, yields

$$y = 2x_1^{0.5}x_2^{0.25} \tag{6.91}$$

which is the production function used in the primal problem. [*Note:* Recall that x_1^c and x_2^c can represent either factor quantities or functions. In equations (6.86) through (6.90) the appropriate interpretation is factor quantity.]

6.5 PROPERTIES OF DUAL FUNCTIONS

Applications of duality theory typically begin with specification of a functional form for an indirect profit function or an indirect cost function, as opposed to beginning with a production function as is done in the primal approach. In derivations in previous chapters and earlier in this chapter, we discovered that certain properties must exist in production functions and in factor demand and product supply equations—properties that were a consequence of theoretical derivations and not functional form (e.g., symmetry), properties required to apply the calculus (e.g., differentiable functions), and properties needed if solutions to first-order conditions were to give an optimum (e.g., concavity). Thus, it should come as no surprise that, in an initial phase of a duality application, one needs to ask: Are there any special properties that an indirect function should possess if resulting economic derivations are to be consistent with their primal counterpart? Several theorems in duality literature address this question; motivation and/or proof is provided for the most important properties.[3] To simplify notation, the proofs are given for the single-product, two-factor case; the proofs can be extended in a straightforward way to the more general case—a task that we leave to the reader.

---

[3]For a rigorous discussion of these theorems, see Diewert (1974).

6.5.a Properties of Indirect Cost Functions

Consider the following properties for an indirect cost function, $\bar{c}(\mathbf{r},y)$ where $\mathbf{r}$ is a *vector* of factor prices:

1. $\bar{c}(\mathbf{r},y) \geq 0$ for $\mathbf{r} \geq 0$ and $y > 0$.

2. $\bar{c}(\mathbf{r}^l,y) \geq \bar{c}(\mathbf{r}^0,y)$ for $\mathbf{r}^l \geq \mathbf{r}^0$.

3. $\bar{c}(\mathbf{r},y)$ is homogeneous of degree one in $\mathbf{r}$; that is, $\bar{c}(t\mathbf{r},y) = t\bar{c}(\mathbf{r},y)$ for $t > 0$.

4. $\dfrac{\partial \bar{c}(\mathbf{r},y)}{\partial r_i}$ is homogeneous of degree zero in $\mathbf{r}$.

5. $\bar{c}(\mathbf{r},y)$ is weakly concave in $\mathbf{r}$ if the explicit production function, $y = f(\mathbf{x})$, where $\mathbf{x}$ is a vector of variable factors, is strictly quasi-concave in the variable factors (or the implicit production function is strictly quasi-convex).

6. $\bar{c}(\mathbf{r},y) = y^{(1/\xi)}\bar{A}(\mathbf{r})$ if the production function is homogeneous of degree ξ in variable factors; further if $\xi = 1$, $\bar{A}(\mathbf{r})$ is the average variable cost function.[4]

Property (1) states that cost should be nonnegative for nonnegative prices and positive output—certainly a reasonable proposition. Property (2) states that variable costs are relatively higher for relatively higher factor prices. This property follows from the fact that the indirect cost function gives the minimum cost of producing alternative output levels for given factor prices. The (minimum) cost must, of course, rise for every output level as factor prices rise. Property (3) makes intuitive sense, because if all factor prices double, we would expect costs to double. For proof of Property (3) for the two-factor case, see Section 3.2.i.

Property (4) follows from (3) in that the derivative of a function that is homogeneous of degree one is homogeneous of degree zero (see Section 2.2.j). The significance of this property is that conditional factor demand equations are homogeneous of degree zero in prices; that is, changing all factor prices by a constant proportion will not change the quantity of input that is demanded, given the output level. Property (4), in addition to Property (3), was proven for the two-factor case in Section 3.2.i.

Property (5) is difficult to intuitively or geometrically visualize, so we offer a mathematical proof for the case of two factors. A function $g(w_1,w_2)$ is weakly concave if $g_{11} < 0$, $g_{22} < 0$, and the determinant of the matrix of second derivatives of g (the Hessian) is nonnegative. First, we establish the sign of g_{11} and g_{22} for an indirect cost function. Consider

$$\bar{c}(r_1,r_2,y) = r_1 x_1^c + r_2 x_2^c \tag{6.92}$$

---

[4]Recall that ξ is the quasi-function coefficient, which is constant and represents the degree of homogeneity *if* the production function exhibits constant proportional returns to proportional variation in the variable factors. Using ξ rather than ϵ (the function coefficient) allows greater generality (i.e., it allows for the possibility of fixed factors as implicit arguments in $\bar{c}$).

From Shephard's lemma, we know

$$\frac{\partial \tilde{c}(r_1, r_2, y)}{\partial r_i} = \tilde{c}_i = x_i^c \tag{6.93}$$

and thus

$$\tilde{c}_{il} = \partial x_i^c / \partial r_l \qquad \text{for } i, l = 1, 2 \tag{6.94}$$

From (6.94), the $\tilde{c}_{ii}$'s, which are the slopes of the conditional factor demand equations, are our equivalent to g_{11} and g_{22}. Assuming that the production function is strictly concave, then the own-price effect is negative (see Section 3.2.j for a proof); that is, $\tilde{c}_{ii} < 0$ for $i = 1, 2$, thus satisfying two of the conditions for concavity.

Consider now the determinant of the matrix of second derivatives of (6.92):

$$|H| = \begin{vmatrix} \dfrac{\partial x_1^c}{\partial r_1} & \dfrac{\partial x_1^c}{\partial r_2} \\[2ex] \dfrac{\partial x_2^c}{\partial r_1} & \dfrac{\partial x_2^c}{\partial r_2} \end{vmatrix} \tag{6.95}$$

Inspection of (6.95) does not reveal anything very enlightening about the sign of H, so we must rely on a trick along with three corollaries of a theorem on determinants in order to determine the sign of (6.95). The first corollary is that if a matrix B is obtained from a matrix A by multiplying a column of A by k, then the determinant of A is the determinant of B divided by k. The second corollary states that if B is obtained from A by replacing a column of A by itself plus another column, then the determinant of A is the determinant of B. The third corollary is that if all elements in a column of A are zero, then the determinant of A is zero.

Now for the trick: multiply the first column of (6.95) by r_1 and the second column by r_2; then add column 1 to column 2 to get

$$|H| = \frac{1}{r_1 r_2} \begin{vmatrix} \dfrac{\partial x_1^c}{\partial r_1} r_1 & \left(\dfrac{\partial x_1^c}{\partial r_2} r_2 + \dfrac{\partial x_1^c}{\partial r_1} r_1 \right) \\[3ex] \dfrac{\partial x_2^c}{\partial r_1} r_1 & \left(\dfrac{\partial x_2^c}{\partial r_2} r_2 + \dfrac{\partial x_2^c}{\partial r_1} r_1 \right) \end{vmatrix} \tag{6.96}$$

Since x_1^c and x_2^c are homogeneous of degree zero in prices, then by Euler's homogeneity theorem

$$|H| = \frac{1}{r_1 r_2} \begin{vmatrix} \dfrac{\partial x_1^c}{\partial r_1} r_1 & 0 \\[2ex] \dfrac{\partial x_2^c}{\partial r_1} r_1 & 0 \end{vmatrix} = 0 \qquad \text{for } r_1, r_2 > 0 \qquad (6.97)$$

thus establishing that $\tilde{c}(r_1, r_2, y)$ is weakly concave. This result holds in the general case as well.

Property (6) is often referred to as the Samuelson–Shephard duality theorem. Before considering the general case, we offer an intuitive proof for the case of constant returns to the quasi-scale factor. In this case $\tilde{c}(y, \mathbf{r}) = y\tilde{A}(\mathbf{r})$. Now, recall that the expansion path for a homogeneous function (assuming constant factor prices) is a ray-line passing through the origin in variable factor space, and that average variable cost is constant for all levels of output. Thus, variable cost along the expansion path, which is reflected in the indirect cost function, will be directly proportional to output. So, if we let $\tilde{A}(\mathbf{r})$ be average cost along the expansion path, variable cost will be $\tilde{c}(\mathbf{r}, y) = y\tilde{A}(\mathbf{r})$. Note that average cost along an expansion path depends on factor prices but not on output in the constant returns case.

For a production function homogeneous of degree ξ in the variable factors, Property (6) can be generalized to $\tilde{c}(\mathbf{r}, y) = y^{(1/\xi)}\tilde{A}(\mathbf{r})$. In this general case, $\tilde{A}(\mathbf{r})$ is no longer average cost, but a proportionality factor that depends on factor prices. To prove this more general case, recall from Section 4.1.d that, given constant factor prices, $\lambda_{vc} = 1/\xi$, where ξ is the degree of homogeneity of the production function in variable factors, and λ_{vc} is variable cost flexibility, defined as $\lambda_{vc} = (\%\Delta VC / \%\Delta y) = (\partial VC/\partial y)(y/VC)$ or in duality notation, $\lambda_{vc} = (\partial \tilde{c}/\partial y)(y/\tilde{c})$. To establish that $\tilde{c}$ is homogeneous of degree $1/\xi$ in y, suppose for the moment that $\tilde{c}$ is homogeneous of degree $1/k$ in y. If we can show that $\lambda_{vc} = 1/k$, then k must equal ξ, the degree of homogeneity of the production function in the variable factors. Letting $VC \equiv \tilde{c} = y^{(1/k)}\tilde{A}(\mathbf{r})$, then $MC = \partial \tilde{c}/\partial y = (1/k)y^{[(1/k)-1]}\tilde{A}(\mathbf{r})$ and $AVC \equiv \tilde{c}/y = y^{[(1/k)-1]}\tilde{A}(\mathbf{r})$. Thus, $\lambda_{vc} = MC/AVC = 1/k$. Since we know that $\lambda_{vc} = 1/\xi$ from above, then it follows that $\tilde{c}$ is homogeneous of degree $1/\xi$.[5]

Note that application of Shephard's lemma to Property (6) implies that conditional factor demand functions, x_i^c, are also homogeneous of degree $1/\xi$ in y. That is,

$$x_i^c = \frac{\partial \tilde{c}}{\partial r_i} = y^{1/\xi} \frac{\partial \tilde{A}(\mathbf{r})}{\partial r_i}$$

[5]For an alternative proof, see Silberberg (1978, pp. 303–307); also see Section 4.1.d of this text.

is homogeneous of degree $1/\xi$ because the partial derivative of $\tilde{c}$ with respect to any variable or parameter, except y, preserves the homogeneity in terms of y.

✳ 6.5.b Properties of Indirect Profit Functions

Now for the essential properties of an indirect profit function, $\tilde{\pi}(\mathbf{p},\mathbf{r})$, where $\mathbf{p}$ and $\mathbf{r}$ are price vectors:

1. $\tilde{\pi}(\mathbf{p},\mathbf{r}) \geq 0$ for $\mathbf{p},\mathbf{r} \geq 0$.
2. $\tilde{\pi}(\mathbf{p}^l,\mathbf{r}) \geq \tilde{\pi}(\mathbf{p}^0,\mathbf{r})$ for $\mathbf{p}^l \geq \mathbf{p}^0$.
3. $\tilde{\pi}(\mathbf{p},\mathbf{r}^l) \leq \tilde{\pi}(\mathbf{p},\mathbf{r}^0)$ for $\mathbf{r}^l \geq \mathbf{r}^0$.
4. $\tilde{\pi}(\mathbf{p},\mathbf{r})$ is homogeneous of degree one in all prices.
5. $\partial\tilde{\pi}(\mathbf{p},\mathbf{r})/\partial p_j$ and $\partial\tilde{\pi}(\mathbf{p},\mathbf{r})/\partial r_i$ are homogeneous of degree zero in all prices.
6. $\tilde{\pi}(\mathbf{p},\mathbf{r})$ is convex in all prices if the explicit production function, $y = f(\mathbf{x})$, where $\mathbf{x}$ is a vector of variable factors, is strictly concave (or the implicit production function is strictly convex).

The first four properties are apparent from previous discussion of properties of indirect cost functions, and Property (5) follows from Property (4). As a proof of Property (6), consider the indirect profit function for the case of a single product and two variable factors:

$$\tilde{\pi} = py^* - r_1 x_1^* - r_2 x_2^* \tag{6.98}$$

For y^*, x_1^*, and x_2^* to give maximum profit, $\tilde{\pi}$, the matrix of second derivatives (Hessian) of (6.98) must be positive semidefinite. The Hessian matrix is

$$|H| = \begin{vmatrix} \dfrac{\partial^2\tilde{\pi}}{\partial r_1^2} & \dfrac{\partial^2\tilde{\pi}}{\partial r_1\partial r_2} & \dfrac{\partial^2\tilde{\pi}}{\partial r_1\partial p} \\[2ex] \dfrac{\partial^2\tilde{\pi}}{\partial r_2\partial r_1} & \dfrac{\partial^2\tilde{\pi}}{\partial r_2^2} & \dfrac{\partial^2\tilde{\pi}}{\partial r_2\partial p} \\[2ex] \dfrac{\partial^2\tilde{\pi}}{\partial p\partial r_1} & \dfrac{\partial^2\tilde{\pi}}{\partial p\partial r_2} & \dfrac{\partial^2\tilde{\pi}}{\partial p^2} \end{vmatrix} = \begin{vmatrix} -\dfrac{\partial x_1^*}{\partial r_1} & -\dfrac{\partial x_1^*}{\partial r_2} & -\dfrac{\partial x_1^*}{\partial p} \\[2ex] -\dfrac{\partial x_2^*}{\partial r_1} & -\dfrac{\partial x_2^*}{\partial r_2} & -\dfrac{\partial x_2^*}{\partial p} \\[2ex] \dfrac{\partial y^*}{\partial r_1} & \dfrac{\partial y^*}{\partial r_2} & \dfrac{\partial y^*}{\partial p} \end{vmatrix} \tag{6.99}$$

Elements of the matrix on the far right-hand side of (6.99) were obtained from the matrix on the left by using Hotelling's lemma, for example,

$$- \partial x_1^*/\partial r_1 = \partial^2\tilde{\pi}/\partial r_1^2 = \left(\frac{\partial}{\partial r_1}\right)\left(\frac{\partial\tilde{\pi}}{\partial r_1}\right) = \frac{\partial}{\partial r_1}(-x_1^*).$$

The Hessian, H, is positive semidefinite if all principal minors of the Hessian matrix are nonnegative. All of the diagonal elements of (6.99) are positive because the assumed shape (strict concavity) of the production function gives an upward sloping product supply equation and downward sloping factor demand equations. Thus, the first principal minor of H, $- \partial x_1^* / \partial r_1$, is positive.

Showing that the second principal minor is nonnegative requires a few tricks. From the first-order conditions for profit maximization, we know that

$$pf_2(x_1^*, x_2^*) - r_2 = 0 \tag{6.100}$$

Differentiating (6.100) with respect to r_1 gives

$$pf_{21} \frac{\partial x_1^*}{\partial r_1} + pf_{22} \frac{\partial x_2^*}{\partial r_1} = 0 \tag{6.101}$$

and differentiating with respect to r_2 yields

$$pf_{21} \frac{\partial x_1^*}{\partial r_2} + pf_{22} \frac{\partial x_2^*}{\partial r_2} = 1 \tag{6.102}$$

Now recall the tricks we used in showing that the indirect cost function was concave. Multiplying the first row of the second principal minor, M_2, by pf_{21} and multiplying the second row by pf_{22}, gives

$$|M_2| = \begin{vmatrix} -\dfrac{\partial x_1^*}{\partial r_1} & -\dfrac{\partial x_1^*}{\partial r_2} \\[2ex] -\dfrac{\partial x_2^*}{\partial r_1} & -\dfrac{\partial x_2^*}{\partial r_2} \end{vmatrix} = \frac{1}{p^2 f_{21} f_{22}} \begin{vmatrix} pf_{21}\dfrac{\partial x_1^*}{\partial r_1} & pf_{21}\dfrac{\partial x_1^*}{\partial r_2} \\[2ex] pf_{22}\dfrac{\partial x_2^*}{\partial r_1} & pf_{22}\dfrac{\partial x_2^*}{\partial r_2} \end{vmatrix} \tag{6.103}$$

Replacing the first row of M_2 by the sum of both rows yields

$$|M_2| = \frac{1}{p^2 f_{21} f_{22}} \begin{vmatrix} \left(pf_{21}\dfrac{\partial x_1^*}{\partial r_1} + pf_{22}\dfrac{\partial x_2^*}{\partial r_1} \right) & \left(pf_{21}\dfrac{\partial x_1^*}{\partial r_2} + pf_{22}\dfrac{\partial x_2^*}{\partial r_2} \right) \\[2ex] pf_{22}\dfrac{\partial x_2^*}{\partial r_1} & pf_{22}\dfrac{\partial x_2^*}{\partial r_2} \end{vmatrix} \tag{6.104}$$

From (6.101) and (6.102) the first element of M_2 is zero, and the second element of the first row is one, so

$$|M_2| = \frac{-\partial x_2^* / \partial r_1}{pf_{21}} \geq 0 \tag{6.105}$$

which is nonnegative since f_{21} and $\partial x_2^* / \partial r_1$ have opposite signs (see Section 3.2.g), if the production function is strictly concave.

As a final step in establishing the convexity of $\bar{\pi}(\mathbf{p},\mathbf{r})$, we must show that $|H|$ is nonnegative. Multiplying the columns of H by r_1, r_2, and p, respectively, and replacing the third column by the sum of all columns, gives

$$|H| = \frac{1}{r_1 r_2 p} \begin{vmatrix} -\dfrac{\partial x_1^*}{\partial r_1} r_1 & -\dfrac{\partial x_1^*}{\partial r_2} r_2 & \left(-\dfrac{\partial x_1^*}{\partial p} p - \dfrac{\partial x_1^*}{\partial r_1} r_1 - \dfrac{\partial x_1^*}{\partial r_2} r_2 \right) \\[2ex] -\dfrac{\partial x_2^*}{\partial r_1} r_1 & -\dfrac{\partial x_2^*}{\partial r_2} r_2 & \left(-\dfrac{\partial x_2^*}{\partial p} p - \dfrac{\partial x_2^*}{\partial r_1} r_1 - \dfrac{\partial x_2^*}{\partial r_2} r_2 \right) \\[2ex] \dfrac{\partial y^*}{\partial r_1} r_1 & \dfrac{\partial y^*}{\partial r_2} r_2 & \left(\dfrac{\partial y^*}{\partial p} p + \dfrac{\partial y^*}{\partial r_1} r_1 + \dfrac{\partial y^*}{\partial r_2} r_2 \right) \end{vmatrix} \quad (6.106)$$

Since x_1^*, x_2^*, and y^* are homogeneous of degree zero in prices, then by Euler's homogeneity theorem the last column of H is all zeros; therefore, $|H| = 0$ and $\bar{\pi}(\mathbf{p},\mathbf{r})$ is (weakly) convex in prices if the production function is strictly concave in $\mathbf{x}$.

Properties of indirect cost functions and indirect profit functions that have been presented hold for any number of factors. Moreover, the properties as well as the envelope theorem hold for the multiproduct, multifactor case under static, deterministic assumptions. For a rigorous discussion of the general case, see Diewert, 1974. The reader should also be aware that duality theory can be applied to consumer behavior (see Silberberg, 1978; Varian, 1978; Diewert, 1974) or to a firm that maximizes a well-defined utility function rather than profit.

6.6 FORMS OF INDIRECT COST AND PROFIT FUNCTIONS

Table 6.1 presents indirect profit and cost functions for the commonly used single-product, multifactor production functions that were discussed in previous chapters. Diligent students are encouraged to derive the indirect profit function for a Cobb–Douglas production function, whereas especially eager students may find great joy in deriving the duality mapping for the CES function. Readers desiring to work with the quadratic production function would make their life much easier by doing all calculations (optimization and derivation of supply and demand functions) in matrix notation.

Indirect profit and cost functions associated with the transcendental production function are mathematically intractable, although they do exist mathematically. The functions are mathematically intractable because one cannot solve an expression of the form, $x^a c^{bx} = g$, explicitly for x except in special (usually trivial) cases.

The functions shown in Table 6.1 can be generalized in a straightforward way to more than two factors, a task which we leave to the reader. It should be pointed out that by no means does Table 6.1 give an exhaustive list of functional forms that can be used to represent indirect cost or profit functions

Table 6.1 Indirect Cost and Profit Functions Associated with Various Production Functions

Production Function		Indirect Cost Function
Generalized Cobb–Douglas[a]	$y = A x_1^{b_1} x_2^{b_2}$	$\bar{c} = [y A^{-1} r_1^{b_1} r_2^{b_2}]^{1/a} \left[\left(\dfrac{b_1}{b_2} \right)^{b_2/a} + \left(\dfrac{b_2}{b_1} \right)^{b_1/a} \right]$
Quadratic[b,c]	$y = a_0 + a_1 x_1 + a_2 x_2$ $\quad + \frac{1}{2} b_1 x_1^2 + \frac{1}{2} b_2 x_2^2$ $\quad + b_3 x_1 x_2$	$\bar{c} = 2(y - \gamma_0)^{1/2} (\beta_1 r_1^2 + \beta_2 r_2^2$ $\quad + \beta_3 r_1 r_2)^{1/2}$ for $y > \gamma_0$
CES	$y = A[b x_1^{-g} + (1 - b) x_2^{-g}]^{-v/g}$	$\bar{c} = y^{1/v} A^{-1/v} [b^{1/(1+g)} r_1^{g/(1+g)}$ $\quad + (1 - b)^{1/(1+g)} r_2^{g/(1+g)}]^{(1+g)/g}$
Transcendental	$y = A x_1^{a_1} e^{b_1 x_1} x_2^{a_2} e^{b_2 x_2}$	Mathematically intractable

Production Function		Indirect Profit Function
Generalized Cobb–Douglas[a]	$\bar{\pi} = (1 - a)[p A r_1^{-b_1} r_2^{-b_2} b_1^{b_1} b_2^{b_2}]^{1/(1-a)}$	
Quadratic[b]	$\bar{\pi} = p \gamma_0 - \eta_1 r_1 - \eta_2 r_2 - \dfrac{\beta_1 r_1^2}{2p} - \dfrac{\beta_2 r_2^2}{2p} - \dfrac{\beta_3 r_1 r_2}{p}$	
CES	$\bar{\pi} = p^{1/(1-v)} v^{1/(1-v)} (1-v) A^{1/(1-v)} [b^{1/(1+g)} r_1^{g/(1+g)}$ $\quad + (1-b)^{1/(1+g)} r_2^{g/(1+g)}]^{-v(1+g)/g(1-v)}$	
Transcendental	Mathematically intractable	

[a] $a = b_1 + b_2$.
[b] Let $A = b_1 b_2 - b_3^2$. Then $\beta_1 = b_2/A$; $\beta_2 = b_1/A$; $\beta_3 = -b_3/A$; $\gamma_0 = a_0 - (b_1 a_1^2 + b_2 a_2^2 - 2 a_1 a_2 b_3)/A$; $\eta_1 = -a_1 \beta_1 - a_2 \beta_3$; and $\eta_2 = -a_1 \beta_3 - a_2 \beta_2$
[c] The indirect cost equation was obtained by integrating the inverse of the product supply equation from γ_0 to y. Note that conditional factor demand equations, which are practically impossible to obtain as relatively simple expressions using the direct (primal) approach, can be obtained by this circuitous route.

for single-product, multifactor production (see, for example, the article by Lau in Fuss and McFadden, 1978).

As noted in Chapter 5, the prospect of specifying a flexible, easy to manipulate production function to represent truly joint production appears to be extremely remote. Fortunately, duality offers more promise for the analyst who is not interested in the production function as such. Table 6.2 presents the generalized Leontief indirect profit function and the translog indirect cost function for multiproduct, multifactor production. Although the production functions associated with these indirect functions are not mathematically tractable, they do exist, and they do have desirable properties if appropriate restrictions on the indirect functions are satisfied. Thus, the functions in Table 6.2 may be useful in empirical studies that are not concerned with the production function itself but are directed toward factor demand and/or product supply functions.

Finally, analysts desiring to empirically apply duality should recognize

Table 6.2 Indirect Profit or Cost Functions for Which the Multiproduct, Multifactor Production Function Is Mathematically Intractable.

Function	Indirect Profit ($\bar{\pi}$) or Cost ($\bar{c}$) Function	Notes
Generalized Leontief	$\bar{\pi} = \sum_j \sum_k a_{jk} p_j^{0.5} p_k^{0.5}$ $- \sum_j \sum_i b_{ji} p_j^{0.5} r_i^{0.5}$ $- \sum_i \sum_l g_i r_i^{0.5} r_l^{0.5}$	1. $a_{jk} \geq 0$ for all j and k, $b_{ji} \geq 0$ for all j and i, and $g_{il} \geq 0$ for all i and l are required for global convexity (and thus for concavity of the implied production function) 2. Some of the a_{jk}, b_{ji}, and g_{il} can be negative and still have local convexity 3. Symmetry requires $a_{jk} = a_{kj}$ for $j \neq k$, and $g_{il} = g_{li}$ for $i \neq l$
Translog	$\ln \bar{c} = a_0 + \sum_i a_i \ln r_i + \sum_j b_j \ln y_j$ $+ \frac{1}{2} \sum_i \sum_l g_{il} \ln r_i \ln r_l$ $+ \frac{1}{2} \sum_j \sum_k f_{jk} \ln y_j \ln y_k$ $+ \frac{1}{2} \sum_i \sum_j h_{ij} \ln r_i \ln y_j$	1. $\sum_i a_i = 1$, $\sum_i g_{il} = 0$, and $\sum_i h_{ij} = 0$ are required for homogeneity of degree one in factor prices 2. $\sum_j b_j = 1$, $\sum_j f_{jk} = 0$, and $\sum_i h_{ij} = 0$ are required for constant returns to scale 3. $g_{il} = g_{li}$ for $i \neq l$ and $f_{jk} = f_{kj}$ for $j \neq k$ are required for symmetry

(handwritten annotations: "OLS will work" and "a, b, g parameters — linear" near the Generalized Leontief row; "linear regression" near the Translog row)

that partial differentiation of an indirect function will not give product supply or negative factor demand equations for problems characterized by certain types of risk aversion (see Pope, 1982) and most types of stochastic multiperiod problems (see Taylor, 1984). For such problems, empirical use of duality is quite complex as compared to the static, deterministic cases discussed in this chapter.

6.7 PROBLEMS

6-1. Derive the indirect cost function and the indirect profit function associated with the two-factor Cobb–Douglas production function.

6-2. Derive the indirect profit function associated with the two-factor quadratic production function. (Refer to Tables 3.1 and 4.1.)

6-3. Derive the product supply function for a firm that operates in a competitive product market and whose production is characterized by the indirect cost function,

$$\bar{c} = y^2 (r_1 r_2)^{1/2}$$

6-4. Derive the production function associated with $\bar{c}$ in Problem 6-3.

6-5. Find the production function associated with each of the following cost functions:

(a) $\tilde{c} = (r_1 r_2)^{1/2} e^{y/2}$

(b) $\tilde{c} = r_2[1 + y + \ln(r_1/r_2)]$

(c) $\tilde{c} = y(r_1^2 + r_2^2)^{1/2}$

6-6. Consider $\tilde{c} = r_1 y^2 x_2^{-1/2} + r_2 x_2$, where y is output, $\tilde{c}$ is short-run indirect cost, and x_2 is the level of a factor that is fixed in the short run. Find the long-run indirect cost function, say $\tilde{\tilde{c}}$, for this problem. Find short-run and long-run conditional factor demand equations, unconditional factor demand equations, and the product supply equations. Find the production function equation associated with $\tilde{c}$ and $\tilde{\tilde{c}}$.

6-7. Show that $(\partial \tilde{R}/\partial p_i) = y_i^c$, where $\tilde{R}$ is an indirect gross revenue function and y_i^c is the ith conditional (conditional upon fixed levels of the factor) supply function.

6-8. Prove the product supply property of Hotelling's lemma using

$$\pi = \sum_j p_j y_j - \tilde{c}(r_1, \ldots, r_n, y_1, \ldots, y_m)$$

and

$$\bar{\pi} = \sum_j p_j y_j^* - \tilde{c}(r_1, \ldots, r_n, y_1^*, \ldots, y_m^*)$$

6-9. Show that the indirect gross revenue function, $\tilde{R}$, is weakly convex when the production function, $0 = F(y_1, y_2, x)$, is strictly quasi-convex.

6.8 SELECTED BIBLIOGRAPHY

Blackorby, C., D. Primont, and R. R. Russell. *Duality, Separability, and Functional Structure: Theory and Economic Applications.* Amsterdam: North-Holland, 1978.

Diewert, W. E. "Applications of Duality Theory" in *Frontiers of Quantitative Economics*, Vol. II, edited by M. Intrilligator and D. Kendrick. Amsterdam: North-Holland, 1974.

Diewert, W. E. "Duality Approaches to Microeconomic Theory" in *Handbook of Mathematical Economics*, Vol. II, edited by K. J., Arrow and M. D. Intrilligator. Amsterdam: North-Holland, 1982.

Epstein, L. "Duality Theory and Functional Forms for Dynamic Factor Demands." *Rev. Econ. Stud.* 48(1981): 81–95.

Fuss, M., and D. McFadden eds. *Production Economics: A Dual Approach to Theory and Applications.* Amsterdam: North-Holland, 1978. This book is an excellent collection of articles dealing with duality.

Laitinen, K. *A Theory of the Multiproduct Firm.* Amsterdam: North-Holland, 1980.

Pope, R. D. "To Dual or Not to Dual?" *West. J. Agric. Econ.* 7(1982): 337–351. This paper provides a brief but rather comprehensive review of duality theory, then discusses the empirical usefulness of that theory. Some cases where duality fails are also discussed. The reference list of this paper cites much of the relevant literature dealing with duality theory and its applications.

Shephard, R. *Theory of Cost and Production Functions.* Princeton, N.J.: Princeton University Press, 1970.

Silberberg, Eugene. *The Structure of Economics: A Mathematical Analysis.* New York: McGraw-Hill, 1978.

Taylor, C. R. "Stochastic Intertemporal Duality Theory." *Amer. J. Agric. Econ.* 66(1984): 351–357.

Varian, H. F. *Microeconomic Analysis.* New York: Norton, 1978. This textbook develops the theory of the firm largely from a dual standpoint.

INDEX

Where the reference is in a footnote, the page number is followed by n.